Brewing better BEER

master lessons for advanced homebrewers

Gordon Strong

brewers
publications

A Division of the
Brewers Association
Boulder, Colorado

Brewers Publications
A Division of the Brewers Association
PO Box 1679, Boulder, Colorado 80306-1679
BrewersAssociation.org

Printed in the United States of America.

10 9 8 7 6 5 4 3 2 1

ISBN: 0-937381-98-5
ISBN-13: 978-0-937381-98-4

Library of Congress Cataloging-in-Publication Data

Strong, Gordon, 1962-
Brewing better beer : master lessons for advanced home brewers / by Gordon Strong.
   p. cm.
Includes index.
ISBN-13: 978-0-937381-98-4
ISBN-10: 0-937381-98-5
1. Beer--Amateurs' manuals. 2. Brewing--Amateurs' manuals. I. Title.

TP577.S795 2011
641.8'73--dc22

2011003301

Publisher: Kristi Switzer
Technical Editor: Joseph A. Formanek, Ph.D.
Copy Editing and Index: Daria Labinsky
Production & Design Management: Stephanie Johnson Martin
Cover and Interior Design: Julie White
Cover Photography: Jon Edwards Photography

*To Joe Frisbie and Ken Weems, who first got me
interested in craft beer and homebrewing,*

and

*To my wife, Karla, and my daughter, Katya,
for putting up with me ever since.*

table of contents

Part III: Applying Your Knowledge

acknowledgements

Since this book is personal and somewhat autobiographical in nature, I must thank those who have played a part in my development as a brewer. I met the people who showed me how to brew all-grain through the DRAFT homebrew club; thanks to Steve Zabarnick, Ted Holloway, Mike Boetger, and Steve Bertolo for showing me different methods and approaches. I also met two professional brewers with strong homebrewer roots, Doug Beedy and Eric Asebrook, who gave me critical early advice and support.

As I got more involved in judging and competing, I met some great brewers who are still close friends—Joe Formanek, Jamil Zainasheff, Frank Barickman, Keith Kost, and Paul Shick. They've always been good for swapping beers and stories, and in sharing information about brewing.

More recently, I've learned the most from fellow members of the Saint Paul Homebrewers Club—Curt Stock, Kris England, Thomas Eibner, and Steve Fletty. These are the guys who have pushed me the most to succeed in the last few years.

Dennis Hall taught me how to properly appreciate and taste wine, which gave me skills that I've used continuously. I also learned a great deal from technical discussions over the years with A. J. deLange, Al Korzonas, Pete Devaris, Alan McKay, Jeff Sparrow, Steve Hamburg, and Martin Brungard. Regnier de Muynck showed me much about Belgium.

I want to thank those who allowed my work to be enjoyed by a wider audience: Justin Crossley and Chad Moshier from The Brewing Network, who have had me on their shows several times, and magazine editors Jim Parker, Jill Redding, Betsy Parks, and Greg Barbera for publishing my articles.

Thanks to Joe Formanek for his technical review. Nothing helps like a second set of eyes from a fellow Ninkasi winner who also happens to be a Ph.D. food chemist. Sincere thanks go to Jamil Zainasheff, Peter Symons, and Randy Mosher, who all reviewed the draft and provided very helpful comments.

My biggest thanks go to Michael Ferguson for his heartfelt foreword. Little did I know when I suggested that he write the foreword, that I would get such a ringing endorsement from a true industry legend and brewing badass. Mufasa is well respected among homebrewers for his honest, straightforward, knowledgeable, and humorous talks, and for his inspiration to us all to advance our skills.

Finally, thanks to Kathryn Porter Drapeau for suggesting that I write this book, and to Kristi Switzer, my publisher, for her support and understanding as I wrote it. Kristi, since I like to use quotes, I'll close with one more from Douglas Adams: "I love deadlines. I like the whooshing sound they make as they fly by."

foreword

There are basically two reasons to read a foreword. You have either already bought the book and are looking to get everything out of it you can, or you are contemplating buying the book and are looking for insight into whether or not you should spend the money. Forewords to books are like book reviews and often are written by an industry peer. Reading the foreword of a book is a way of preparing to read the book in question.

Well, let's just cut to the chase. For those of you who have purchased this book, you are way ahead of the game. As for the contemplators; just buy the book. You will not be disappointed.

There are plenty of how-to books out there. How to brew, how to use yeast, how to imitate classic styles; the list is quite long. Most are decent, and some are great. It is my opinion, however, that there are enough technical how-to books on the market, and I'm sure more are coming.

This book, however, is not a how-to book; it's a "do you want to" book.

Huh?

Let me explain.

The questions you need to ask yourself are: Do you want to pursue the mastery of homebrewing? Do you want to have a conversation with someone who is considered a Master at homebrewing? Do you want to gain insight into what it takes to be a Master at homebrewing? Do you want to win more awards? Do you want to know if you have what it takes? Do you want to understand the commitment it takes to go to a level that few of us ever attain?

Do you want to have a conversation with Gordon Strong?

You get the picture yet?

It probably sounds like I'm talking about a self-help book. Maybe it is, in a way. Gordon has taken his life experiences and channeled them into becoming a Master at his craft, and even though my life experience is diametrically different, I found myself saying out loud: "Gordon. Get out of my head." So much of what he says in this book parallels my own philosophy on brewing. The same thing will happen with most of you who have devoted your life to brewing.

Don't get me wrong; I'm not saying that this book is only for those who want to become Masters or who want to devote their lives to brewing like some secret society acolyte. There is something here for everyone.

Gordon would say that this is for the experienced brewer already brewing all-grain recipes. I say that this is a book for anyone who has ever contemplated or attempted homebrewing, from the newbie looking in through the window to the professional brewer who has returned to his or her roots, not unlike what I have done.

Without hyperbole I can say this book has something for everyone. It is like the *Zen and the Art of Motorcycle Maintenance for Brewing*. I see the "Metaphysics of Quality" all throughout this book. There was a definite metaphysical shift in Gordon's life experiences, which helped him understand where to focus his energy. Fortunately, we don't need a near-death experience to find this understanding. All we need to do is read this book and take the lessons learned to heart.

I remember my first attempt at homebrewing. There were no homebrew shops. There were no online stores. Hell, there was no on line! The "recipe" was from a high school buddy, who got it from his uncle, who used to brew various concoctions while in the military. Dry bakers' yeast and lots of sugar were just two of the many ingredients that we used to make perhaps the worst alcoholic beverage ever brewed.

I was pretty sure at this point that I wanted nothing to do with homebrewing even when it started to become legal around the country. I simply was not invested. Add to it the disappointment, when the first brewpubs started to pop up, of finding that there were some amazingly bad beers out there in the mix. It just didn't seem possible to become inspired about home- or craft-brewing. I have always loved beer, from the first taste I received at an early age from my father to the young adult that enjoyed the revitalization that Fritz Maytag brought to the Anchor Brewing Company. I just didn't think I could brew it!

That was a very long time ago, and after 20 years in the industry I finally see what it was that I was missing back then. I was missing somebody to point me in the right direction. I was missing that person to point me toward Charlie Papazian's book. I needed a mentor.

This book is just like having a mentor. Mentors use their own life experiences through stories and allegories that motivate you to learn and gain your own experience. That is at the core of what this book does. You are being mentored by Gordon Strong when you read this book. And that is a very good thing.

Brewing Better Beer is the personal journey of a homebrewer and homebrewing, with frequent stops at award-winning recipes and techniques along the way. Gordon's use of analogy and allegory is never farfetched and always on the mark, though it might take a little thought to catch up with the mind of a Master. These comparisons create a philosophy of thought as it relates to Homebrewing and its mastery.

I often use analogies when relating the philosophies of brewing during my talks and classes and in articles I've written. When creating your own beer style and philosophy, think of the jazz musician who considers covering a song. He doesn't strike out immediately into ad lib willy-nilly. The great ones study the melody and practice it exactly as written until they have mastered the nuance, intent, and emotion of the original piece. Then and only then will they expand and extend on the piece and make it their own.

This book flows along the lines of analogy, technique, and practice. It discusses the tools available without judgment and examines the reason why they help support your own senses and abilities of evaluation. When delving into techniques Gordon delivers a conversation couched in philosophy as well as technical detail. That is the real charm of this book. It doesn't preach or proselytize; it doesn't set you up for a punchline or lofty point. It has a logical flow without reading like a textbook. It almost tricks you into learning and introspection. The fact is, it's a good read: part novel, part informational prose, a little autobiographical, and a lot conversational.

I am impressed with the way Gordon blends science and technique with art and craft to give the reader a clear vision of how to navigate the brewing process. Like in *Zen* he examines the gestalts or the romantic view of homebrewing, as well as the detail-oriented mechanics and rational analysis. This is a microcosmic view of the brewing collective consciousness.

Brewing Better Beer does make some major assumptions, the biggest of which is that it's a book of and for all-grain brewing. Yes! All-Grain-Brewing! That's right. Baking from scratch, y'all.

Those of you who know me know that I am a staunch proponent of all-grain brewing. I believe that extract brewing is akin to making Kool-Aid. Just add water. I think this is the real reason why I was picked to write this foreword. I see no reason to continue extract brewing once you get the basics under your belt; sanitation, bottling, carbonating, and the like.

I believe the most important part of brewing a great beer takes place in the mash. This is really where beer is made. Sure, yeast, fermentation profiles, and sanitation play major roles in creating the final product, but actual wort production is the key to how well these other parts work in the end. If your wort is wrong, then yeast and fermentation profiles won't help much at all. Satisfaction is increased with all-grain brewing. Just ask any of us who brew all grain, and the answer will be the same.

Extract brewing is like painting by the numbers. All-grain brewing is painting from the heart . . . the true artisanal craft of brewing. Decoctions, no-sparge, and step mashes are wonderful techniques to experiment with and only possible with all-grain brewing.

So there you go. All the mistakes have already been made and documented. All the insight is laid out for you in a comprehensive format that includes tips, hints, examples, techniques, recipes, analogy, and allegory. *Brewing Better Beer* is the one book the experienced homebrewers need to up their game. It's the book that less experienced brewers need to decide how far they want to go with this hobby, which can so easily turn into a way of life. It is the book that can show something new to every brewer out there.

I am fond of saying that we all should learn something new every day and that we will learn how to die on our deathbed. After all, isn't that what life is, or at least should be?

It is my hope that you will enjoy this book as much as I did on my first read and will continue to enjoy it on successive reads. I already consider it one of the base books in any brewer's library, professional and homebrewer alike. There is just too much going on here not to appreciate it for years to come.

Einstein said, "If I have seen farther than others, it is because I was standing on the shoulders of giants."

Here is your chance to stand on the broad shoulders of a brewing giant. *Brewing Better Beer: Master Lessons for Advanced Homebrewers* is a roadmap into how we can all Brew Strong!

Brew long and prosper. Prosit!

Michael "Mufasa" Ferguson
Director of Brewery Operations
BJ's Restaurants Inc.

introduction

A smart man learns from his mistakes,
but a truly wise man learns from the mistakes of others.
– Variation of Publilius Syrus

Blown Up, Sir

There's something about almost dying that tends to focus your attention on what's important in life. In early June 2007, I had a near-death experience while working on a homebrew club project with a friend. We were preparing a bourbon barrel to be filled with 50 gallons of English barley wine, which our club made on National Homebrew Day, when it suddenly exploded, severely injuring us both.

We had done this before, so we thought we knew what we were doing. We were trying to kill any mold in the barrel using a smoldering sulfur stick, a common winemaking technique. But apparently there were too many bourbon vapors still in the barrel, and the sulfur stick ignited them. Flames shot out the bunghole, charring my friend's hand. The pressure was too great to be contained and blew out the head of the barrel. Unfortunately for me, I was standing right next to it.

I was scorched by the flames, hit by at least four heavy pieces of oak, and knocked back a good fifteen feet by the blast. The barrel was left burning on the deck, while pieces of it were later found more than a hundred feet away. The emergency room staff kept questioning us like we were terrorists, until we finally convinced them that we were just a couple of homebrewers who were having a bad day.

It took us both more than eight weeks to recover, but we both felt incredibly fortunate to have not been injured more seriously. After recovering, I took some time to reflect on what had happened. For some reason, I kept thinking of that phony motivational poster from *despair.com* titled "Mistakes" that showed a sinking ship with the caption, "It could be that the purpose of your life is only to serve as a warning to others." I didn't want that to be the purpose of my homebrewing life; I wanted to be known for something more positive.

I previously had been very successful in brewing, and in winning competitions, but I never competed at the national level or wrote much about my approach to brewing. That all changed after the accident. I reassessed my priorities and decided that a job was just a way to get paid, but homebrewing was my passion, and I wanted to pursue it with a newfound purpose and focus. I wanted to achieve more from brewing and to see how far I could go if I really tried. That's when I started competing seriously in the National Homebrew Competition.

After some successes at the national level, I began to get more questions from homebrewers about my approach to brewing and the secrets of my success. After answering these for a while, it dawned on me that I should collect all these tidbits and organize them into a coherent book on my brewing philosophy. This will let me share my experiences with the widest possible audience and make a lasting contribution.

I've always believed in lifelong learning and in giving back as a way to honor those who had shared so much information with me. I see writing a book as the best way to help people brew better beer and to help everyone to share in the same enjoyment that I get out of brewing.

I began writing this book after I had won my second Ninkasi Award, and developed it during the 2009-2010 brewing season, while I was preparing for the 2010 National Homebrew Competition.

This is the recipe we were making during The Big Bang. It's one I've made several times and is a local favorite. It is meant to taste like an aged *J.W. Lee's Harvest Ale*, one of my favorite beers. When young, I find *J.W. Lee's* to be cloyingly sweet, but after several years it takes on a beautiful, malty complexity. I was trying to skip the extensive aging and find something that is drinkable within six months.

It's called Old Draft Dodger after my local homebrew club, the Dayton Regional Amateur Fermentation Technologists (DRAFT). I know this is a complicated recipe, but see what you have to look forward to in this book.

Old Draft Dodger—English Barley Wine

Recipe for 6 gallons (22.7 liters)

10 lbs. (4.5 kg) Maris Otter malt

10 lbs. (4.5 kg) Vienna malt

2 lbs. (907 g) amber malt

1½ lbs. (680 g) malted wheat

2 lbs. (907 g) Victory malt

1½ lbs. (680 g) CaraPils malt

3 lbs. (1.4 kg) 60 °L crystal malt

¾ lb. (340 g) 12 °L crystal malt

1 lb. (450 g) muscovado sugar

½ oz. (14 g) Tomahawk whole hops, 16% alpha acid, at 60 min.

½ oz. (14 g) East Kent Goldings whole hops, 6% alpha acid, at 45 min.

½ oz. (14 g) Fuggles whole hops, 4% alpha acid, at 30 min.

1 oz. (14 g) East Kent Goldings whole hops, 6% alpha acid, at 5 min.

Yeast: WLP002

1 tsp. calcium chloride in mash

Mash-in at 152° F (67° C).

Collect 8 gallons (30.3 liters).

Boil hard for 90 min.

Oxygenate.

Ferment at 68° F (20° C).

OG: 1.120

FG: 1.034

35 IBU

11.3% ABV

J.W. Lee's is available aged in several types of barrels. This recipe will likely do well treated in the same manner. I'm obviously not an expert on using barrels, but I've done it enough that I can offer some tips on how to handle them:

- It's much harder to get beer out of a barrel than it is to fill it. Have a plan for removing the beer before you fill it.

- Build a stand to hold the barrel; the stand should be above the height of a carboy or keg, unless you use a pump.

- Plan to install a spigot in the barrel; racking from a barrel is very difficult unless you use a pump.

- Pick up your barrel right before you fill it. Don't let it sit around, particularly in direct sunlight or high temperatures.

- Get the barrel from a place that has rinsed it and checked it for leaks. If you don't, be sure to rinse it out yourself with boiling water, and to spray down the exterior with water to make sure the wood doesn't dry out.

- Place the fully prepped barrel in its final cellar location before filling it; you won't be able to move it after it's full.

- Keep any fire or heat source well away from your barrel. It's not necessary to use a sulfur stick.

- Check the character of the beer regularly (monthly, at least). Remove it from the barrel when it has the desired character.

You can reuse the barrel, but you should rinse it, unless you want some carry-over in flavor. You can also try a solera approach, where you remove a keg's worth of volume at a time and refill it with fresh beer. This is an interesting way to get an aged, blended character or to adjust the balance; it is a traditional method for producing aged, fortified wines such as sherry, madeira, port, and marsala.

The Journey Is the Reward

Writing a book is something that I've always wanted to do. But like everything else I do, I want to do it my way. I didn't want to write yet another book on the basic mechanics of brewing that covers the same old topics in the same old way. The basics are well known and are described in literally dozens of books. I wanted this book to be something special that takes a fresh look at all-grain brewing and discusses the choices that an advanced brewer makes and how new skills are mastered and internalized.

There are many ways to brew successfully, so don't be fooled into thinking there is only one way to do it. I'll talk about the way I brew, but that's not the main point of this book. The goal isn't for you to learn how to brew like me; it's to use my experiences as an example, so you can develop your own personal style that works on your system. I'll consider it a success if you start thinking about how you brew and thinking about new ways of combining techniques and ideas so that you can brew better beer.

By now, you should be realizing this is not your average book on brewing. I'm not going to simply present information and leave it to you to figure out what to do next. It's more about lessons learned, tips, and strategies for applying the information, and how to think about beer and brewing in new ways. If you learn how to adapt new brewing information, you'll be able to apply the lessons in this book even after state-of-the-art advances in the future. The knowledge base can change, but the way you go about learning can still be applied.

So if this isn't your average brewing book, what exactly is it? I think it's helpful to first describe what it isn't before I discuss what it is.

First of all, this isn't a textbook or a purely technical brewing book. I'll discuss brewing at a relatively advanced level, but I won't spend much time deriving basic information or discussing the science behind the concepts. If I want that information, I'll look in the brewing reference textbooks, such as those from major brewing universities and researchers—De Clerck, Kunze, Narziss, Briggs, Bamforth, and Lewis. My favorite technical brewing books are ones that are more directly written for homebrewers, such as those from Fix and Noonan. I also enjoy digging through online technical studies by A.J. deLange and Kai Troester that describe practical experiments, particularly those that investigate common brewing practices or dogma.

This also isn't a scholarly study; I'm not using many footnotes, and I'm certain that I've learned and adapted ideas and concepts from a great many sources, most of which I can't identify. Most individual techniques aren't original, but the way I combine them and use them is my own. It's my goal that you will use this book as an example of how to learn and how to develop your own way of brewing based on your system, your common ingredients, and the experiences you've had in your brewing career. The focus is on thought processes and choosing between alternatives, not providing a complete treatise on brewing.

This is not a recipe book, but I provide many of my award-winning recipes. I'm using recipes to illustrate points and to add color to the stories. If I'm looking for a new recipe, I often look at books by Zainasheff/Palmer, Noonan, or the Classic Styles Series published by Brewers Publications. This book is not focused on recipe formulation, but I do include a long chapter on how I approach that topic. If I'm looking for ideas on formulation, I'll look to Daniels and Mosher.

This is not a basic brewing book and it doesn't discuss extract brewing at all; that's not how I brew, and I assume you are well past that level as well. I won't teach you how to get started brewing or give you step-by-step procedures for basic brewing processes. There are many great sources for this information (Palmer, Korzonas), and I don't have anything new to add.

All those sources I've discussed and more have been influential to me. I have learned from them and continue to use them, and many of their thoughts are likely to appear in my methods.

What this book does is fill an unaddressed niche in homebrewing literature. It describes how to think about brewing, how to select and apply proper techniques, and how to continue to learn and develop your own brewing style. I talk about how to integrate tips, best practices, and modern advice into your brewing routine. It's like Maslow's Hierarchy of Needs[1] applied to brewing; once you have achieved the basic brewing needs and can make good beer, what motivates you to reach for self-actualization, to achieve your full potential, and to be the best brewer you can be?

This is the book for the experienced all-grain brewer looking to develop advanced skills, make better beer, win competitions, become a mentor, and add to the knowledge base. I'm sharing my experiences and lessons learned. I learn the most when I have open and honest discussions with my closest

[1] Maslow's Hierarchy of Needs is a theory in psychology to describe human behavior. Often represented as a pyramid, it contains levels (from low to high) for physiological, safety/security, love/belonging/social, esteem, and self-actualization. The theory is used to understand human motivation, where lower-level or basic needs must be satisfied before people will seek fulfillment of higher-level needs.

brewing friends, who all brew at a very advanced level. That's what has helped me improve the most, so I'm going to use the same techniques, but in print.

When sharing information and learning from each other, it's important to remember that no one person knows everything about brewing. There is always something to learn. Don't take what someone tells you on blind faith— test ideas for yourself. What you ultimately adopt and incorporate into your standard practices is up to you.

Finally, keep in mind that I'm a homebrewer, not a professional brewer. I talk about hand-crafting beer on a homebrew scale with homebrew equipment, and not all these ideas are necessarily applicable on a large production scale.

Structure of This Book

I was thinking about all the various questions people have asked me, what they want me to show them when we get together to brew, and how I explain brewing to someone. I tried to encapsulate those lessons in this book. As in the medieval guild system, you mostly have to learn from a craftsman who has mastered the skills. I have organized the topics into the various lessons that I have discussed with other brewers.

Chapter 1 presents the themes of the book and my general philosophy about brewing. I talk about the way I think about brewing and how I go about learning and enhancing my knowledge. This provides the context for much of what is discussed in this book and gives you an opportunity to understand my approach to brewing.

Chapters 2 through 4 discuss the brewing background you should master, along with my tips and commentary. I cover it in a different order than other, more straightforward brewing texts. I talk about process first, and equipment and ingredients afterward. This is because I expect readers to have a background in all these areas, so I don't need to introduce the topics. These topics could really be discussed in any order, so you might want to consider them to be parallel discussions. Understanding these sections is necessary before getting into the rest of the book.

Chapters 5 through 9 apply the fundamental knowledge to brewing better beer. As with Chapters 2 through 4, these chapters can be studied in parallel.

Chapters 5 and 6 talk about how to think about beer styles, evaluate beer, and build recipes.

Chapters 7 and 8 discuss dealing with problems that arise with your beer and getting your beer ready to drink.

Chapter 9 is about competition brewing and deals with making your best effort to get your beer ready for a specific event.

Chapter 10 presents my concluding thoughts and the major lessons I've learned, which I'd like you to think about.

Using This Book

I discuss experiences on my system using ingredients with which I'm familiar. My techniques will likely need to be adjusted and adapted to other systems; that's normal. Learning how to apply ideas from others to your own system is one way you demonstrate mastery of the brewing process.

I frequently use stories, recipes, and anecdotes to illustrate points. I want this to be something special and to tell a personal story. How I brew is based on the experiences I have had, the information I've learned, and the tips I have learned from others. This book is about how to make choices and how to approach brewing, which should be quite individualized. I'm not trying to convince you to make the same choices that I did but to make your own, based on your own experiences and personality, and to develop your own style.

Analogies are used liberally, particularly in how someone masters other fields. Cooking is another passion of mine, so I use those examples frequently. Your own experiences will guide what analogies or influences you use to think about brewing and how you can learn and apply the same information.

I often state strong opinions, but they are based on my experiences with brewing and seeing problems other people have while brewing. I don't claim they are universally true, just that they work for me. As I said earlier, I'm not trying to write a textbook or a research paper; I'm trying to take my experiences and relate them in a way that can help you brew better beer. I know the difference between facts and opinions; you don't have to agree with my opinions to get something out of this book.

I look at this book as a conversation with you, the reader, and I, the author, and have freely used the words "you" and "I" while writing. This is a personal, conversational tone and is entirely intentional. As I'm writing, I'm imagining that we're talking, recalling the countless conversations I've had with other brewers who have asked me questions over the years. If I'm discussing a scientific or academic point, I might drop into a drier tone. But I want this work to be engaging, so I hope you are not put off by my less-than-formal style.

But Why Nothing on Extract Beers?

OK, I said I was going to have strong opinions, so here's my first one: there's nothing in this book on brewing extract beers because making extract beers isn't really brewing any more than heating up TV dinners is cooking. When you outsource wort production, you are removing much of what the brewer does. You can make beer that way, but you won't be able to make the best beer possible or get the full value from this book unless you make the commitment to learn the complete brewing process.

You can make good extract beers but you can't make all the styles. You have to make compromises; you know you're cutting corners. You don't have full control over your system or ingredients. You can still have good results, and you can make beer quickly, but you really haven't mastered brewing. If all you want to do is make good beer quickly, and you are only interested in making a subset of the styles, then by all means remain an extract brewer.

I'm not saying there is anything wrong with making extract beer. We all started that way. I made 23 extract beers in my first year-and-a-half of brewing. I entered 11 of them in 13 competitions, and won four best-of-shows and more than 25 medals. Six batches didn't turn out very well, and one was dumped (thus, I learned lessons in humility and persistence). Along the way, I learned how to pay attention to sanitation, avoid oxidation, manage a fermentation, and use different forms of ingredients. All of those were useful skills, but I had learned about as much as I could and couldn't do all the things I wanted to do. I had hit a plateau and knew I had to step up to all-grain if I was to keep moving ahead.

Once I moved to all-grain, I had so much more to learn, but I got more enjoyment out of it. Finally, I could make a proper *Kölsch* and a *hefeweizen* that wasn't too dark. I could make a Belgian *dubbel* and other beers that use dark Munich malt. I could get the proper attenuation in a Düsseldorf-style *altbier* using a step mash. Finally, I felt like I was brewing. I no longer felt like I was sitting at the kiddie table when I talked to other brewer friends. As I write this, it has been more than 12 years since I made that step, and I have not regretted it once.

The biggest reason why I'm not writing an extract book is because I don't brew that way. If you're reading this book because you know something about me and what I have achieved, then you don't want to hear about extract, because that had nothing to do with those successes except to get me started. The recipes in this book are the ones I've made; I don't include extract versions because I haven't made them that way and can't vouch for their accuracy. You may be able to convert them, but they will be approximations at best.

PART I
philosophy

Talking about the philosophy of brewing likely strikes most people as odd, since it isn't immediate apparent what that means. Is it part of a joke ("Two philosophers walk into a bar …")? Is it a metaphor for rambling while drunk (think Peter O'Toole in *My Favorite Year*)? Is it a pompous attempt to attach more importance to the subject than is due? Hopefully, it's none of these—this isn't a joke, I'm not drunk, and I hope it isn't arrogant or condescending.

A **philosophy of brewing** is simply how a brewer thinks about and approaches brewing. One definition of philosophy is "a view or outlook regarding fundamental principles underlying some domain." That's pretty much what I mean. It's a very personal subject for brewers, since it touches on deeply held beliefs and personal attitudes and preferences. I will talk about my experiences and brewing philosophy, how I learned and continue to learn, but these are only examples of how to develop your own belief system. I'm not trying to indoctrinate you, so keep the big picture in mind.

This chapter talks about the themes for the book as I work to explain my personal brewing philosophy and lead you on a discovery of your own. I discuss the following topics:

- How I approach brewing, an overview of my personal philosophy.

- My story, the background that led me to where I am.

- Channeling influences. How to take ideas from non-brewing fields and apply them to brewing. Finding your own influences.

- Becoming a master. What does that mean? What is a master?

- Developing your own style. The approach for finding your own voice.

the philosophy of brewing

The reward of a thing well done is to have done it.
– Ralph Waldo Emerson

Courage is grace under pressure.
– Ernest Hemingway

I did it My Way.
– Frank Sinatra

I have several beliefs about brewing that affect how I look at it and how I practice it. These aren't right or wrong; you will likely have different views. I certainly believe that those who take a more rigorous, scientific approach to brewing will object. But that's what's great about calling it your personal philosophy—it's yours!

I think there is a certain elegance in **effortless excellence, quality, and style.** Think James Bond or Frank Sinatra; they would just roll in and own the place. It's my goal to make something hard look easy, so I don't waste time and effort. If you know what you're doing, you won't thrash or panic. Proper preparation and thinking several steps ahead allows you to adjust as you go. Knowing your control points allows you to focus your efforts on the areas where they have the most benefit. I see brewing as a series of small course corrections; stay calm and just deal with problems as they arise.

I've always been interested in the **intuitive way of brewing**. I like to understand cause and effect and how to influence processes to favor the outcomes I want. Done right, it almost has the feel of stacking the deck in your favor. There is a fairly large margin of error on the homebrew scale, so exploit these opportunities to control processes based on observation and judgment.

When I took economics in college, it was presented as a rigorous discipline heavy with math. However, the more I paid attention to how economics worked, the more it seemed like a pseudoscience to me. Economists had formulas but didn't evaluate them; they just used them to determine how one variable influenced the direction of another. When I say homebrewing has a margin of error, it means that I think of it in somewhat the same way. There is real science and math underneath what we do, but we don't have to access it directly to be successful. Understanding what factors move you in the right direction may be enough, as long as you can use your senses to determine when you've reached the right goal (like a chef salting to taste rather than measuring the salt).

Maybe it's the way I think, but I love using analogies and **channeling influences** from nonbrewing domains. I'll have more to say about that subject later in this chapter, but the essence is that you can use knowledge and information from any topic to help you better understand brewing. If you can tap and apply knowledge you've already learned, you can make faster progress in picking up brewing skills. Learning is not a straightforward path for me; as long as I'm acquiring usable knowledge and can store it in a meaningful framework, then I'm advancing.

I'm not into meditation or Eastern philosophies, but I do like to **understand what matters** and focus my energies accordingly. I see this as a way of prioritizing and making the best use of limited resources. I often call this the *Zen of Brewing*.

If you develop sufficient skill, you should be able to trust your judgment. Your palate is an outstanding tool; use it. You can often approximate solutions using your judgment, and your palate and other senses can substitute for direct measurements in many places. Taking measurements while learning to calibrate your senses reinforces the learning process. This is very much how I developed and apply my skills.

I manage complexity through **abstraction** to avoid information overload. Think about processes as black boxes that do certain functions and give known outputs based on certain inputs. You don't always have to know why or how the black boxes function to understand the overall process. Managing the scale of a complex process allows you to think about one part of it at a time without losing your bearings. Just be sure you have an accurate model of your complex processes. The Internet is a source of much disinformation and oversimplification, and it is easy to misuse. Watch how you take advantage of unproven data.

Brewing is a creative endeavor that allows you to **develop your own style**. I think too many brewers lose their artistic side in favor of their scientific side. Each has its place, but if you don't make your own mark, I don't see how you can express yourself in your beers. The best artistic works resonate with the passion and soul of their creator.

Everyone Has a Story

Many people have asked me about how I got started in brewing and what led me to where I am. I didn't discover craft beer until after college. While I had tried different beer, I didn't really like it. I never knew what I was going to get when I ordered a beer at a bar; this must be why most people are single-brand drinkers. Two friends from college taught me the basics of beer styles and how to appreciate the different flavors in beer.

A few years later, I tried some homebrew from those same friends. It was outstanding, and I thought homebrewing didn't sound too hard, if you knew what you wanted to do. One of them loaned me a copy of *The New Complete Joy of Homebrewing*, I bought a brown ale kit at a local homebrew shop, and I jumped in. That was in September 1996.

I had some early successes that helped boost my confidence. I won my first best-of-show with my fifth batch of beer, a Christmas ale (see the recipe in Chapter 4). I also had some early failures, most notably a horribly oxidized beer, probably from squeezing hops trying to extract more yield. I didn't know what was wrong, or why my beer tasted like wet paper. That taught me some humility and inspired me to become a beer judge.

Studying for the Beer Judge Certification Program exam led me to greatly expand my brewing library and to read every technical and style book I could. I took the BJCP exam at the American Homebrewers Association conference in 1997 and started judging immediately. I entered and judged at all the competitions within driving range, which helped me understand how beers are evaluated and showed me how good homebrewed beer could be.

Membership in a local homebrew club helped my brewing tremendously in the early years. I went to club brewouts and watched others brew. I examined their systems, asked questions, and saw how the processes worked. These brewouts gave me the confidence to make the transition to all-grain brewing in April 1998, my batch no. 24—a Belgian *dubbel*.

Continuing to leverage my club membership, I found more experienced all-grain brewers and asked to brew a batch with them. These experiences were invaluable, since many of the processes must be seen to be understood properly. I quickly came to realize that there are many ways to brew good beer, since none of these brewers used the same systems or methods.

As I started brewing all-grain, I realized I had so much to learn again: recipes didn't work the same, water profiles became important, and there were many more ingredient choices. I kept fiddling with my system, as I added pieces and upgraded components. I moved from a 20-quart stovetop pot to a 9.5-gallon pot for full boils. I stopped using ice baths for cooling and bought a chiller. I moved from using a Gott cooler with Phil's Phalse Bottom to using a rectangular picnic cooler as a mash tun and using the Gott cooler to lauter. I moved from brewing in the kitchen to brewing outdoors.

In September 1999 I bought my current brewing system, a three-vessel half-barrel Pico system from Pico Brewing Systems. I have made some enhancements and modifications to this system over the years, many of which are described in the Mastering Equipment chapter. Once again, I found that I had to relearn techniques and adapt to my new system before I could surpass my previous results.

I switched to kegging at about the same time I got my full system. It took me some time to get the same competition results with kegged beer as I had with bottled beer.

I took up meadmaking in 2000, little knowing how much it would later influence me. Through attending AHA conferences and judging, I became friends with Ken Schramm, who offered some early advice. I began judging mead best-of-show at the National Homebrew Competition in 2001 and would do that every year until 2007, when I first entered. My early successes in mead mirrored those I had in beer; I won the Mazer Cup in 2002.

By 2003, I felt as if I had hit a plateau. I had won many awards and was satisfied with my brewing. I was a BJCP Grand Master judge and felt that I had pretty well mastered the subjects necessary to do what I wanted in brewing. Yet I eventually noticed I wasn't brewing as much any more. It might have had something to do with being involved with a rewrite of the BJCP Style Guidelines, but my interest in making beer had waned.

A fortuitous turn of events happened in September 2003. Ray Daniels asked if I would like to be technical editor for Randy Mosher's *Radical Brewing*. The more I worked through that book, the more I was inspired. I began to see new ideas and think about brewing again. I brewed five times in six weeks while working on that book. It relit a fire that had almost gone out.

I think many brewers can go through a midlife crisis. Once you've achieved your initial goals, what continues to push you? Do you retire and work for yourself, or do you take it up a notch and push yourself harder? Many people told me that once you learned how to brew all-grain, you were pretty much done unless you wanted to go pro. I now see that isn't true; there is plenty more to learn and achieve at the homebrew level.

I took on leadership roles with the AHA Governing Committee and the BJCP staff (and later board). I continued to meet people from outside my local area by attending National Homebrew Conferences. Rather than being a big fish in a small pond, I was entering the larger pond and getting to learn a whole new set of skills. The new friends I met turned out to be outstanding brewers and good people. Friendly rivalry, peer pressure, and better knowledge networks drove me to new heights.

I had developed a friendship with several members of the Saint Paul Homebrewers Club through several NHC events, and began sitting with them at the awards banquet. They always had the best beer and mead to sample, so that was another attraction. At the 2006 conference in Orlando, some of them jokingly told me that if I wanted to sit with them next year, I had better enter the national competition. I was a member of their club, so it wasn't hard for me to do, but I never really liked to ship my entries, so I always declined. But faced with a possible cutoff of quality mead and the chance to pull a joke on them, I decided to enter the NHC in 2007.

My only intent in entering the NHC was to help my adopted club in its quest to win the Club of the Year award. Once I told them I had entered, they told me that the stakes were raised and that I'd have to medal to sit with them. Fortunately, I had several entries advance to the finals. It was in the time between the first round and the second round in 2007 that the infamous bourbon barrel accident happened.

I could barely walk at the NHC in Denver that year, but I did limp on stage to accept my first NHC medal (a silver medal for a melomel) and to join my club as Club of the Year. Reassessing what I wanted to do with my life, I decided to make yet another push and see how far I could go. That has carried me to where I am today.

My brewing story has shown how experiences have made a big difference in my life and in my brewing career. But every brewer has similar influences that drive advancement, lead to new discoveries, and spur on continued commitment. Reflecting on my story and how it might apply as a general case led me to ask several questions about brewers and how they develop: Who taught them? Who gave them advice? What books did they read? What did experience teach them? How can we model this? What decisions did the brewers make? What information did they unlearn or exclude? What events or influences drove them to achieve more?

You can take many roads to becoming a great brewer, as long as you keep an open mind and keep moving in the right direction. Your personal story documents your journey and plays a strong role in developing your own brewing philosophy.

Channeling Influences

As I thought more about my approach to brewing, I pondered how I learned or thought about new material—not just with brewing but with any hobby or skill. I realized I was taking experiences from other parts of my life and using them to help me either to understand brewing or to experiment with new methods.

Applying knowledge and techniques from one domain to another is one way to be an innovative thinker. Taking different approaches can yield novel results and is a hallmark of open-ended creative thought. Innovations come from breakthrough thoughts, not incremental refinements of existing work. These new approaches might not always produce good results, but you can't innovate without making some mistakes.

Each person will have different life experiences and influences to draw upon. I'll use my own experiences as an example. I have an educational background in computer science and have studied and used engineering disciplines in various jobs. As a nerd, I've been exposed to my share of technology and science fiction writing. I am a beer judge and have some training in wine tasting. I like to cook, which ties in well with beer and wine tasting. I've done some carpentry around the house and some woodworking projects for enjoyment. It's not a major hobby of mine, but I've done it enough to understand it. I see how I've used all of these disciplines in brewing:

Think like an engineer. I can see how my engineering background leads me to think about processes and process control, breaking down complex systems into manageable components and looking at the interfaces between systems. So I use this part of my background, but not the more rigorous side with its formulas, calculations, obsession with details, and detailed logging. I guess that's why I majored in computer science and not electrical engineering. I see the engineering influence expressed more in those with a German way of thinking about brewing—tight process control, brewing a very specific way with rigid limitations, attempting to perfect something that has been done before. This isn't really the way I brew; it might make sense for professionals on large systems with limited portfolios, but it doesn't sound like much fun to me.

Think like a carpenter. I'm an engineer by training, but this perfect view of the world came to a crashing reality the first time I attempted carpentry. You can't assume everything is a right angle, is square, or is true. Reality is messy. Assuming that you can cut a piece square and it will fit against another piece will produce sloppy results. You have to measure, adjust, and make it fit. If there's a problem, you have to know how to hide it, correct it in a later step, or draw the eye away from it. The same is true in brewing. You don't have the full control that you think you do, and you have to adjust to reality, not try to live in an idealized world.

Think like a judge. Becoming a beer judge was one of the best things that happened to my brewing. It taught me how to taste critically, objectively evaluate beer against reference standards, and diagnose problems. But I don't just apply these skills to the finished product; I use them throughout the brewing process. I can begin making better decisions earlier in the brewing process than I would have thought possible, because I understand how those choices will affect the final product.

Think like a chef. This one is my personal favorite, and the one I use most often when explaining brewing. A master chef has a creative concept, selects techniques from alternatives, knows how to control the processes to get a particular result, knows how to fix problems and adjust on the fly, understands when the finished product is what was intended, and doesn't serve anything unless it meets his or her standards. Chefs take the same basic tools and apply them creatively to produce something unique. This is basically how I approach brewing.

Think like a Jedi Master. The Jedi Master (or Zen Master for those less geeky) is perhaps the most appropriate analogy for the overall philosophy. It's taking all the influences and letting them wash over you and become you. Mastering balance with these forces and influences is the goal. Know your limitations and what you can influence. Keep working towards a vision. Don't compromise.

Understand how you can use influences, knowledge, and techniques from beyond the world of brewing for new inspiration, for deeper understanding, and for incorporating the lessons of brewing into an overall framework of wisdom. As you learn and expand your knowledge, keep an open mind about new insights; these influences can come from any direction.

After I had formed these concepts, I heard Randy Mosher give a talk on recipe formulation, during which he kept describing his way of thinking about beer using terms like contrast, balance, proportion, depth, and perspective. I realized that his background was in art, and he was thinking like an artist when talking about beer. I didn't have that background, so I didn't think of it that way, but his perspective gave me new insight. I encourage you to find your own influences and work them into your brewing; the results will certainly be interesting.

Mastering Skills

Add the word "master" to a title and what does it imply? It's deeper than just having practiced a skill for more than a certain amount of time. It means that you have mastered the body of knowledge for a subject; that you are fluent in it and know how to quickly retrieve any information you need. Think of it in the traditional guild sense; that you are a leader and a teacher, that you can work alone and be responsible for creating something, that you are an example to others, and that you can add to the body of knowledge. It's not a term to be thrown around lightly.

In the book *A Pattern Language*, architect Christopher Alexander contrasts the work of a 50-year-old carpenter with the work of a novice. The experienced craftsman does less planning, because he has learned to do things in a way that lets him make small mistakes. This gives his work "unconcerned simplicity." The author describes it best:

> *The experienced carpenter keeps going. He doesn't have to keep stopping, because every action he performs is calculated in such a way that some later action can put it right to the extent that it is imperfect now. What is critical here is the sequence of events. The carpenter never takes a step that he cannot correct later, so he keeps working, confidently, steadily.*
>
> *The novice by comparison spends a great deal of time trying to figure out what to do. He does this essentially because he knows that an action he takes now may cause unretractable problems a little further down the line; and if he is not careful, he will find himself with a joint that requires the shortening of some crucial member at a stage when it is too late to shorten that member. The fear of these kinds of mistakes forces him to spend hours trying to figure ahead; and it forces him to work as far as possible to exact drawings because they will guarantee that he avoids these kinds of mistakes.*
>
> *The difference between the novice and the master is simply that the novice has not learned yet how to do things in such a way that he can afford to make small mistakes. The master knows that the sequence of actions will always allow him to cover his mistakes a little further down the line. It is this simple but essential knowledge that gives the work of a master carpenter its wonderful, smooth, relaxed, and almost unconcerned simplicity.*[1]

[1] Christopher Alexander, et al., *A Pattern Language* (New York: Oxford University Press, 1977), 964.

21

This almost exactly captures my approach to brewing and is something I feel every brewer should work toward.

Mastering a skill is something many people aspire to but not everyone can do. The book *Outliers* by Malcolm Gladwell makes the point that you need to repeatedly practice a task to master it completely; he says that 10,000 hours are needed to reach the top of your field. While you can become a great homebrewer with much less practice, this does stress the need for practical hands-on experience, not just "book smarts." To obtain practical skills, you need to learn from others and see how it's done. You should be humble and understand that you always have more to learn, and realize that the subject can advance over time and that you need to stay current.

If you're trying to master brewing, you can't treat it like Neo jacking into the Matrix ("whoa, now I know how to fly a helicopter"). You can't just transplant all brewing knowledge into your head and be successful. Study and research is important, but it's only part of the solution. Work at it, apply it, see the limitations of the information and how it affects actual processes. Adapt to your system and develop your own techniques. You can use other people's methods, but keep an open mind about changing them to suit your needs so they give you the best results.

Developing Your Own Style

I'm a firm believer in the creative side of brewing, and that once you have mastered the basic skills you should work on developing your own individual, distinctive character. What's the point of just being a clone of someone else? Sure, that's a reasonable way to start, but once you reach a certain level of ability, you tend to feel a need to solo.

I've seen too many people jump in quickly and attempt to learn advanced parts of brewing, or attempt complicated and creative experiments, without having an adequate grasp of the basics. That's a big mistake. You might have limited successes, but you don't actually learn this way. So rather than trying to make an imperial peanut butter smoked black rye IPA, why not learn how to make a decent American pale ale or brown porter first? To use an example from the guitar world, learn how to play the chords to "Smoke on the Water" before attempting the solo from "Sweet Child o' Mine."

Think about your own style being your framework for brewing. You'll fill out the details as you learn and grow in your abilities. Select the tools and methods you want to use and learn. Work towards mastering a core set of skills that let you make the beer styles you enjoy most. Develop abilities through practice and repetition, then branch out and develop new skills after you have mastered the first set.

You don't have to incorporate every skill or technique you learn into your brewing routine. You can be successful with only a subset of techniques mastered and knowledge of a certain set of ingredients. Learn the minimum to make good beer, and then repeat it before going into too much depth. Understand how to treat a smaller set of ingredients before introducing more variables. What you are able to accomplish will also depend on the equipment at your disposal. Reconsider what you are able to do whenever you make modifications to your system.

When I was learning how to brew all-grain, people taught me their techniques and showed me how they used their systems. I didn't directly adopt any of them completely, but I did pick pieces of what several brewers taught me to integrate into my own framework. I reflected on what I was shown and compared it against information I had read. I practiced and tested theories on my system and adjusted techniques based on my own experience. If I found a recipe I liked, I asked for it and then tried to brew it. Once I had a good result, I tried to improve it and give it my own twist.

There will always be people who can brew as well as you or better. You'll always have something new to learn, so keep an open mind and ask others what they are doing. The state of the art continues to advance, so even if you know everything (and you don't), the subject changes. Stay current; continue to learn and improve. Even if you don't integrate every new change into your routine, you should at least review and consider it.

You'll need to push yourself to advance your skills. You might advance in stages, and need a new push every so often to make the next leap forward. If you don't try something and fail, you don't know your limitations. Failure often teaches vital lessons and can teach you to deal with issues that arise. You don't have to personally fail; you can also learn from the failures of others.

When you do start developing your own style, think about the beers you are making. Do you want them to have a certain house character or feature a signature ingredient? Will you use these on all styles or only certain ones? For instance, one of my signature moves is to include a little bit of honey in pale ales and IPAs. I know of other brewers who like to use an uncommon malt, such as amber malt, pale chocolate, special pale, or honey malt in many of their beers. Some brewers will always use one or two types of yeast or ferment them in a certain way. Contemplate whether you'd like to have a specific signature to your beers or if you'll make each style differently.

Consider the styles you'll make. Do you want to make every style, or do you want to be known for certain types of beers? While it's nice to be able to brew any style, it's hard to have a mastery of all of them. If you don't have the time to continually re-brew and investigate individual styles, you may not learn to appreciate their range. It's a good thing to have at least one go-to recipe for each style, but I also like being able to draw from a selection of recipes for a single style. Given that some styles have considerable breadth, being able to brew all the different common variations is a good skill.

Finally, don't be afraid to reinvent yourself. Think of how Madonna has changed her routine over the years. If you find your routine is getting stale or boring, shake things up. This will often give you the necessary kick to get the creative juices flowing again. Don't let the fact that you have developed a personal style keep you from innovating, because eventually you (and others) will grow tired of it. As Alfred Hitchcock said, "Self-plagiarism is style."

mastering your craft

Facts do not cease to exist because they are ignored.
– Aldous Huxley, *Proper Studies*

Anyone looking to master the craft of brewing should first work to get the fundamentals right. Before you can begin improvising and being truly creative and inventive, you should take the time to understand the proper way of doing things. This involves understanding essential brewing techniques, knowing how your equipment works, and being able to make intelligent decisions about ingredient selection. Once you understand these essential elements, you can start making smart choices to achieve your desired results.

In the next three chapters, I will review the stages of brewing, the choices to make, identifying the critical control points, and what your choices will imply later. Understanding the cause-and-effect relationships and tradeoffs inherent in brewing is an important step in mastering the craft, since you need to understand how the choices you make influence the beer you are producing. I will give you practical advice and lessons on how to take advantage of the skills you already have, and will round out your skill set by discussing some modern brewing practices and unusual techniques that may not be discussed in basic or traditional brewing books.

I assume that you already understand how to make all-grain beer. If not, there are many good references available. My favorites are John Palmer's *How to Brew* and Greg Noonan's *New Brewing Lager Beer*. Noonan's book is more advanced and is really a great reference text. I also like Al Korzonas' *Homebrewing:*

Volume I as a source of useful information, although it doesn't cover all-grain brewing. For a person first learning to homebrew, I still like *Dave Miller's Homebrewing Guide*. All of these books have given me information that I still use today.

Rather than simply laying out the choices and letting you decide, I will try to lead you through the decision process and discuss some of the choices I have made in developing a personal brewing style. The goal isn't to have you emulate how I brew, but to use how I brew to help you develop your own way of brewing. Being a master means that you understand the body of knowledge and how to apply it, and that you are able to blaze your own path. You can't really do that if all you are doing is trying to emulate someone else. Don't strive to brew like I do; strive to brew better than I do.

Some words of advice for those trying to master the craft. Measure carefully, and closely monitor each step as you are learning a process. Make sure you understand how something works, and verify frequently with well-calibrated instruments. Then learn what the proper steps look, smell, and taste like as you go. Use your senses, not just the instruments. As you develop advanced skills, you will find you are often using your senses first, with instruments being used just to verify and validate your intuition or to check the few critical process steps. This helps you anticipate problems and make minor adjustments in brewing without being too paranoid.

Paying close attention to details when you are learning and mastering the craft is important. But once you've learned the lessons, you can relax and have fun. If you learn the few critical control points during which you have to monitor your work carefully, and you organize your work to avoid wasted effort, you really can make brewing look effortless. This shouldn't be about drudgery, tedious calculations, and endless measuring and fiddling. After all, this is a hobby and you are *making beer*. How cool is that?

CHAPTER 2
mastering techniques

Ability will never catch up with the demand for it.
– Malcolm Forbes, American capitalist

When thinking of mastering the techniques of brewing, I often am drawn to the analogy of a master chef learning the techniques of cooking. When a chef is given a piece of meat, he envisions a final dish and selects the appropriate cooking process (sauté, roast, braise, etc.) to achieve his or her vision. If a chef sautés, he doesn't measure the heat of the pan. A chef puts the meat in and listens for the right tone of sizzle. While he can check doneness with a thermometer or by cutting into the meat, a chef is much more likely to just touch it and know from the firmness whether it's ready. Experience, practice, and repetition have given the chef that insight. In the same way, given ingredients, a brewer must decide on a target beer and select the mash technique, the lauter technique, how to use hops, and other choices that bring the envisioned beer into being. The specifics are obviously different, but the same kind of thought and decision processes are being used, the same effort must be put into mastering and practicing the basics, and the level of mastery demonstrated is often based on how well the brewer chooses and controls his or her techniques.

The primary work of the brewer in the brewhouse is wort production, so the techniques I'm describing focus on that aspect of brewing. I'm assuming that ingredients have been selected, prepared, and are ready for use in brewing. The decisions on ingredients, preparation, and equipment are discussed in subsequent sections. Yes, they are all part of the brewing process (as are fermentation and packaging, stages occurring after wort production), but I think the brewer should learn about proper brewhouse techniques—mashing, lautering, boiling, and hopping—before giving attention to the other topics. I'll also cover some unusual techniques that may be handy for certain types of beers; having knowledge of multiple brewing techniques will allow you to select the proper one for your particular brewing situation.

When learning the techniques, remember that you need to select and hone the methods on your own system. You can't just blindly follow instructions. Some measurements are approximate and should be adjusted as you learn how your specific system works. There are many variables to consider when brewing—water absorption rate of grain, evaporation rate of the boil, system efficiency, etc.—that you can either pay careful attention to or approximate. You can tune your variables with ProMash, BrewTools Pro, BeerSmith, or some other brewing software. But before you jump into that level of detail, understand what's happening. Learn your system. Recognize the steps. Develop an intuitive feel for how beers will turn out based on your past experience. This is the effort that must be invested to develop proper brewing skills. Once you develop this level of understanding, you are on your way to becoming a master brewer.

Transforming Grain

The process of transforming grains and malts into wort is the process that has always felt to me like the essence of brewing. I guess I'm a firm believer in the old adage, "Brewers make wort, but yeast make beer."

The goal of this phase of brewing is to take the grain-based raw ingredients (mostly malted barley, but also other malted and unmalted grains) and transform them into wort. Starchy grains and malts must be *mashed*—crushed, combined with water in specific ratios, and rested at various temperatures to allow enzymes to convert starches to sugars—in order to make the sugars available, but some grains can simply be *steeped* (soaked in water) to extract their goodness. The sugars extracted from this process are what yeast consume to make alcohol. The grains help contribute color, flavor, aroma, and body to the finished product.

Mash Fundamentals

If you're an all-grain brewer, you already know how to mash. I'm not going to lecture you about the basics or go into textbook depth—I just want to cover some important process control points and talk about some of the frequently misunderstood science behind the process. Then we can get into the different types of mashing and why you would want to use those methods. It's important to understand what is happening and why, so you can better understand how to control the conditions of a mash and to troubleshoot problems.

Mashing is mixing crushed malted cereal grains (the *grist*) with water at a certain ratio for specific times at specific temperatures (the *rest*). Enzymes—complex organic catalysts in the grains developed during the malting process—systematically break down complex carbohydrates in the grains to produce fermentable sugars and other desirable compounds. Mashing is an indirect control method—as the brewer, you are creating the conditions for enzymes to do their work. Since malts contain a great number of enzymes that work best in different temperature and pH ranges, you have several decisions to make about which enzymes you want to work.

One of the biggest misconceptions about enzymes is that they work like transistors or diodes—that they just switch on or off under specific conditions. Don't think of a switch, think of a bell curve—there is a region where the enzymes are most active, but they are still functioning outside the prime temperature range. However, once enzymes are heated beyond their normal functioning range, they begin to *denature* (or break down), an irreversible process. This process doesn't happen instantly; hotter temperatures (more outside the desired range) cause enzymes to denature faster. Due to the denaturing process, enzyme activity is reduced more quickly on the hot side of the normal range than on the cooler side.

Enzymes are highly specific—they tend to operate on very few (perhaps only one) substrate, speeding up very specific reactions. They are usually identified by the suffix "-ase," and the substrate they act upon is usually the root for the word. Some enzymes have co-factors, or substances that help them work more efficiently. Calcium is an important co-factor for the amylase enzymes, and also helps protect α-amylase at normal mashing temperatures. Mash-related enzymes require water and certain concentrations of enzymes to substrates—thus the importance of water-to-grist ratios for mashing. If you have too dilute a mash, the enzymes won't be concentrated enough to do their work.

Traditional and historical brewing texts often talk about the need for brewers to do more work in breaking down malts. However, modern malts are very well modified and are designed for rapid saccharification. The maltsters have done much of the work that used to be performed by the brewers. The need for a β-glucanase rest[1] is pretty much gone. Amino acids are well developed, so lower temperature protein rests tend to do more harm than good (they can ruin head retention and thin the body). The malting process creates the enzymes and allows them to work, breaking down much of the cellular structure in the grains. Proper kilning then suspends the enzymes, which then lie dormant until properly hydrated and in the appropriate temperature and pH range.

Common Mash Rests

The mash programs a brewer selects will consist of one or more mash rests, typically chosen from the following list:

Protein rest. Designed to allow proteolytic enzymes to work, principally proteases and peptidases (there are many types of each). These generally work in the range 104 to 140° F (40 to 60° C), but are most active between 122 and 131° F (50 and 55° C). Avoid 122° F (50° C) with well-modified malts; a rest at that temperature favors creation of amino acids (which the maltster has likely done already) at the expense of medium-weight molecular proteins[2]. A rest at 122° F (50° C) can be appropriate with undermodified malts or with starchy adjuncts. A short rest (10-20 minutes) at around 131° F (55° C) can help reduce chill haze and improve head retention by developing medium-weight molecular proteins. I find that I can skip this with British and American malts, but that German and Belgian malts (especially Pils malt) can benefit from this rest. When I use a protein rest, it is most commonly at 131° F (55° C) for 10-15 minutes.

β-amylase rest. This is the primary saccharification (sugar-producing) rest. It generates the highly fermentable disaccharide *maltose*. A lower pH mash will improve wort fermentability and extract, since β-amylase works best in the pH

---

[1] A mash rest at 95-113° F (35-45° C) to help break down viscous gums, which could cause lautering and clarity problems, and to improve extraction.

[2] Medium-weight molecular proteins help contribute body to beer and (in particular) provide good head retention. Degrading these proteins too much will result in beer that tastes thin and insipid.

5.0 to 5.6 range—5.3 is best, in my opinion. The β-amylase enzyme is active in the 131 to 150° F (55-66° C) range, and 142 to 146° F or 61 to 63° C is optimal. It creates maltose by snipping maltose molecules off the ends of longer-chain starches (the straight-chain *amylose* and the branched *amylopectin*). Longer rests in the lower temperature range can create highly fermentable wort, although the amylopectins won't be fully reduced.

α-amylase rest. The other saccharification rest produces dextrins (unfermentable sugars), and works best in the 154 to 162° F (68-72° C) range with a higher pH (5.1 to 5.9). The α-amylase rest is used to build body in the beer or to provide a higher finishing gravity. α-amylase is active over a fairly wide temperature range, but it works somewhat slower than β-amylase.

Lauter rest (mash-out). Normally performed at 168 to 170° F (76-77° C). This isn't a step where enzymatic activity is being encouraged—it is the point where all mash enzymes will be denatured. If no enzymes are active, then the wort composition is fixed and will not continue to change. The other benefit of this rest is that it dissolves the wort sugars to facilitate lautering.

Other rests. There are some other mash rests that may be used for certain beer styles or when using specific ingredients:

- *Weizen* beers may benefit from a short (10-minute) *ferulic acid rest* at the 111 to 115° F (44-46° C) range (113° F or 45° C is optimal) to develop ferulic acid, which is metabolized by *weizen* yeast to produce the clovelike 4-vinyl guaiacol.

- Beers with a lot of starchy adjuncts (unmalted or flaked wheat, rye, oats) may benefit from a *β-glucanase rest* (98-113° F or 37-45° C, 20 minutes) and a short protein rest at 122° F (50° C) to help break down some of the gummy bits.

- Traditional mash programs with undermodified malts may have used an *acid rest* at 86 to 126° F (30-52° C) to develop *phytase*, which would lower mash pH. Virtually all brewers today achieve the same result using water treatments or acidulated malt; there is no need to worry about acid rests.

Doughing-In

The process of initially combining the milled grain with the strike water is called *doughing-in*. It can also be called *mashing-in*, but that tends to gloss over the importance of this step. The real reason for performing the step is to properly hydrate the starches in the crushed malt, which leads to increased mash efficiency. To dough-in, combine the crushed grain with the strike water, thoroughly stirring to get the grain uniformly wet. It's important to avoid clumping (or balling) of the grain, since those starches won't get converted. It's a good idea to avoid excessive aeration when stirring to avoid oxidizing the mash.

The thickness of the mash (expressed in terms of water-to-grist ratio) is more important for getting a uniform temperature distribution in the mash, facilitating stirring, and protecting enzymes than it is for increasing wort fermentability. With today's well-modified malts, mash thickness has little impact on fermentability. A thicker mash can better protect the enzymes, since the thin liquid portion of the mash is where the enzymes are concentrated. A thinner mash, using rice hulls, and increased stirring can help even out temperature distribution throughout the mash tun. You'd be surprised how much the temperature can vary within your mash—get a long probe thermometer and check for yourself. I particularly like the idea of adding rice hulls, since it not only helps even out the mash temperature, it also gives you additional insurance for a smooth lauter.

English brewers traditionally used a thicker mash (1.0 to 1.25 quarts per pound, 2.1 to 2.6 liters per kilogram) since they used a single unheated vessel as a combined mash/lauter tun. A stiffer mash is harder to stir but allows infusions to be used without overly diluting the mash. German brewers traditionally used thinner mashes (1.75 to 2.5 quarts per pound, 3.7 to 5.3 liters per kilogram) with their directly heated systems, often using decoction, pumping, and stirring systems. German brewers also tend to use a thinner mash for lighter-colored beers than for dark beers. I find 1.5 quarts per pound (3.2 liters per kilogram) to be a good compromise for the homebrewer, maybe bumping it up somewhat if decocting. If I'm using limited sparging (batch sparging or no-sparge), I often use a thinner mash.

If you are going to use a protein rest, doughing-in at 122° F (50° C) or 131° F (55° C) is appropriate. However, with today's highly modified malts, doughing-in above the protein rest temperature is more desirable, since you don't want to risk reducing the head-forming and body-building proteins. Most homebrewers prefer to dough-in at the primary saccharification temperature for most beer styles.

Single-Infusion Mash

A *single-infusion mash* (or single-step mash) is the traditional English way of brewing, and is most popular among modern craft brewers and homebrewers for most beer styles made with well-modified malt. It uses one mash rest only in the saccharification temperature range. Rather than doing separate β-amylase and α-amylase rests, the single-infusion mash uses a combined saccharification rest in the 148° F (64° C) to 158° F (70° C) range (most commonly in the 151-154° F or 66-68° C range). This allows both diastatic enzymes to work.

Targeting the lower end of the temperature range (150° F or 66° C and less) produces a beer with less body, more fermentability, and thus higher potential alcohol. Mashing at the higher end of the single infusion range (156° F or 69° C and up) produces a chewier, sweeter beer due to the increased quantity of dextrins. Adjusting the mash temperature is one way of controlling the attenuation of the beer (another way is using more or less dextrinous malts). A higher mash temperature will tend to produce a beer with a higher apparent extract or final gravity, and thus lower alcohol.

The single-infusion mash is the fastest, easiest, and most economical mashing technique. It uses the least amount of energy and equipment and is well suited to a variety of mash tun designs. Basically anything that is moderately well insulated, can hold the entire mash volume, and can withstand the mash temperature is fine. When I first started brewing all-grain, I mashed in a rectangular picnic cooler and transferred the mash to another cooler with a false bottom for lautering. Now I use a three-vessel, half-barrel system with a combined mash/lauter tun. Both work fine, although I prefer the newer system, since I can directly heat the mash tun. When using a picnic cooler for mashing, it's important to calculate your water volumes and temperatures properly, since it's difficult to raise the temperature of the mash once in the cooler.

When using modern well-modified malt, the single-infusion mash is quite logical. The maltster has already done much of the work for you. Your control points are mostly the mash temperature and rest time but also the mash thickness. I tend to use about 1.5 quarts per pound (3.2 liters per kilogram) water-to-grist for most beers and have started using some rice hulls (1 pound/454 grams per 5-gallon/19-liter batch) to help keep an even mash temperature. (Thanks to Mike McDole for that suggestion.)

The mash pH should be in the 5.2 to 5.5 range with a target of about 5.3. Note that mash pH is measured at mash temperatures, not cooled. If you cool the mash, the pH will read about 0.35 higher than at mash temperature. Most pH strips are designed for room temperature, but some pH meters will work with higher temperatures. Read the instructions to make sure you don't ruin your equipment. ColorpHast strips in the narrow range (4.0 to 7.0) work well for brewing but are designed to be used at room temperature (68° F/20° C), so remember to subtract 0.3 from the reading to get the pH at mash temperatures. Given a choice, good pH meters are always more accurate than strips and rely less on a subjective appraisal of color, (which can introduce quite a bit of error and are impacted by lighting conditions). A good bench-type pH meter is a solid investment and should be something every advanced brewer considers owning.

All this talk of mash pH probably has you thinking this is complicated and requires a lot of fiddling. Actually, it doesn't. For the most part, the mash pH regulates itself, as long as your water is reasonable. Calcium in the water reacts with phosphates in the grain husks to release phytic acid, which lowers the mash pH naturally. We'll talk about this more when we discuss water, but as long as your water has some calcium and isn't excessively high in carbonates, you'll likely be fine. Measuring mash pH is not something you have to do regularly unless you're trying something unusual, you aren't sure of your ingredients, or you are trying to troubleshoot a problem. Once you understand your water profile and water treatments, you likely won't worry about mash pH at all.

Mash Temperatures, Final Gravity, and Maltsters

Different malts have different degrees of modification and diastatic power (ability to convert starch to sugar). Because of these differences, brewers may get different results when switching base malts and even maltsters. Brewers typically use mash temperatures to control the amount of dextrins in the beer and the final gravity (apparent extract) target. However, the same mash temperature could give different results based on whether you're using Brewer's two-row malt or Maris Otter, for example. You may also see differences between maltsters, say Crisp Maris Otter versus Munton Maris Otter.

Since barley is an agricultural product, it can vary from season to season or year to year. Maltsters will use their own quality standards and shouldn't pass along inferior grain, but you can encounter differences. There can even be lot-by-lot variation (particularly in floor-malted grain), although maltsters should try to adjust their processes to minimize these differences.

Brewers cannot always predict how their malt will perform, so it's best to pay attention to the details and keep careful notes. If you notice differences in your target beer from batch to batch, check to see if you used a different maltster, type of malt, or malt from a different lot or year. It might not be your process; it could be your ingredients. My best advice is to find certain types of malt and maltsters that you prefer based on taste and availability, and then understand how they perform. Adjust your recipes accordingly to hit your target results.

Step Mash

The *step mash* (or step-infusion mash) is a variation of the single-infusion mash using two or more mash rests. The steps are always done in the same mash tun and are always progressively increasing in temperature. The change in temperature may be accomplished either with an infusion of boiling water or through direct heating of the mash tun. This technique is frequently used by modern German brewers instead of a decoction mash to give German lagers that malty-but-attenuated character.

The step mash allows higher attenuation and mash efficiency, particularly in grists containing starchy adjuncts or not fully modified malts. This mash method doesn't require any more equipment than a single-infusion mash, but it does take more time. If direct heating of the mash tun is being done, it's helpful to recirculate the wort to avoid scorching and to even out the temperature throughout the mash. This is the principle behind the Recirculating Infusion Mash System (RIMS), which can be done easily with a pump if your mash tun can be heated.

Personally, I like to use this technique in *altbier, Kölsch*, Belgian ales, and sometimes IPAs and double IPAs. I also like to use it combined with a decoction mash to speed up the brew day, so it may show up in my lagers as well. Anytime I'm using starchy adjuncts, such as in an oatmeal stout, I'll add a protein rest as a mash step. I would not use a step mash with highly modified malts, particularly English malts.

There are many possibilities for steps, depending on what you want to accomplish. The step mash technique allows you to select a specific step for a given purpose, so choose from the list depending on your recipe objective. I will often do a step mash at 131° F (55° C) and then at 149 to 155° F (65-68° C) when brewing with Pils malt. When I want an attenuated German lager and don't feel like decocting, I'll generally use 131-145-158° F (55-63-70° C). In almost all my recipes, I use a step to mash-out at 170° F (77° C).

A modern German brewing practice is to use a *Hochkurz* (high short) mash. Mash-in around 145° F (63° C; but 142-146° F [61-63° C] will work), then hold for 30 to 40 minutes. Step up to 158° F (70° C), and hold for 30 to 50 minutes. Mash-out at 168 to 170° F (76-77° C) for 20 minutes. Use a water-to-grist ratio of 2 quarts per pound (4.2 liters per kilogram). This is very much like what I use, except I often add a 10- to 15-minute rest at 131° F (55° C). It's a good alternative to using a decoction mash.

Step Mashing for Attenuation Technique

For a long time, I didn't really like Belgian *tripels*. I found them too heavy, sweet, and boozy. But then I went to Belgium and learned what they really should taste like. Many American microbreweries don't seem to understand that a *tripel* needs to be highly attenuated and fairly bitter—it's not a pale Belgian barley wine. Here is my version, which was inspired by my favorite beer from the trip, *La Rulle's Tripel*. Step mashing and the use of 20 percent sugar provide the attenuation.

Tripwire—Belgian Tripel

Makes 6.5 gallons (24.6 liters)

15 lbs. (6.8 kg) Dingeman Pils malt
1 lb. (454 g) Durst Vienna malt
4 lbs. (1.8 kg) white beet sugar
1 oz. (28 g) Newport whole hops, 9.8% alpha acid, at 60 min.
1 oz. (28 g) Newport whole hops, 9.8% alpha acid, at 30 min.

1 oz. (28 g) Amarillo whole hops, 7% alpha acid, at 10 min.

1 oz. (28 g) Styrian Goldings whole hops, 4% alpha acid, at 5 min.

White Labs Bastogne yeast, WLP510

Step: 131° F (55° C) for 15 minutes, 138° F (59° C) for 15 minutes, 145° F (63° C) for 45 minutes, 157° F (69° C) for 15 minutes, 168° F (76° C) for 10 minutes. I step using slow, direct heating of the mash tun with recirculation.

Use RO water treated with ½ tsp. calcium chloride and ½ tsp. calcium sulfate in the mash. Adjust RO water for sparging with phosphoric acid to pH 5.5. Batch sparge, draining first runnings, refilling, then draining enough to collect preboil volume.

Start fermentation at 62° F (17° C), and let rise to wherever it wants to go. Rouse yeast if necessary to get full attenuation.

Collect 8.5 gallons (32.2 liters).

Boil 90 min.

FV: 6.5 gallons (24.6 liters)

OG: 1.080

FG: 1010

9.1% ABV

Decoction Mash

The final mash technique is the *decoction mash,* the most complicated, time consuming, and resource-intensive program. It's a traditional German and Czech method for developing a more elegant, refined malt flavor with better efficiency when using undermodified malts. The technique uses more vessels, since a decoction (a removed portion of the mash) must be heated separately from the main mash. The decoction is heated, rested, and boiled, which creates rich flavors and a darker color. It is then recombined with the main mash to cause a temperature increase, similar to a step mash. Decoction mashes always involve multiple rest temperatures. Decoction mash programs typically involve one, two, or three decoctions, and are called single- , double- , and triple-decoction mashes.

Boiling the mash encourages the *Maillard reaction,* which creates Maillard products (complex, richly flavored compounds—like the end piece of roast beef) and *melanoidins* (brown-colored but flavorless substances). Note that this is not the same as *caramelization,* a related process involving the melting and browning of sugar. The Maillard reaction involves amino acids (which contain nitrogen, coming from malt or proteins), reducing sugars[3], moisture, and heat. Sugars are carbohydrates and don't contain nitrogen.

Decoction mashing is good for undermodified malts but also for malts without a lot of diastatic power, such as Munich malt. Decoction mashing takes the malt through saccharification temperature rests multiple times, and also boils grain, thus bursting starch granules and making the starches more accessible to enzymes. A higher temperature rest for the initial decoction can also result in more attenuation, since the α-amylase enzyme is more active at higher temperatures and pH ranges (breaking down complex starches into dextrins gives more surface area for the β-amylase enzymes to work once the mashes are recombined).

Many people believe that you can get flavors identical to those developed during decoction mashing by grist reformulation: for example, using a higher percentage of Vienna or Munich-Type malts, by adding aromatic or melanoidin malt, or by limited use of caramel malts. However, there is more to matching the style than simply cloning the flavor profile. Single-step mashing won't always sufficiently break down the branched amylopectin starches. If you change the malts trying to match a decoction flavor profile, you may wind up with a beer that has more body or sweetness than you intended. You may also need to change the mash program—for example, using a step mash to get the right attenuation.

I happen to believe that decoction mashing does make a difference, and that it helps to make beers maltier but drier. I like getting better attenuation without sacrificing malt flavor. I also think it's fairly important in my German wheat beers (where it breaks down complex starches) and beers with a high percentage of Munich malt (where full conversion could be an issue). But you can certainly get similar flavors by playing around with the grist. I have done that as well when I don't have the time for a decoction mash. I find that I tend to combine step mashing with decoction mashing to try to get the flavor benefits of decoction with the time savings of a step mash.

If your goal is to boost the malt flavors in your beer, you have more than these two choices. You could do both; you can add aromatic or melanoidin malt and decoct. Be careful about trying to develop too many Maillard products; I've

---

[3] A reducing sugar is a sugar that contains an aldehyde or ketone group. Reducing sugars cause chemical compounds to be reduced during a redox reaction. Examples of reducing sugars meaningful in beer include glucose, fructose, and maltose. Most significantly, sucrose (table sugar) is not a reducing sugar.

judged some beers that have an almost beef brothlike flavor that I associate with overdecocting, or using too much darker Munich-type malt. Another technique you may wish to try for boosting maltiness is the no-sparge technique. I think that gives a bigger flavor boost than decocting. Of course, no-sparge is a lauter technique, so it can be combined with any of the mashing methods to vary the final malt profile. So you have three choices for increasing maltiness that can be used independently: grist reformulation, decoction, and no-sparge. Try them all for the ultimate in maltiness.

Now that we've discussed the results and alternatives to decocting, let's look at how it's actually done. Decoction mashing involves hitting certain rest temperatures, and there are often two separate components being heated to different rest temperatures. Multiple decoctions can be performed during a mash program. When pulling decoctions, always pull a thick decoction (i.e., separate out the grain portion of the mash) except for the last one. The enzymes are found in the thin, watery portion of the mash, so you want to retain these in the main mash to protect them from being denatured by higher temperatures in the decoction. The grain contains the amino acids, and thus will form the Maillard reaction products and melanoidins. The main mash in a decoction mash program is thinner than typical mashes, about 2 quarts per pound (4.2 liters per kilogram). The thick decoction won't be dry; it should have a consistency similar to an English single-infusion mash (1.25 quarts per pound/2.6 liters per kilogram).

Decoction and Tannins

Some people wonder why grains can be boiled in a decoction without extracting harsh, astringent tannins. After all, aren't we told that sparging with hot water will do exactly that? This is where pH comes into the equation. The pH of the mash is well below 6.0 (typically in the 5.2 to 5.5 range), which prevents the tannins from leaching out. So you can boil your mash as much as you like and not get harshness (unless you scorch it, but that's another issue entirely).

When pulling a thick decoction, don't worry about squeezing out water—you need to have some liquid in the decoction to keep it from scorching. I use a 2- to 3-quart, short kitchen saucepan for this step. Scoop the decoction like you're trying to get all the good parts out of a big pot of soup, letting most of the liquid drain out; however, the first scoops should have more liquid in them. You can use brewing software to calculate the size of the decoction to pull, although it's somewhat difficult to measure. I normally use about 33 to 40 percent of the mash for the thick decoction and whatever liquid I can get as the thin decoction. Rather than scooping the thin decoction, I drain it from my combo mash/lauter tun. When scooping the grain, try to avoid excessive splashing and aeration.

Don't preheat the pot where you will be boiling the decoction; you don't want the grains to sear and stick when transferred. You will need to keep stirring constantly once you start heating the pot, so don't turn on the heat until the transfer is done. Watch out for grain sticking to the bottom of the pot—you can usually feel if it's happening with your spoon (wooden or metal). Heat slowly to avoid scorching, maybe raising the decoction 2 to 4° F (1-2° C) per minute. If the grain starts sticking, back off the heat and add a little water (pH adjusted to 5.5) and keep stirring. When the grain boils, the bubbles rising from the decoction can splash around—be careful, it burns!

Common decoction mash programs:

- Single decoction, boiling thin. Mash-in at 131° F (55° C). Step to 149° F (65° C) to 158° F (70° C). Pull thin decoction, boil, remix to hit 168° F (76° C). Use with well-modified malt where minimal color development is desired.

- Single decoction, boiling thick. Mash-in at 131° F (55° C). Pull thick decoction, step to 158° F, rest, boil, remix to hit 149° F (65° C) to 158° F (70° C). Step to 168° F (76° C) to mash-out. Use for fairly well-modified malt or where additional color and flavor is wanted.

- Double decoction, traditional. Mash-in at 122° F (50° C) to 133° F (56° C). Pull thick decoction, step to 158° F (70° C), rest, bring to boil, remix to hit 149° F (65° C) to 158° F (70° C). Pull thin decoction, boil, remix to hit 168° F (76° C). Use with undermodified malts or starchy adjuncts, or if you want even more flavor and color.

- Double decoction, *Hochkurz*. Mash-in at 131° F (55° C). Step to 142° F to 146° F (61 to 63° C). Pull thick decoction, step to 158° F (70°

C), boil, remix to hit 158° F (70° C). Pull thin decoction, boil, remix to hit 168° F (76° C). Fine for most beers today. I usually follow this program, although I often step to 170° F (77° C) rather than boiling a thin decoction.

- Triple decoction. Mash in at 97° F (36° C). Pull thick decoction, step to 158° F (70° C), boil, remix to hit 122° F (50° C). Pull thick decoction, step to 158° F (70° C), boil, remix to hit 149° F (65° C) to 158° F (70° C). Pull thin decoction, boil, remix to hit 168° F (76° C). Old school, for sure. Only use with undermodified malts when trying to replicate a classic style that was traditionally triple decocted, such as Bohemian Pilsener or Munich *dunkel*.

In these mash programs, the length of the decoction rests and the main saccharification temperature are not specified, since they are style-dependent. Most decoction rests (including the boil) are usually 10 to 15 minutes in length, although they could be longer in the boil if more color development is needed. Paler beers may use shorter boils. The primary conversion temperature will be based on the desired body and final gravity in the finished beer, higher temperatures giving more body. The time spent resting or boiling the decoction is usually less than it takes to slowly heat the decoction to the rest temperature—that's what takes the most time in a decoction mash program.

Personally, I almost always decoct my German lagers and wheat beers. Joe Formanek told me that he likes to use decoction on nontraditional styles to get a different malt profile. It's certainly fun to experiment.

Hochkurz Double Decoction Mash Technique

This is probably the first lager I ever brewed, based on a recipe from Brian St. Clair. I asked for the recipe after scoring it a 48 at the Ohio State Fair in 1998. He suggested the high-temperature decoction mashing technique as a compromise between getting a well-developed malt flavor and getting done in a reasonable amount of time. It's become one of my standard methods, sometimes modified by adding a short 131° F (55° C) protein rest to improve clarity. Thanks also to Ted Holloway, who first brewed this with me and demonstrated the proper decoction technique.

Procrastinator—Doppelbock

Recipe for 5 gallons (19 liters)

5.25 lbs. (2.4 kg) Weyermann dark Munich malt

5.25 lbs. (2.4 kg) Durst light Munich malt

5.5 lbs. (2.5 kg) Weyermann Pils malt

1 lb. (454 g) Durst CaraMunich malt

1 lb. (454 g) DWC CaraVienne malt

1 lb. (454 g) DWC CaraPils malt

½ lb. (227 g) Crisp crystal 80° L malt

1.4 oz. (40 g) Crystal pellet hops, 3.2% alpha acid, at 60 min.

1.8 oz. (51 g) German Tettnang whole hops, 2.8% alpha acid, at 60 min.

Wyeast 2206

4 gal. (15.1 L) spring water (moderate carbonates) + 3.3 gal. (12.5 L) RO water (or all RO water with 1 tsp. $CaCO_3$)

Dough-in at 144° F (62° C). Rest 20 minutes.

Pull one-third thick decoction, boil 15 minutes.

Remix, hit 154° F (68° C). Rest 45 minutes.

Boil thin part of mash 10 minutes.

Remix, hit 170° F (77° C) for mash-out.

Recirculate until clear.

Sparge with RO water treated with ½ tsp. phosphoric acid.

40-minute lauter.

Collect 8 gallons (30.3 liters).

90-minute boil.

Ferment at 48° F (9° C) for 6 weeks., Rack, lager 2 months minimum.

OG: 1.087

FG: 1.019

8.9% ABV

Step and Decoction
Mashing Techniques Combined

I've been using decoction mashes for *hefeweizens* since I first read Eric Warner's *German Wheat Beer* Classic Styles Series book. This recipe is a variation of one I've been using for at least the last ten years. It combines step mashing with a single decoction. I've also done this one as a double decoction, but I try to keep the boil time on decoctions down, because I don't want too much color development. This beer took a gold medal in the 2009 AHA NHC finals.

El Hefe German—Hefeweizen

Recipe for 5.5 gallons (20.8 liters)

6 lbs. (2.7 kg) Durst wheat malt

4 lbs. (1.8 kg) Durst Pils malt

$^2/_3$ oz. (19 g) Sterling whole hops, 6.2% alpha acid, at 60 min.

Wyeast 3068

Using RO water, add 1 tsp. calcium chloride to mash. Dough-in at 111° F (44° C), and hold for 15 minutes. Step to 131° F (55° C), and rest 10 minutes. Pull thick decoction and slowly heat to 158° F (70° C), and rest 20 minutes, then bring to a boil and boil 10 minutes, stirring constantly. Meanwhile, ramp up main mash to 149° F (65° C) and hold. Recombine to hit 158° F (70° C). Rest for 10 minutes. Mash-out at 170° F (77° C). Sparge, collecting 7 gallons (26.5 liters). Boil 90 minutes. Chill to 58° F (14° C) before oxygenating and pitching. Ferment at 65° F (18° C).

OG: 1.050

FG: 1.014

4.7% ABV

Handling Dark Grains

Brewing with dark grains is in many ways like brewing coffee. There are many kinds of coffeemakers—percolators, drip filter, French press, espresso machines—which all handle coffee differently. Those that expose coffee to higher heat over a greater period of time tend to produce coffee that is more bitter, acrid, and acidic. There is a big difference in quality between coffee that has been sitting around for hours on an electric hot plate and coffee freshly made through a drip filter that is then stored in a vacuum-insulated carafe. Dark grains are much the same; longer exposure to higher temperatures results in increased bitterness, acidity, and harshness.

Dark, roasted grains and malts—such as chocolate malt, black patent malt, and roasted barley—do not need to be mashed. The high roasting temperatures denature the enzymes and break down the proteins and starches. The grains can simply be steeped to release their character. If dark roasted grains are included in the mash, they aren't really being mashed—there is nothing left to convert. The mash is essentially a long, high-temperature steep of the dark grains. There are several options for using dark grains and malts, including the traditional mash, adding them during the vorlauf (recirculation step), and steeping them.

Traditional mash. In the traditional mash, dark grains are milled and mashed along with the rest of the grist. They are not treated differently at all. This approach can lead to harsher, more astringent flavors in the finished beer, particularly if the water chemistry isn't handled properly (alkaline water, high bicarbonates, pH is too high). However, dark grains can serve a useful purpose if your brewing water has high levels of carbonates; the higher acidity in the darker grains will help lower the mash pH. Regardless, the dark grains are exposed to the most heat during this method, and that can lead to a harsher bitterness in the finished beer.

Adding at vorlauf. Rather than keeping the dark grains with the rest of the grist, they can be milled separately and added during the vorlauf (recirculation). By waiting until the mash is complete and adding the grains at mash-out, the long, hot steep during the mash is avoided. The husk material is not kept in contact with hot water for very long, which removes the main source of astringency. The recirculation process also helps derive the character from the dark grain in a manner similar to a drip coffee maker. However, the liquid extracted from the dark grain will still be boiled with the rest of the wort, which can provide some harshness.

Crystal malts can also be added at this time. There is no real disadvantage to mashing crystal malts, although some may prefer to add the more highly kilned crystal malts (greater than 100° Lovibond, 197 EBC) along with the darker grains.

Steeping. I first learned of this method from an article by Mary Anne Gruber of Briess Malting. The method is intriguing, since it has such strong parallels to coffee making. The process begins with the dark grains being milled separately from the rest of the grist; they can even be finely ground. The steeping options to consider are a hot steep, a cold steep with no boil, and a cold steep with a short boil.

The mix ratio for all methods is 1 pound (454 grams) grain to 2 quarts (1.9 liters) water. The water should be like any other water you'd use for brewing—clean, good-tasting, and not containing any chlorine. I use reverse osmosis (RO) water, but filtered water (as through a Brita) would also work well. The extract yield is about what you'd see from mashing—roughly 45 to 50 percent.

Hot steeping is almost like making coffee. The ground dark grains are mixed with 165° F (74° C) water and steeped for five minutes, then strained using a fine mesh bag, a coffee filter, a kitchen strainer, or a chinois. If not using immediately, chill in an ice bath, cover, and refrigerate. The dark grain extract can be added to the wort in the fermenter.

Cold steeping takes more time. The dark grains are mixed with cold water and left at room temperature for a full day. They are then strained as with the hot steeped grains. The dark grain extract can be made in advance and chilled, then added to the fermenter when needed.

Cold steeping with a short boil is like cold steeping, except the dark grain extract is added to the brew kettle during the last 5 to 10 minutes of the boil. Obviously, the extract would have to be made in advance.

Tasting results from Briess indicated that black malt tasted best using the cold-steeping method, while roasted barley tasted best with both the hot steep and the cold steep with a short boil method. I know from experience that roasted barley treated with only the cold-steeping method has a flavor like cold coffee, which isn't as appealing as the other methods.

The amount of dark grain extract that can be added to your beer can be precisely controlled. You can add it in batches, and see how well the flavor balance and color work. Using the hot steep or cold steep methods allows you to use the dark grain extract at any time, even after fermentation is complete. Just be careful about introducing oxygen if you do it this way.

The dark grain extract is stable, so it can be made in advance and stored. Any left over from a batch of brewing can be saved as well. Simply heat to 150° F (66° C), chill, cover, and refrigerate in a mason jar.

Steeping the grains and avoiding most of the boil results in less astringency and harshness, less acidity, and a little less color. The downside is that another process must be managed, and you have to blend the products to taste. This is one of my favorite methods for making darker beers that don't have a high level of roasty bitterness, such as sweet stout, *schwarzbier,* and oatmeal stout.

Cold-Steeped Roasted Grains Technique

Sweet stout is a style that features a large dark-grain character without the associated roasted harshness. This is based on a recipe I originally got from Rick Georgette, but I cranked it up a bit to give it a higher starting gravity. I've also used this beer as the base for a braggot made with buckwheat honey.

Headlights On Sweet—Stout

10-gallon (37.9-liter) recipe

19 lbs. (8.6 kg) Maris Otter malt
2 lbs. (907 g) Quaker Oats
2 lbs. (907 g) crystal 60° L malt
1 lb. (454 g) CaraPils malt
1 lb. (454 g) flaked barley
½ lb. (227 g) Briess Special Roast malt
1½ lbs. (608 g) Munton's roasted barley
¾ lb. (340 g) Weyermann Carafa III malt
¾ lb. (340 g) Munton's chocolate malt
¼ lb. (113 g) Briess black patent malt
2 lbs. (907 g) lactose, last 15 min. of boil
3 oz. (85 g) East Kent Goldings whole hops, 5.9% alpha acid, at 60 min.
Wyeast 1968

OG: 1.072

FG: 1.024

About 30 IBU

About 6% ABV

Cold steep dark grains (roast, Carafa, chocolate, black) in 8-quart (7.6-liter) pot using RO water. Steep 24 hours. Strain carefully. Yields about 1 gallon (3.8 liters) liquid.

Mash remaining grains at 154° F (68° C) for 1¼ hours using RO water with 1 tsp. calcium carbonate and 2 tsp. calcium chloride. Sparge with RO water treated with phosphoric acid to pH 5.5. Collect 12.5 gallons (47.3 liters). Boil hard 90 min. FV: 10.5 gallons. Add dark liquid at 5 minutes. Wait 5 minutes after knockout. Force chill, oxygenate. Ferment at 70-72° F (21-22° C).

Unusual Technique: The Overnight Oven Mash
by *Joe Formanek*

Basically, this process was developed to help split up the day to allow family time, while at the same time being able to keep up with a busy brewing schedule. Brew when the kids go to bed, and finish up early the next day.

I am fortunate in that, after our second daughter, Hannah, was born in 2002, we built another kitchen in the basement to allow me to be able to brew year-round without impacting the normal function of our regular kitchen.

The mashing step is as you would normally conduct the process—infusion, step infusion, single, double, or triple decoction—it doesn't matter. Personally, I use an oven to hold the mash at conversion temperature, using 8-gallon (30.3-liter) canning pots for my mash kettles, which fit in the oven nicely. Of course, an oven typically doesn't hold temperatures much below 150° F (66° C), so for temperatures below those for conversion, such as when using step conversion or multiple decoctions, I just keep the kettle on the stove and adjust the temp accordingly.

The boiling step is also the same as you would do with a normal brewing process. However, the difference is in the middle. Once you complete the mash, you just mash-out and collect the sparge for boiling some hours later. Considering the temperature of the wort at this point (about 175° F or 79° C), and the amount present (5+ gallons, 19 liters), the heat capacity of that amount of liquid keeps the temperature of the wort quite high for an extended period of time. You can use that to your advantage, being able to safely wait to boil for an extended period of time—in this instance, overnight!

After 7 to 8 hours, the temperature of the wort decreases to around 120° F (49° C). Over most of that time period, the temperature is significantly above that, maintaining an environment inhospitable to microbial growth. If there is some inoculation when the wort is at lower temps, that threat is neutralized by the boil, giving you a wort as clean as if it were boiled immediately after the sparge.

This process can also give some advantages when conducting more time-consuming processes during the boil, such as multiple-decoction mashes or caramelization of wort for beers such as Scottish ales and wee heavies. You are able to split up the time necessary to conduct the complete brewing process while using these time-consuming techniques, making the overall process seem less daunting. Having this extra time also helps greatly when that inevitable stuck sparge occurs due to ingredient experimentation! Bananas, pumpkin, and potatoes can certainly gum up the works!! Just let it drain overnight, and you're ready to boil that wacky wort the next morning like you would any other brew.

Lautering

Lautering is the process that filters sweet wort from spent grain; think of it as the "straining" or "separating" step. Many confuse lautering with sparging—they are *not* the same thing. *Sparging* is the rinsing of the grains; think of "spraying" or "sprinkling" as the translation. Sparging is often used as part of lautering, but it is not always required. If a dedicated brewing vessel is used for this step, the container is called the lauter tun. On some systems, the mash tun does double duty in this role. The lauter tun is the one piece of brewing equipment where a false bottom (or similar screenlike device) is essential.

Lautering is performed after the mash is complete, the desired sugar composition is fixed, and the mash is at the appropriate temperature (typically 168-170° F or 76-77° C, called the *mash-out*[4] temperature). The mash is typically in a vessel with a false bottom (mash tun or lauter tun). The sweet wort has been recirculated (vorlauf is the common brewing term for

[4] Some homebrewers skip the mash-out process at the expense of slightly reduced efficiency and a little more work in calculating sparge water temperatures.

this step) back through the mash until it is clear, which establishes the grain bed as a filter. Be sure to perform the vorlauf without excessive splashing to minimize oxygen uptake, which can cause the beer to prematurely lose its peak flavors.

Preparing to Sparge

Before you sparge, ensure that your mash is fully converted. If you have doubts, you can always perform an iodine test (careful: iodine is poisonous). Simply take a small sample of the mash liquid, taking care not to pick up any husks, and put it on a white plate. Place a few drops of iodine next to the liquid, then tilt the plate to allow the liquids to merge. Look for a color change; if you see any purple color, starch remains in the mash. Discard the test liquids; do not put them back in the mash. However, once you do a few mashes, it becomes much easier to just sense when it is done. Look at the liquid on the surface of the mash. Is it cloudy or clear? Completed mashes have a clear, bright (but dark) look, while starch will appear hazy, white, and reflective. Smell and taste the mash; a completed mash will be sweet. Once you learn these clues, you won't need to do iodine tests again.

Sparging involves gently rinsing the mash with hot water to dissolve the converted malt sugars so they can easily be run off. Sparge water should be at about 168 to 170° F (76-77° C) when it hits the lauter tun. If you lose heat during transfer, remember to raise the temperature of your hot liquor tank to compensate. Lower temperatures aren't as efficient in dissolving the sugars and don't fully denature the enzymes. Higher temperatures can extract unwanted flavors if the pH is also too high, and can burst starch granules (liberating starch with no enzymes present to convert it), causing a slower and more difficult lautering process.

Sparge water should be treated to have a pH lower than 5.8 to 6.0 (5.5 is a good choice) *at sparge temperature* to reduce the chances of extracting harsh and astringent tannins from the grain; pH has a *much* greater effect on tannin extraction than temperature. Some people mistakenly think adding gypsum to the sparge water will achieve this goal since gypsum "lowers pH." Gypsum only lowers pH in the mash by reacting with phosphates in the grain husks. It won't change the pH of brewing water at all. Use either the same water profile as your strike water, or use reverse osmosis (RO) water.

Adding phosphoric acid is the easiest way to lower the pH of sparge water without adding undesirable flavors. Lactic acid is a distant second choice. However, there is no simple formula for achieving this goal. It depends on the pH and alkalinity of your water. In general, it is easier to adjust water that contains fewer carbonates, since they tend to buffer pH changes. I use RO water and adjust it for my strike water, then save some for the sparge. Assuming I haven't added carbonates (which I rarely do), I find that ¼ teaspoon (1.25 milliliters) of phosphoric acid will lower the pH of 5 gallons/19 liters of RO water[5] at 77° F (25° C) from about 6.5 to 5.7. Test your water with a pH meter or test strips and find a dosage that achieves your desired pH target on your system, and then use that as your standard water treatment. Keep in mind that pH changes based on temperature, with the room temperature sample reading about 0.3 pH higher than the same sample at mash temperature and 0.4 pH higher at mash-out/sparge temperature. So a pH of 5.7 at 77° F (25° C) is like 5.4 at 149° F (65° C) and pH 5.3 at 169° F (76° C).

Lautering Options

The goal of lautering is to run off the sweet wort into the kettle, where the wort will be boiled and hops will be added. The method used to get the wort into the kettle is a decision point for the brewer: Will sparging be used, and if so, what technique? We examine the techniques of continuous sparging, partigyle brewing, batch sparging, and the no-sparge method.

Continuous sparging. The modern form of sparging involves adjusting the lauter tun runoff rate and the sparge rate, so as to maintain a constant, approximately one-inch layer of water on top of the mash. The runoff rate should not be too fast, since that encourages channeling through the grain bed. The lautering continues until the desired kettle volume is achieved. This is sparging as practiced by most professional breweries today, and it is sometimes called *fly sparging* or *continuous sparging*. Most brewers would just call this method "sparging," but we use the term "continuous sparging" to clearly differentiate it from the other techniques.

[5] When I performed this test, my RO water had 20-30 ppm of total dissolved solids (TDS), most likely carbonates, based on my water supply. I ran similar tests with other water samples. RO with 0 ppm TDS went from pH 6.1 to 4.1 with ½ tsp. phosphoric acid. RO with 120 ppm of TDS went from pH 7.4 to 7.1 with ½ tsp. phosphoric acid. I was using food-grade 10% phosphoric acid. When adding acid to water with carbonates, the acid will first neutralize the carbonate alkalinity (this is the "buffering" part of alkalinity) before lowering the pH. Note also how the pH of my source RO water varied as the amount of carbonates increases. This is likely due to how recently the RO machine was serviced. Note also how RO water with 0 ppm TDS is nearly in the desirable pH range for sparging; only minor adjustment is needed. I tend to use ¼ tsp. phosphoric acid per 5 gallons of RO water, then measure the pH to see if it is in an acceptable range (between 5.5 and 5.8).

Continuous sparging yields the highest efficiency of any lautering method, but it also tends to take the most time and requires careful monitoring of the runoff pH, the sparge water temperature, and the overall flow through the grain bed. Adjusting the sparge water pH to approximately 5.5 (or better yet, to the actual mash pH) greatly reduces the concern of oversparging. Channeling—where sparge water follows narrow paths through the grain bed—can occur, reducing efficiency. Sparging slowly and preemptively cutting a tight checkerboard pattern in the grain bed with a thin spatula can reduce this problem. Running off too quickly or using high proportions of gummy grains (oats, rye) can also compact the grain bed and cause a stuck sparge. Using rice hulls can help prevent this problem.

Parti-gyle brewing. The *parti-gyle* technique is a historical English brewing method in which the same mash is used to produce multiple worts, which might then be blended to create different beers. This came from the era when it was possible to build larger wooden mash tuns than direct-fired kettles. So the breweries of the time would produce two or three distinct beers from the same mash by sparging the mash and running off the sweet wort into different brew kettles for boiling. Brewers later learned to use this technique to more efficiently use their equipment to make a variety of products simultaneously. The highest-strength beers would be made exclusively from first runnings, while other beers would be made by blending the separate worts or beers in different proportions. The easiest way to remember it is this: brewing a single beer from a single mash is *gyle* (or *single-gyle*) brewing; brewing multiple beers from a single mash is *parti-gyle* brewing.

Homebrewers typically use parti-gyle brewing to produce two different beers: the first runnings are run off for the initial beer, and the second runnings are run off for a smaller beer. Anchor produces its *Small Beer* in this way from the second runnings of *Old Foghorn*. Historically, English brewers might have repeated the process a third time, although this seems like dubious advice for homebrewers to follow today, since third runnings contain very little sugar. Fuller's continues to use true parti-gyle techniques today to produce *Golden Pride, ESB, London Pride,* and *Chiswick Bitter*, which involve blending of the separate beers.

Since the grains used for the second runnings have already been mashed, the subsequent sparge water is simply used to rinse the grains to remove the remaining sugars. You may also add additional malts that don't need to be mashed at this point, such as crystal malts and roasted malts. The sparge water will dissolve their sugars and flavors and run them off along with the second runnings of the main mash. If I'm adding additional malts, I like to stop the lautering to give the sparge water a little time to dissolve the converted sugars, facilitating runoff. Remember, if you mix the mash, let rest for about 10 minutes, then vorlauf it to allow the grain bed to reform.

The parti-gyle technique is useful for making two or more different beers from a single mash, or for not letting converted sugars go to waste when making a high-gravity beer. If you use this method, carefully taste the wort and beer produced from the second runnings and see if it is to your taste. I find that it produces a beer with a pronounced grainy flavor, which I don't particularly like. Adding additional crystal and dark malts can help mask that flavor, but let your own palate be the judge. Perhaps this is why the English blended the various batches, to help provide additional maltiness and flavor to the smaller batches. In any event, batches made with a high proportion of second runnings might need to be blended to have a suitable flavor.

Parti-gyle beers may be sparged using a variety of techniques. Batch sparging is easiest, but continuous sparging is more efficient. When using parti-gyle techniques, the grains do not need to be "re-mashed"—all the conversion has already taken place. However, if the mash is capped with additional grains (crystal or roast), then continuous sparging is preferred, unless the grains are mixed in and allowed to rest a bit to let the sugars dissolve before lautering.

If you do intend to blend batches, consider blending the wort either before or after boiling rather than the beer after fermentation. The first and second runnings have a different composition, and not just of sugars. The various salts, lipids, proteins, and such can cause a poor break in the small batch, or a weak fermentation. However, you should experiment and see what works for you. My biggest advice is to avoid a pure second runnings beer, since I find that it has an unpleasantly grainy flavor. Either blend with the first runnings, or add additional malts during the second running sparge.

Parti-Gyle Technique Producing Two Beers

This parti-gyle recipe was the first batch I brewed on my current system from Pico Brewing. I was shooting for an English barley wine like *Thomas Hardy's Ale* with the first runnings, and a nice session English brown ale from the second runnings. The barley wine ages very well (mine is currently seven years old), but the session beer can be enjoyed right away. I also like using the parti-gyle technique for making a strong Scotch ale and a dark mild.

Seven-Year Itch—English Barley Wine

5-gallon (18.9-liter) recipe

31 lbs. (14.1 kg) Crisp Maris Otter malt
3 oz. (85 g) Northern Brewer whole hops, 8.5% alpha acid, at 60 min.
1 oz. (28 g) Challenger hop plugs, 7% alpha acid, at 30 min.
1 oz. (28 g) Fuggles whole hops, 4.5% alpha acid, at 10 min.
1 oz. (28 g) Crystal whole hops, 3.2% alpha acid, at 10 min.
Dry hop ½ oz. (14 g) Hallertauer
Dry hop ½ oz. (14 g) East Kent Goldings
Wyeast 1028
Use RO water with 1 tsp. calcium chloride and ½ tsp. calcium sulfate.
Mash 90 minutes at 150° F (66° C).
Mash-out at 170° F (77° C).
No-sparge, collect 8 gallons/30.3 liters at 1.082.
Boil fairly hard 120 minutes.
OG: 1.123
FG: 1.034
11.7% ABV

Session Slammer—Northern English Brown Ale

6.5-gallon (24.6-liter) recipe

1½ lbs. (680 g) Crisp crystal 80° L malt
¼ lb. (113 g) Crisp chocolate malt
¾ oz. (21 g) Northern Brewer whole hops, 8.5% alpha acid, at 60 min.
½ oz. (14 g) East Kent Goldings whole hops, 6.2% alpha acid, at 10 min.

Wyeast 1028

Add additional grains to previous mash.

Use 170° F (77° C) water, fill mash tun, steep 30 minutes.

Collect 7.5 gallons (28.4 liters) at 1.040.

Boil for 75 minutes.

OG: 1.046

FG: 1.012

4.5% ABV

Batch sparging. Many homebrewers use a variant of the parti-gyle method for sparging, called *batch sparging*. There are two basic ways of doing a batch sparge, and the choice is often dictated by the capacity of your lauter tun. The first version adds all the sparge water (at 5.5 pH) at once, hitting the mash-out temperature of 168 to 170° F (76-77° C). Stir the mash thoroughly, let it rest for about 10 minutes to allow the grain bed to form, vorlauf until clear, then run off into the brew kettle. You will need to determine the volume and temperature of the sparge water to hit your final desired kettle volume on your system. If you have already raised the mash to the mash-out temperature, it is easier to determine your sparge water temperature.

The second way of performing a batch sparge is almost exactly like parti-gyle brewing, except the first runnings and the second runnings are both sent to the same brew kettle. You can also combine the mash-out step with the first runnings by heating some of your sparge water (again, at 5.5 pH) to boiling, then adding it to the mash to hit the mash-out temperature. Mix, rest the mash for 10 minutes, vorlauf until clear, then run off normally. Meanwhile, heat the rest of the sparge water to a temperature that will allow it to be 170° F (77° C) when combined with the mash (that's 185° F or 85° C on my system). When the first runnings are run into the kettle, close the lauter tun valve and add the second batch of sparge water. Mix thoroughly and let rest for 10 minutes. Vorlauf until clear, then drain into the kettle. Proceed with the boil.

Batch sparging is preferred by many homebrewers, because it is relatively fast and is an easy process to control. The first approach requires a larger lauter tun that can hold the entire volume of sparge water. It also may make it more difficult to establish a grain bed and keep it from compacting due to the greater volume of water. The second approach might be of concern to some, since it exposes the grain bed to additional oxygen. This effect is likely minimal, but it can't be entirely discounted.

Batch sparging generally is less efficient than continuous sparging. You will likely need to adjust your recipes slightly to hit the same gravity targets. The effect will vary by systems and methods, but efficiency may be reduced by between 5 and 10 percentage points. Homebrewers may not find this a problem, but for professional brewers this represents lost profits.

No-sparge brewing. The final form of sparging is called the *no-sparge* method, in which you mash as normal (with a normal water-to-grist ratio, mashing-out with an infusion of boiling water or through direct heat), then simply drain the lauter tun into the kettle without sparging at all. This method will not likely give you sufficient preboil volume, unless you are making a very high-gravity beer. Simply make up any volume shortfall by adding brewing liquor (water prepared for brewing) directly to the kettle. Then proceed with the boil as normal. Using parti-gyle terminology, you are making a beer solely from first runnings. Anchor produces *Old Foghorn* barley wine and Fuller's makes *Golden Pride* barley wine in this manner.

This is the least efficient and most expensive (but fastest) method, requiring an increase in your grist of about 33 to 40 percent. However, the main benefit of this approach is that it yields a richer, more intense, higher-quality malt flavor with the least harshness of any technique. The resulting beer is also a little deeper in color and a little lower in acidity. This can be a useful approach when making a very special beer or a beer in which you are looking for the best possible malt flavor. Of course, you will also need to use the freshest, highest-quality malts when using this technique. No-sparge brewing maximizes malt flavor, but it can't create flavor that isn't already in the malt.

Determining your system efficiency when using the no-sparge method is a little tricky, since it depends on the mash thickness and the way mash-out is performed. It's best to measure the gravity and volume of your first runnings when complete to decide how much water to add and how to conduct your boil to hit your target gravity and volume. Once you have used the technique, calculate your actual efficiency and then use that number in your calculations for subsequent batches. Start first with a one-third increase in your grist, and see what numbers you achieve.

You can always sparge the mash to produce a second beer using the parti-gyle approach, if desired. This may be something you want to try when making large beers (like barley wines, Scotch ales, or imperial stouts) but may not be worth the effort if your primary beer is of average strength. You may not recover enough gravity points for making a full batch of beer, although you can always use the sparged wort for starters or for yeast storage. In general, the second runnings yield about half the gravity points of the first runnings.

No-Sparge Technique

This recipe was something I put together for the 2002 Real Ale Festival in Chicago, modeling it somewhat on Fuller's ESB. I put it in a pin cask and served it on hand pump. I was very happy to see several English gentlemen standing around my keg most of the evening. It came in fourth place in the People's Choice award, which Ray Daniels said was quite an accomplishment for a beer that wasn't "big or goofy." The WLP002 yeast is a wonderful choice for cask-conditioning; after rolling around in a van on a six-hour drive, the second pint pulled bright after letting it sit cold overnight.

Pride of Warwick—Strong Bitter

5.25-gallon (20-liter) recipe

13 lbs. (5.9 kg) Maris Otter malt
1/3 lb. (150 g) Victory malt
½ lb. (227 g) flaked maize
¾ lb. (340 g) Crisp crystal 80° L malt
1 oz. (28 g) black patent malt
1 oz. (28 g) East Kent Goldings whole hops, 4.5% alpha acid, FWH
½ oz. (14 g) Challenger plugs, 8.3% alpha acid, at 60 min.
½ oz. (14 g) Fuggles plugs, 4.6% alpha acid, at 30 min.
1 oz. (28 g) East Kent Goldings whole hops, 4.5% alpha acid, at 3 min.
1 oz. (28 g) Styrian Goldings pellets, 4% alpha acid, at whirlpool
White Labs WLP002 yeast

No-sparge method

Strike water: 10 gallons (37.9 liters) RO + 2 tsp. calcium sulfate + ½ tsp. calcium chloride + 2 tsp. calcium carbonate

Mash 90 minutes at 152° F (67° C).

Mash-out with 1 gallon (3.8 liters) boiling water.

Collect 6 gallons (22.7 liters) wort without sparging, dilute kettle volume to 9 gallons (34.1 liters) using RO water.

Boil hard for 90 minutes.

Collect 5.5 gallons (20.8 liters).

Ferment at 66° F (19° C).

OG: 1.052

FG: 1.016

4.7% ABV

Managing the Boil

Once the lauter is complete and the wort is in the brew kettle, boiling can commence. In general, the boil is a fairly simple process to manage, but I would like to mention the key control points and talk about a few useful tips and techniques. Note that a discussion of handling hops is done separately.

Skimming. Like a chef might clarify a stock, the brewer can remove impurities by skimming the wort as it comes to a boil. Depending on your system, you might prefer to have less hot break in the kettle. The foamy material—consisting mostly of proteins and unconverted starches liberated when the starch granules burst—can be skimmed off with a large slotted spoon and discarded. This helps reduce the chances of a boilover in addition to clarifying the wort.

Boilovers and break. I tend to avoid adding bittering hops before the break, since they can get bound up in the foam and contribute to a boilover. Yes, the tannins in the hops can help cause the hot break to form. So having some first wort hops is helpful, as is adding a few hops well before the wort is close to a boil. What you want to avoid is tossing in a large amount of hops when the wort is near boiling, since air in the wort is being driven off, and hops can provide nucleation points that cause a rapid release of bubbles (like sprinkling salt in beer). If the break hasn't happened yet, the proteins form a foamy cap that can keep in heat and exacerbate the problem. The proteins tend to become more frothy as the temperature rises and can expand tremendously in volume. If you don't have a lot of extra head space in your kettle, you'll have to watch it carefully. The froth seems to expand quickly right before collapsing; this is the visual indication that the hot break has occurred. Adding the hops after the break occurs might cause some additional foaming, but it shouldn't cause a boilover. Besides, I tend to use 75- to 90-minute boils and no more than 60-minute hop additions, so this schedule works well for me.

Controlling the boil. Managing the rate of boil has several important effects. The most obvious is making sure you don't boil so hard as to cause a boilover. Nobody likes to clean that up. But the rate of evaporation is often one of the more important aspects of your particular brewing system to determine. You can estimate that you will boil off between 1 and 1.5 gallons (3.8-5.7 L) an hour, but it's best to measure it, then plan for it in your recipes. Similar to determining your system's efficiency, calculating your average evaporation rate is important for the all-grain brewer.

Since one of the purposes of conducting a boil is concentrating the wort, it's important to measure the preboil gravity and kettle volume of your wort. Not properly measuring kettle volumes is one of the typical mistakes of a new full-boil brewer (which usually happens when becoming an all-grain brewer), which results in missing your target gravities and getting a beer that might not match your expectations.

Before you first use your kettle, you need to calibrate it. I prefer to use a measuring stick, such as a wooden dowel. First, set up your kettle as you would for brewing, including any submerged parts (false bottom, hop strainer, etc.). Next add 5 gallons (19 liters) of water to the kettle. Then lower the measuring stick until it touches the top of the water. Mark the stick with a permanent marker. I use a thick mark for full gallons; write the number next to it. Always measure from the same reference point (such as a notch or weld or other permanent fixture at the top of your kettle). Then repeat the process, adding a measured half-gallon of water at a time. I use thinner marks for half-gallons, and only write the numbers for the full gallons. Repeat this until you have filled your kettle. Now you have a calibrated measuring stick for your system. You will use this every time you brew—once before the boil and once when the boil has finished. Brewers using the metric system would follow the same process, measuring in liters instead of gallons, and marking the stick at two-liter intervals.

Use your measuring stick to know when to stop lautering, or when to stop filling your kettle. Record your preboil volume (for example, 7). Take a gravity reading using a hydrometer or refractometer, being sure to adjust for any temperature differences. If you take the gravity points (suppose your preboil gravity is 1.050—those are 50 gravity points) and multiply them by the wort volume, then you will have the total gravity points in your wort (in our example, it would be 7 x 50 = 350). You can then estimate the final gravity for your target volume by using algebra. Assume you want five gallons of beer at the end of the boil; your final gravity would be 350/5 = 70, or 1.070. Total gravity points are a constant; as you change the volume of the boil, you change the gravity of your wort.

You can use your measuring stick to measure the volume during the boil, but be aware that wort expands during the boil, so you will get a higher reading. If you take the boil down to a simmer, you will get a more accurate reading. If you find that you have boiled down too far, you can add water back to the kettle. If you have boiling water to add, it will be an easier process, since you won't have to drive off the additional air in the water, and you lessen the risk of boilover. Adding boiling water at the end of the boil is another solution and lessens the risk of infection. Just know that you will have slightly lower hop utilization, since you are boiling at a higher gravity than expected. Be careful adding water after the boil; you may be adding bacteria, oxygen, chlorine, or some other unwanted substance. Think about your water before mixing it in.

If you take a preboil gravity reading and find that you don't have enough gravity points to hit the target, you have two choices. You can either increase the gravity points in the kettle by adding some form of fermentable sugar (sugar, malt extract, honey, molasses, etc.), or you can boil down to a lower final volume. Most people will choose to add additional fermentables. A pound of sugar or dry malt extract adds about 45 gravity points per pound, while liquid malt extract adds about 36 gravity points per pound (since it also contains water). Sanitize the added ingredients by boiling for five minutes with enough of the wort to dissolve. Obviously, perform this correction before pitching any yeast.

Intentional caramelization. Some styles, such as strong Scotch ale, may rely on a strong kettle caramelization. I have done this two ways. The first is to collect the first runnings (up to a gallon, perhaps) and then boil them down separately in a small stockpot. Boil hard, and look to reduce the volume by perhaps 75 percent (boil a gallon down to a quart). The second way to do this is to turn on the flame under your brew kettle before running off the wort from the lauter tun. This way is easier, but it's harder to judge the amount of caramelization. It also can cause scorching on the bottom of your kettle, which could lead to burnt flavors. Be careful.

Caramelized first runnings have a deep flavor, but some judges may confuse caramel-type flavors with diacetyl. Keep in mind that you can get deeper caramel flavors by layering different crystal malts, particularly some of the darker varieties. See which you like best. I like the rich flavors of caramelized first runnings, but I have been dinged by confused judges for it.

Intentional Caramelization Technique

This was a huge Scotch ale that took nearly a year to come into balance. Be sure to give it time. It took a silver medal at MCAB in 2003. I rarely entered it because it tasted so good I wanted to save it for my friends. The basic concept was a classic Scotch ale based on the beers described in Greg Noonan's *Scotch Ale* book, hence the grist of mostly pale malt with a bit of roasted barley for color and dryness in the finish. I like Scotch ales to be malty and rich, with the perception of sweetness coming more from low hop bitterness than from underattenuation or incomplete fermentation. I use a half-barrel system, and this pretty much filled my mash tun. I used a no-sparge technique to increase the maltiness and didn't need to dilute the kettle volume. The long boil, no-sparge technique, and boiled first runnings increased the gravity greatly. I made a 1.040 dark mild with the second runnings (with the addition of crystal 80° and chocolate malt).

Gunn Clan Scotch Ale—Strong Scotch Ale

Recipe for 5.5 gallons (20.8 liters)

15 lbs. (6.8 kg) Pauls Mild malt
15 lbs. (6.8 kg) Crisp Maris Otter malt
6 oz. (170 g) roasted barley

1.5 oz. (42 g) Northern Brewer whole hops, 8.5% alpha acid, at 60 min.

0.5 oz. (14 g) Northern Brewer whole hops, 8.5% alpha acid, at 30 min.

White Labs WLP028 Edinburgh ale yeast

Mash at 158° F (70° C) for 2 hours. No-sparge technique, collect 9 gallons (34.1 liters). Boil first gallon or so of first runnings hard in the kettle. 2½-hour boil.

Ferment at 60° F (16° C).

OG: 1.130

FG: 1.035

32 IBU

6% ABV

Boil length. The length of boil can have several important effects on the beer. We have already discussed concentrating the wort to achieve the final target gravity and kettle volume. But the boil also develops the necessary hop characteristics, so it must be at least as long as your first hop addition. A full rolling boil helps create a hot break, which aids in clarification, but that happens within the first 15 minutes. Likewise, the boil sterilizes the wort by killing off anything biological that got into the kettle, but that happens in the first 5 or 10 minutes. The wort pH drops during the boil, typically a full point from the mash pH; this is important for keeping the finished beer stable and free from infection. All of these effects are fairly routine and don't require much additional thought.

Some of the effects that you do want to consider when choosing your boil length include controlling DMS (dimethyl sulfide), developing color and flavor, and controlling hop harshness. Longer, more vigorous boils will cause more color development, melanoidin production, and caramelization. They can also cause the hop bitterness to take on additional harshness, particularly if boiled for longer than 90 minutes. If you are planning a long kettle boil, be sure to add your hops working back from your expected end time.

Pilsener-type malts contain about eight times more SMM (s-methyl methionine)—the precursor to DMS, the compound that tastes like cooked corn or cabbage—than pale malts. Heat converts SMM to DMS, but DMS is volatile and is driven off during the boil. A longer, more vigorous boil drives off more DMS from Pils-based beers; I use 90-minute boils for these beers. Rapid cooling then will prevent DMS from reforming. During both boiling and cooling, allow the vapors to escape; don't cover the kettle! Fermentation will also scrub out some of the residual character, but the primary control of DMS in these beers is the boil. Decoction mashing also helps reduce DMS, due to boiling of the grains.

In paler beers without much Pils malt, I might use a 75-minute boil. I estimate 15 minutes to form the hot break, then 60 minutes afterward. I do shorter and slightly less vigorous boils in these situations to avoid color development. Keep in mind that if you use a less vigorous boil, your evaporation rate will be lower.

In beers where I am trying to get a lot of kettle caramelization (for example, strong Scotch ale, English barley wine, old ale), I will often boil 120 to 150 minutes. The initial kettle volume will need to be adjusted accordingly, or the kettle might need some water additions during the boil to maintain the proper volume.

Clarifying and chilling. There are two clarification processes involved in the boiling phase, the hot break and the cold break. The hot break occurs at the start of the boil and has already been discussed. The cold break occurs after the boil has finished but before fermentation starts. Cold break generally forms with the rapid cooling of the wort and has the look of egg drop soup. Kettle additives (also called copper finings, not because they contain copper but because the English term for brew kettle is "copper") can be added in the last 15 minutes of the boil to enhance this process; some common examples include Irish moss, Breakbright, and Whirlfloc. These are negatively charged and bind to the positively charged proteins in the wort, causing them to precipitate. Beer clarifies more rapidly in a lower pH range (4.2-4.4).

The various break material (proteins, tannins) and hop debris are known as *trub*. Trub must be separated from the wort to produce a clear, stable, and good-tasting beer. One method for separating the kettle trub is simply to let the wort rest after the boil before running it off into the fermenter. As turbulence from the boil subsides and the wort cools, the particulate matter will naturally precipitate. An immersion chiller can aid this process by cooling the wort faster. If you slowly swirl the wort in one direction, you can help the particulates fall into a cone in the center—this is the same effect you get from using a whirlpool. Rack the chilled wort out of the kettle, or run off if you have some kind of screen or filter system.

Letting the wort rest for 10 to 20 minutes has a visible effect on clarity. However, I also worry about losing volatile hop compounds, causing additional hop utilization and allowing DMS development by keeping the wort hot. I haven't really noticed those other effects when letting wort cool in this manner, but I do watch for them.

Hot break material and hop debris can be separated from the wort by either filtering it out, whirlpooling it to remove it, or by letting it settle and gently racking the wort off it. My kettle has a false bottom, so I use whole hops to form a natural filter bed. Similar to lautering, the hops help filter the trub before running the wort through a counterflow chiller. The hot wort could also be run through a hopback before the chiller, which would provide some filtration. A whirlpool could also be used; the wort could be pumped into another vessel with the wort being injected tangentially (i.e., with the hose pressed against the inside wall, and pointed parallel to the ground). The wort is recirculated, forming a whirlpool; once finished, the wort rests and the trub is left in a cone-shaped pile in the center. The wort is then drawn away from the outer rim, away from the trub.

A counterflow chiller can help crash cool the wort and form a good cold break, but all the break material is carried over into the fermenter. Some of the cold break material can actually help the yeast, but too much can contribute off-flavors. You can remove more of the break material by using a settling tank. If you run the chilled wort into a carboy and let it sit for several hours (particularly if at near-freezing temperatures), the break and remaining trub can settle out. Rack the wort into a primary fermenter, warm to pitching temperature, and proceed with fermentation. When I use this method, I tend to blanket the wort with CO_2 to reduce staling.

All of these methods will work, but I prefer to use two methods of direct chilling in the kettle and removing all break material before running it into the fermenter. One method uses an immersion chiller, and the other uses a counterflow chiller. Both require a pump, and both also perform the function of a whirlpool.

The first approach uses an immersion chiller in the standard configuration, but the wort is recirculated while the immersion chiller is operating. The biggest drawback to using an immersion chiller was always that it worked using direct contact with the wort. Wort next to the chiller would be cooled, but the rest of the wort would remain hot for quite some time. By recirculating the wort, the entire volume of the wort would be run past the chiller. Pump the wort out of the kettle and then back in the top, taking care to position the wort outflow so that it re-enters the kettle next to the chiller. Monitor the temperature of the wort, and stop recirculating when you have hit your target temperature.

The second approach uses a counterflow chiller in the standard configuration but also recirculates the wort back into the kettle. Since the chiller is external, the wort can be redirected back into the kettle in any manner. I prefer to run it in tangentially, giving the whirlpool effect as previously described. The net effect is the same as with the immersion chiller but uses different equipment. Open your lines and run them full open to get maximum circulation. Again, monitor the temperature and stop recirculating when you have reached your target temperature.

Either approach also could incorporate a hopback for continuous hopping and filtration, although I tend not to use this method. If you add hops directly to the kettle when you start the chilling, it has the same effect as whirlpool hopping. Once chilled, the wort can be racked off or run off, separating the trub using any of the previously discussed methods. Since the wort has cooled to pitching temperature, I prefer to simply let it rest for 10 to 20 minutes and allow the trub to settle out, then slowly draw off the wort. I avoid excessive splashing and oxidation while at hot temperatures and oxygenate the wort in the carboy.

I like these two methods because they rapidly chill the wort, which preserves hop character and reduces DMS formation. They are similar to methods used in commercial kitchens for cooling soups and stocks. You could also combine them if you have the equipment. For cooling to colder temperatures than your supply water, you can use another heat exchanger (immersion chiller or plate chiller) packed in ice on your supply line—think of it as a jockey box for your cooling water.

Using Hops
Hops provide bitterness, flavor, and aroma contributions to beer. A full discussion of hops, including selecting particular varieties, can be found in

the chapter on ingredients. This section is mostly concerned with how the hops are used in the brewing process. Aside from selecting the varieties, your brewing choices include picking the form of hops, how much of each variety to use, and what technique will be used during and after the boil.

The form of hops (pellets or whole/plugs) selected will often depend on your system, especially how your kettle is constructed. My kettle has a false bottom that assists with filtering, so I need to use some whole hops. I have seen other systems incorporate a type of whirlpool in the kettle to separate hops, so pellet hops are fine. I like using whole hops because they are less processed, but not all varieties are available in this form. Regardless of the form, hops should always be fresh and stored well (I keep mine in the freezer).

Water chemistry can have a significant impact on hop character. At a general level, low-to-moderate sulfates in water tend to bring out the hop character, increasing the perceived bitterness and dryness in beer. At higher levels, sulfates cause the hops to develop a harsher bitterness as well as giving a negative sulfur character. Adding gypsum (calcium sulfate) is the primary way to increase sulfates in water, since calcium is obviously beneficial to brewing. Magnesium sulfate (Epsom salts) is another way, although magnesium can produce sour flavors. Carbonates and higher pH in water tend to bring out a harsh character in hop bitterness, and in my opinion are best avoided. Calcium chloride in moderation gives a rounder, sweeter hop character. As general advice in adjusting water for hoppy beers, I tend to use calcium sulfate in English styles, calcium chloride in German and Belgian styles, and a mix of the two in American styles. I try to avoid sulfates when using noble hops.

Traditional Hopping

We all know the traditional role of hops in providing bittering, flavor, and aroma to beer, along with some preservative qualities. Bittering hops are traditionally added in the last 30 to 90 minutes of the boil, with 60 minutes being the most common. Flavor hops additions are considered to be in the last 10 to 20 minutes of the boil, while aroma hops are added with 10 minutes or less. These are all true statements, but keep in mind that you will get some bitterness, flavor, and aroma contributions from hops no matter when you add them in the boil. It's not like hops magically cease providing their character when added outside the traditional range. Also be aware that some hop varieties (like Chinook) have flavors and aromas that will linger longer than others, while some varieties (like Magnum) are very clean and neutral.

Using some of the modern hop varieties with both strong aromatic qualities and higher alpha acid levels can pose a quandary for brewers. How do you get their aroma and flavor qualities without getting an excessively bitter beer? If traditional hopping can't get the character you want, consider using all-late hopping and/or first wort hopping techniques.

All-Late Hopping

The all-late hopping method was something I first heard about from Peter Zien, brewmaster for AleSmith Brewing Company, at the AHA NHC in Las Vegas 2003. He said it produced a much smoother and cleaner bitterness with very low harshness in highly hopped beers, while giving a huge but smooth late hop flavor and aroma. His beers certainly had that quality, which was somewhat hard to find in other commercial examples of the time. Since a harsh finish is something I absolutely hate in a beer, this technique quickly became a staple of my repertoire.

In a nutshell, the technique involves adding all your hops within the last 20 minutes of the boil, adjusting your amounts to compensate for the reduced utilization. Similar to the technique of handling dark grains, less contact time with heat extracts fewer tannins, which makes for a smoother beer. You will want to watch out for excessive vegetal and grassy flavors coming from the increased hop material (as well as the volume loss due to absorption). The advice to keep your total hop bill to less than 8 ounces (227 grams) per 5-gallon (19-liter) batch still applies.

Estimating hop bitterness is something best done in brewing software. Just know that whatever you do, you're likely to be off from the actual value. You have no way of calculating all the factors that go into actual utilization. For instance, you know the alpha acid value of the hops when tested, but you don't know how much they've degraded since then. If you have a choice of IBU estimation methods in your brewing software, choose the Tinseth method. It has been tested to be more accurate in estimating actual IBUs than other common methods. Here is a table of hop utilization for whole hops and pellet hops using the Tinseth method in 1.050 wort with a full boil; the pellet hop correction factor is 1.24. These factors are used in the IBU estimation formula.

The relevant point here is to compare the differences in utilization; a 15-minute hop addition will give you roughly half the IBUs of a 60-minute addition, and a 5-minute hop addition will give you roughly a quarter.

Hop Utilization

Time	Pellets	Whole
60	28.6%	23.1%
30	21.9%	17.7%
20	17.4%	14.0%
15	14.1%	11.4%
10	10.4%	8.4%
5	5.7%	4.6%

I like the all-late hopping technique a lot, but some may find the lack of harshness means that the perceived IBUs are lower than measured; you may need to increase the IBU target of your recipe to compensate. Try both methods and see for yourself if you need more IBUs. The water chemistry can have an effect on the hop bitterness impression. Bumping up the sulfates could achieve the same effect as increasing the IBUs. Think of it as the difference in perceived bitterness in Bohemian Pilseners (made with low-ion water) and German Pilseners (made with sulfate-rich water). Bohemian Pilseners have more IBUs but seem less bitter (partially due to less attenuation, but also due to the water profile).

I find this technique gives a much more floral and fragrant finish to the beer due to the increased amount of late hops present. Given that the late hop character is featured so prominently, I suggest that you pick your late hops based primarily on their flavor and aroma contributions. For very highly bittered beers (more than 50 IBUs), adding some hops at the start keeps them from having an overwhelming hop flavor as well as helping with break formation. You might also need more wort volume to compensate for losses due to using more hops.

First Wort Hopping (FWH)

First Wort Hopping (FWH) is a historical German brewing technique that was largely forgotten until it was rediscovered by Brauwelt and published in a 1995 article that the late George Fix publicized. Originally, it was meant as a way to increase hop utilization in bittering additions. However, it was described as having a much more elegant and refined bitterness and late hop character as well. The actual phenomenon is not well understood, but it may have to do with introducing hops at the higher mash pH rather than the lower boil pH. The hops are steeping at 60 to 70° C (140-158° F) in pH 5.2 to 5.5 for an extended time.

The technique involves adding some hops to the kettle just prior to lautering. When the wort is run off from the lauter tun, the hops steep in the hot wort until lautering is complete and the boil begins. The rest of the boil is conducted normally, with other hop additions being added at their traditional times. The German literature discusses adding no more than one-third of the total hop charge as first wort hops.

The interesting thing about first wort hopping is the perceived effects. While measured bitterness is tested at perhaps 10 percent greater than that obtained from a 60-minute boil, the actual perceived bitterness seems lower to me because it has a smooth character. Some sources have suggested that a FWH addition should be calculated as providing the IBU contribution of a 20-minute hop addition. Since the actual measured bitterness is higher, I'd be concerned that this approach would throw off the balance of the beer. Calculate the bitterness as a 60-minute boil, but understand that it might seem lower to some palates.

The literature is somewhat divided on the other perceptual effects. Some sources say that FWH introduces a refined, elegant hop aroma, but my observations have found very little aroma contribution. Yes, what is there is refined, smooth, and pleasant, but it is very low in intensity. The flavors are elegant and strong but seem to be better blended in with the flavor profile than a traditional flavor addition.

For recipe formulation purposes, I don't consider FWH as providing any aroma at all. However, I do find a huge hop flavor contribution from FWH. The flavor I get is higher than an equivalent 20-minute addition. Since I think of bittering and aroma hops more in terms of ounces than IBUs, I tend to consider FWH hops as providing as much as 50 percent more flavor than the same amount of 20-minute hops. For example, if I want the flavor contributions from 1.5 ounces of hops at 20 minutes, I'll use an ounce of first wort hops.

Considering the sensory profile of first wort hops (not much aroma, tons of flavor, very smooth and clean bitterness), I try to select varieties based on their flavor profile and to use them in beer styles with a pronounced hop flavor. I think they are a good idea for German Pils-based beers, using high-quality noble hops like Hallertauer and Tettnang. I've used them in English beers, which in the United Kingdom have a very large flavor dimension; East Kent Goldings are the obvious choice, but I've also used Styrian Goldings. I prefer the floral English varieties rather than the earthy English hops (like Fuggles). I also like them in hoppy, bitter American beers where you don't want excessive harshness (pale ale, IPA, amber ale, brown ale). I like using Cascade, Centennial, Amarillo, and Simcoe, but there are many other flavorful varieties that will work well (Citra, Summit, Sorachi Ace). My basic rule of thumb is that if you like the way a hop variety tastes and it doesn't seem harsh, then try it in first wort hopping.

First Wort Hopping and Late Hopping Techniques Combined

This is a one of my standard pale ale recipes. It uses some modern techniques, including first wort hopping and late hopping for bitterness. It also uses a richer malt base and some newer hop varieties. I particularly like the combination of Amarillo and Simcoe, but you could also go "old school" and use Cascade and Centennial.

Avant Garde—American Pale Ale

Recipe for 5 gallons (19 liters)

6.5 lbs. (2.9 kg) Maris Otter malt
1 lb. (454 g) Vienna malt

¾ lb. (340 g) crystal 40° L malt

¼ lb. (113 g) crystal 80° L malt

½ lb. (227 g) malted wheat

1 lb. (454 g) white sugar

1 oz. (28 g) Amarillo whole hops, 8% alpha acid, FWH

½ oz. (14 g) Tomahawk whole hops, 14% alpha acid, at 20 min.

½ oz. (14 g) Tomahawk whole hops, 14% alpha acid, at 15 min.

½ oz. (14 g) Tomahawk whole hops, 14% alpha acid, at 10 min.

½ oz. (14 g) Simcoe whole hops, 12% alpha acid, at 5 min.

1 oz. (28 g) Amarillo whole hops, 8% alpha acid, at 2 min.

½ oz. (14 g) Simcoe whole hops, 12% alpha acid, at 0 min.

WLP060 American Blend

OG: 1.060

FG: 1.012

45 IBUs

SRM: 10

6.3% ABV

Mill grains and dough-in using RO water until a medium-thickness mash is achieved. Treat mash with 1 tsp. calcium chloride. Hold mash at 150° F (66° C) until conversion is complete. Add first wort hops to kettle. Sparge slowly with 170° F (77° C) RO water treated with ½ tsp. phosphoric acid, collecting 6.5 gallons (24.6 liters) wort. Bring wort to a boil.

After the hot break, add the sugar. Boil for 75 additional minutes, adding the hops per the hopping schedule. Chill rapidly to 68° F (20° C). Rack to fermenter, leaving break material behind. Oxygenate, pitch the yeast, and ferment at 70° F (21° C). Fermentation should be done in less than a week, but don't rush it. After the beer has dropped bright, rack to keg and force carbonate. Target a carbonation level of 2 to 2.5 volumes.

Post-Boil Finishing Hop Methods

There are a wide variety of options for introducing additional hop aroma and flavor into beer after the boil. I tend to group the techniques into two main groups, depending on whether they are conducted at hot or cold temperatures. The hot techniques are performed right after the boil completes, before the chilling. Cold techniques generally are deferred until after fermentation has finished.

The first post-boil method is adding hops at knockout in the kettle. Sometimes called the zero-minute addition, this has the advantage of simplicity, since you simply add hops when you turn off the burner. You use the latent heat in the kettle to extract the hop character and have control in your methods of how fast you chill the wort. There is still some loss of aromatics and character change due to the heat, but the effect is not nearly as strong as during the boil. This technique can be used with whole hops or pellet hops, but I tend to use whole hops. If you use pellet hops, you might want to put them in a mesh bag to make it easier to remove some of the hop mass.

Hops can also be added to the whirlpool, a hot temperature technique most commonly used by craft brewers. Pellet hops are often used in this method. Homebrewers can create a whirlpool by pumping the wort from the kettle back into the kettle along the inside with the hose outlet set parallel to the bottom of the kettle. This encourages circulation and settles the hops and other trub in the center. If you don't have a pump, you can do this manually with a large spoon and some elbow grease. After recirculating for 10 to 20 minutes, let the wort rest for another 10 to 20 minutes to allow the hops to drop out. You can combine this method with chilling as described in the boiling section.

The hopback method is another hot temperature technique. The hopback is an inline container sitting between the boil kettle and the chiller. It contains whole hops (typically, although it could contain pellets if contained in a tight-enough mesh), which filter the hot wort on the way to the chiller. The nice benefit of this method is that the hop character is kept within the wort, since the system is sealed and the wort is rapidly chilled after contact. The heat takes away some of the raw hop character, but the aroma impact is very bold.

Dry hopping is the most common post-boil technique that brewers will recognize. This is a cold technique in which the hops are added after primary fermentation has finished. The hops may be added in the primary fermenter, in the secondary, or even in the serving vessel (a common cask technique). Dry hopping produces additional hop aroma, with a very fresh quality, and might add to the perception of body. However, it can also produce a lingering grassy, vegetal note that some may not like.

Some brewers use a variation of the dry-hopping technique during dispense, using a device popularized by Dogfish Head Brewing Company and nicknamed the Randall. Homebrewers can make an equivalent device using a cartridge-type water filter with the cartridge replaced by a hop-straining device (like a screen or a pipe with tiny holes drilled in it), and adding hops (or fruits, spices, herbs, etc.) into the chamber.

In recent years, I have gotten away from dry hopping many of my beers. I prefer the more refined aroma that you get from using a hopback or from adding hops at the end of the boil or in the whirlpool (all hot methods). Giving the hops some heat helps remove those raw aromatics, but you have to cool the beer rapidly from this point, so as to keep the liberated aromatics within the beer.

If you do dry hop, here are some tips. Rack the beer from the primary to remove most of the yeast. Keep the beer cool, in the 60 to 68° F (16-20° C) range. Watch out for oxidation; you might consider blanketing the surface of the beer with CO_2 after adding the hops. Two days before removing the hops, crash cool the beer to 32° F (0° C) to help drop out suspended particulates. Always keep the beer and hops under CO_2 to avoid oxidizing any of the hop compounds.

I prefer to limit the contact time of dry hops in beer to 3 to 7 days to cut down on grassy, vegetal flavors, although some say that 10 to 14 days is the upper limit. Usage rates are typically between 0.5 ounce and 2 ounces per 5-gallon batch, although some extreme styles can use much more. Keeping the hops in contact with the beer will aid in extraction, so rousing the hops (without introducing oxygen) is a good idea.

Sierra Nevada uses an innovative dry-hopping technique called the *hop torpedo*. Think of it as a recirculating cold-side hopback. I'm not sure how practical it would be to do something like this at home. However, if you want to try, the first thing you'll need to figure out is how to set up a closed system to recirculate the beer through a hopback stuffed with fresh, whole hops. Purge the entire system with CO_2 to remove any oxygen, particularly from the hopback. Then slowly push the beer through for up to a week at cool temperatures.

In summary, the key decisions in post-boil hopping involve deciding what kind of hop character to impart, how to prevent the loss of volatile hop oils, how to keep the hops from oxidizing, and how to separate the hop mass from the beer. Common elements among the methods are to cool the beer as quickly as possible, to keep the hops in as much contact with the beer as possible, and to avoid introducing oxygen.

Multiple Additions

Using multiple additions of hops can add a nice, layered complexity. However, beware of mixing too many different varieties of hops. Some of the flavors might clash. You can use multiple additions of the same hop variety or blend of varieties, up to the continuous hopping methods of Dogfish Head Brewing Company. In super-hoppy beers, you may want to try multiple dry-hop additions. Give each batch of hops seven days to work, then remove and hit it with another round of hops.

Some of my favorite hop combinations are using Cascade and Centennial together or using Amarillo with Simcoe. I like to use fewer than four varieties of late hops in most beers, often just one or two. It's fun to make single-hop varietal beers. Nothing will teach you the character of a hop variety better than using nothing but that type of hop in your beer. If you use multiple additions of a single hop, you certainly will get an appreciation for its aroma, flavor, and bittering contributions.

CHAPTER 3
mastering equipment

This is my rifle. There are many like it, but this one is MINE.
My rifle is my best friend. It is my life.
I must master it as I master my life.
My Rifle: The Creed of a United States Marine (first stanza)
–Major General W.H. Rupertus, 1941

In order to be a great brewer, you have to learn your brewing system in detail and make it your own. You have to know its strengths and weaknesses and how it responds to different brewing conditions. You don't have to have a fancy system, spend thousands of dollars, invest in automation, or build a dedicated brewhouse. I know great brewers who have turned out award-winning beer on the most basic equipment. Certainly our forefathers brewed on less advanced equipment, so don't become a gear snob. But whatever system you do have, know it inside and out. You don't have to be able to brew great beer on *every* system, but you should know how to consistently brew great beer on *your* system.

Brewing with others and observing how their systems work is a great way to learn about brewing. However, be careful about drawing too many conclusions about how someone else's methods will work on your system. As Ronald Reagan used to say, "trust, but verify"—take their suggestions, but test them on your system before you accept them as fact. Their methods might not work or might need to be changed to work on your system. Your methods might work better on your system. Have an open mind about making changes, but don't just blindly accept recommendations.

The major topics in this chapter are selecting your equipment, learning your system, and optimizing your brewing. I think of these steps as occurring in phases, although some will be repeated as you enhance your system, learn new techniques, and adapt your procedures. Selecting your equipment is a basic skill, learning your system completely is a more advanced skill, and optimizing your brewing is one of the signs that you have mastered your system.

Matching Equipment to the Task

I'm a firm believer in the design approach that says *form follows function* (a quote attributed to American architect Louis Sullivan, and later promoted by his assistant, Frank Lloyd Wright). Start with what you need to accomplish, then find devices to best meet those needs. There will always be tradeoffs to be made, often involving cost. However, if you always keep the task foremost in your mind, you should be able to assemble and upgrade your system smoothly.

Don't buy equipment or systems without knowing how you're going to use them. Equipment you buy doesn't have to be designed specifically for brewing, but maybe it's better for the task at hand. Maybe you can take another piece of equipment and adapt it. Keep an open mind, and don't be limited by what one store sells. One piece of equipment might be able to handle multiple tasks—that's fine—but understand the impact if you do this. (Is throughput limited? Can it be cleaned as easily? Are you still able to multitask?) Consider your equipment selections along with your process choices.

In this section, I'll walk through the common brewing tasks that require equipment and discuss alternatives and tradeoffs. I'll also describe how I solved the problem on my system. Although I won't mention it in each discussion, cost is an implicit factor with every choice; a brewer with limited resources must decide where to focus those funds for maximum payback. Not everyone will be able to make choices solely on technical merit.

Measuring Ingredients

Accurately weighing and measuring your ingredients is critical for properly making your recipe. Grains and hops need to be weighed, and water needs to be measured by volume.

I've used several types of scales to measure grain. For large amounts of base grain, I used a hanging dairy scale in conjunction with a 5-gallon (19-liter) bucket, for smaller amounts of grain, a kitchen scale that can weigh up to a few pounds. Lately I've switched over to an electronic scale that can weigh up to 13 pounds (5.9 kilograms) in 0.1-ounce (2.8-gram) increments. When selecting scales, consider the following attributes:

- Capacity. What is the total weight it can hold?
- Resolution. What increments does it display?
- Units. How is it marked? Does it display in English and metric?
- Portability. Can it be easily moved?
- Speed. How fast does it take a measurement?
- Calibration. How is it adjusted to match a reference weight?
- Taring. Can it eliminate the weight of the container from the measurement?
- Size. Can it hold your common containers and still allow you to read it?
- Durability. Can it handle your operating conditions, including getting wet?

Think about the different weights you will commonly measure and how accurate you have to be. You might choose a scale that can handle a large quantity, but at a lower resolution, and a smaller scale that is more precise (perhaps 0.1 gram precision) but can't handle large weights. That's what I use; the larger one is for grains, and the smaller one is for hops and additives.

You can approximate bulk weights by using standardized containers and marking them; I use two different scoops, which can hold about 3 pounds (1.4 kilograms) and 1 pound (454 grams), respectively, and use them for transferring grain from sacks to containers for weighing. I use smaller containers for holding hops (little glass bowls for pellet hops and additives, larger plastic bowls for whole hops) while they are being weighed. I weigh directly on the scales, which have been tared.

I use large (2-quart, 1.9-liter) and small (1-pint, 473-milliliter) measuring cups for water, as well as 5-gallon (19-liter) plastic jugs. Mostly I measure water while in a brewing vessel (hot liquor tank or kettle). As described in the techniques section, I use a calibrated measuring stick to take readings of the water level while in the brewing vessels. Some systems have sight glasses to display the water level, which also works well.

Crushing Grain

Grain must be properly crushed in order to be mashed. While grain can be bought precrushed, or can be crushed in most homebrew shops, it's much more convenient to buy grain in bulk and crush it as needed. Crushing grain requires investment in a mill.

The goal of the mill is to crush the endosperm (starchy interior) of the grain without shredding the husk. Some considerations for selecting a mill are:

- Quality of crush. Can the grain be crushed without tearing the husks excessively? What is the performance on different types of grain? Is the mill designed to crush grain or to make flour?

- Adjustability. Can the gap be adjusted? How hard is it to adjust? Can the gap be directly measured? Does it maintain the gap throughout a session, or must it be readjusted? How many rollers are used, and are all the gaps adjustable?

- Capacity. How many pounds of grain can the hopper hold? Is it integrated, or must you add something?

- Throughput. How long does it take to crush the grain? How many pounds per minute can it crush?

- Automation. Can you drive the mill with a motor or drill?

- Output. How is the crushed grain ejected? Is there any form of dust containment?

- Mounting. Can you permanently mount the mill, or must it be set up every time it is used? Does it require any other specific equipment to use?

- Quality. How robust is the manufacturing? What is the expected lifetime of the mill? What replaceable parts are present? How much maintenance (lubrication, etc.) does it require?

There are many different commercial mill manufacturers, all of which appear to make good-quality products. About the only advice I have is to avoid Corona-type mills, which are designed to crush corn. But the rest of them seem very good. If I had to buy new, I'd look for large-diameter rollers and most other features listed above.

I've used the same mill since I started brewing: a Listermann PhilMill I, mounted to a table, fitted with a drill, and modified to use a 5-gallon plastic water jug as a hopper. I can fit more than 20 pounds (9.1 kilograms) of grain in this hopper, which is sufficient for most batches. The crush is adjustable and gives me very good efficiency. I also fitted it with an output chute (a flexible dryer hose) to keep dust down and to direct the crushed grain into a 6-gallon (22.7-liter) bucket. This is probably the most heavily modified piece of equipment I own, but it performs so well I don't want to replace it.

The table where I've mounted the mill is in the garage next to my grain storage. The table also holds my various scales and measuring devices that I use for working with grain. It's next to the workbench, so I have access to tools if I need them, and electricity is available for the drill (a half-inch Porter Cable model). Good lighting, extra storage space, and a writing surface are a bonus. I like to check off grains from my recipe as I weigh them and add them to my hopper. Tools are handy for opening new sacks of grain (utility knife) and making any adjustments or repairs to my equipment (wrenches, screwdrivers, etc.).

Moving Liquid

Water and wort have to be moved between vessels during brewing. This is generally accomplished manually, with gravity, or with pumps. To me, this decision, along with the number of brewing vessels, is what drives the overall design of your system. A brewing sculpture is designed to use gravity to move liquid from one stage to another. A manual system might use grants to collect liquid and manual lifting to move them to another stage. A system with pumps can move the liquid from one vessel to another in any configuration.

You can view each phase of the brewing process as discrete and handle it separately, or you can look at brewing as a continuous process with each step linked with the next. The phases that are important in this step are how water gets into the hot liquor tank, how brewing liquor is added to the mash tun, how sparge water is added to the mash tun, how the outflow of the lauter tun is directed to the kettle, and how the boiled wort is moved to the fermenter.

- Safety. How likely are you to injure yourself while using the equipment? Can you be burned, electrocuted, or hurt your back while lifting?

- Automation. Is work involved in each step, or can it be automated?

- Effort. Can liquids be moved mechanically to a higher level, or must they be lifted?

- Ease of use. If using pumps, are they self-priming? Can they handle the full temperature range of liquids? Can controls be used with one hand? Are controls nearby when brewing? How much reconfiguring is necessary to support the different phases of brewing? Are the hoses capable of withstanding heat?

- Flow rate. Can the flow rate be adjusted? What is the maximum flow rate? Can it be turned off? Do the connectors allow full bore flow through?

- Integration. How integrated is the solution with the rest of your system? Are pieces of equipment dedicated or single-purpose? How much effort is required to change the equipment to support the next phase of brewing?

- Safety. How likely are you to injure yourself using the equipment? Can you be burned, electrocuted, or hurt your back lifting?

I've known brewers who carried buckets of near-boiling water up ladders to start their sparge. I never felt safe doing that, but I did use gravity for years until I bought a more automated system. Gravity-based systems start with equipment from one phase raised higher than the next phase's equipment. Some systems are configured with each phase higher than the next, while others have only two levels, and liquid is manually raised at the start of each phase. Now I use two March pumps on my system, so I can do two tasks simultaneously (like pump sparge water onto the mash and pump mash runoff into the kettle). March pumps can handle the near-boiling temperatures but unfortunately are not self-priming, so generally need to be mounted low or be removable. Flow rates are not adjustable by the pumps, but by valves where the pumps connect to the brewing system. No liquids have to be raised higher than chest-level, and then only to initially fill the hot liquor tank. The pumps can be easily switched on and off and either the pumps or hoses can be moved from one part of the system to another with quick-connects.

Managing Heat

This activity is considered along with moving liquid as part of the core system design. Together they identify how many brewing vessels are used, what materials are used in their construction, and how they are linked together.

- Heat source. What type of fuel is used to supply the heat? How easy is it to obtain, and how easy is it to use? Are there any special safety considerations? How many heat sources are used, and are they restricted to being used with only specific vessels?

- How applied. Can you directly heat the brewing vessels, or must you heat the ingredients (mash, water) separately?

- Control. Can you adjust the level of the heat applied? How do you maintain a specific temperature?

- Conservation. How do you keep heat from dissipating? Are any of the vessels insulated?

This step drives how you will mash, sparge, and boil. Which size vessels you use depends on how you can heat them. Will you be direct-firing kettles or adding hot water boiled on another source? If you miss your mash temperatures, can you adjust them with your system, or do you have to move the grain to another vessel? How many burners will you have? How many vessels will you have, and are any of them reusable in other roles?

When I first started all-grain brewing, I was using picnic coolers and heating hot water on the stove. That generally worked, although it was a pain if I missed mash temperatures because infusing boiling water didn't always raise the temperature enough; I was also concerned about the consistency of the mash changing. So I found that I would often have to decoct my beers (pull grain out, heat it in a separate pot) to get to desired temperatures. Coolers did a good job of maintaining temperatures because of their insulation, however.

I've since moved to a three-vessel, half-barrel system, with three kegs serving as brewing vessels, each with its own individually adjustable burner. This gives me total control and allows me to work on multiple brewing steps at once. If I'm making a second batch, I can start on the process while the first batch is still being brewed. I use propane burners, since tanks can easily be refilled or exchanged. I've developed insulated wraps for my mash tun and hot liquor tank to help retain heat (uninsulated, I would often lose 10° F /4.5° C or more in an hour; insulated, I lose perhaps 1° F/ 0.5° C an hour).

I use one vessel as a hot liquor tank, one as a mash and lauter tun, and one as a boil kettle. If I need to decoct, I use an external pot and the burner from one of the unused vessels (typically the boil kettle, which is easy to move since it's empty during the mash). My vessels have lids, which also help conserve the heat. I can direct-fire them and can maintain temperatures by also using the pumps to recirculate liquid while the burners are lit.

Mashing

A separate vessel is needed for mashing; it may or may not be used for lautering. The basic requirement is that it be large enough to hold all your crushed grain and water, and that it do a decent job of maintaining a temperature for an hour.

If you are using a complete or turnkey system with a dedicated mash/lauter tun, you probably don't have any other choices. The mash tun comes with your system. If you are putting together your own system, you do have some choices. I see three basic options for most homebrewers:

- A large, rectangular picnic cooler

- A 10-gallon (37.9-liter) cylindrical Gott water cooler

- A large metal pot (9 gallons/34.1 liters or larger) or cut keg (half-barrel)

If you use a cooler as a mash tun, then you cannot directly heat it. You will have to understand how to hit your mash temperatures, which may involve preheating the mash tun with boiling water or carefully measuring temperatures and volumes of water (brewing software can help). Metal pots can be direct-fired to change the temperature. Keep in mind that larger pots typically won't fit on most kitchen stoves and likely have to be put on an outdoors burner.

Think about the size of your batches when choosing a mash tun. Can you make a 5-gallon (19-liter) batch? Can you make a 10-gallon (37.9-liter) batch? Can you make a 5-gallon batch of your highest-gravity beer? I find that my half-barrel mash tun tops out at about 32 pounds (14.5 kilograms) of grain, which can make a very high-gravity, 5-gallon batch. Even if you regularly make 5-gallon batches, having a half-barrel system gives you the flexibility to make huge 5-gallon batches or easily make a 10-gallon batch to split with a brewing friend or to use in a side-by-side experiment.

If space and budget are an issue, picnic coolers are a good approach. They hold temperatures very well, but it takes practice to hit mash temperatures.

They can be used as lauter tuns, although that also takes some effort in some configurations. (More on that in the next section.)

If you are going to decoct, you'll need an additional pot. It doesn't have to be as big as your mash tun, since you are typically using only 30 to 40 percent of the grain mass, and it won't have a false bottom. A large kitchen stockpot will typically do well, especially if it has a heavy bottom (this reduces the chance of scorching).

Wherever you mash, you'll need to have some way of transferring the grain. I typically use a kitchen saucepan as a scoop. It holds grain and liquid and is a maneuverable shape.

Lautering

Lautering can take place in the same vessel as the mash tun or a separate vessel. So the first choice to make is whether or not you will use a separate lauter tun. In a well-designed complete system, the mash tun and lauter tun are usually combined. If you're using a picnic cooler, you have choices. The thing to keep in mind is how manipulating the grain during mashing will impact lautering. If you have to stir your grain, will that somehow clog your lautering system?

When I first started brewing all-grain, I was using a 10-gallon (37.9-liter) Gott cooler with a Phil's Phalse Bottom. I found that I was frequently getting stuck sparges but could reduce the problem if I held down the false bottom with my mash paddle when adding grain and then underlet the water. Even then I had to be very careful when stirring, because it was easy to get grains under the false bottom, which would then clog the outlet.

Later, I switched to using a rectangular cooler as a mash tun and lautering in the Gott cooler. I thought this worked much better for lautering, since I didn't have to stir the grain once it was in the lauter tun. I had fewer stuck sparges but was losing temperature moving between vessels, and I had to mash-out with near-boiling water to raise the temperature back up.

Now, with my three-vessel system, my mash tun has a tight-fitting false bottom that doesn't float, so I don't have either of these problems. I have also seen other solutions for lautering that work very well. If you have a slotted pipe system or a bazooka screen-type system installed in your rectangular cooler, you can get very good results. Without a false bottom, stirring isn't as much of a problem, and these systems don't clog as much.

Whichever system you have, decide how you are going to vorlauf and sparge. Vorlauf is fairly easy on any system, since it doesn't involve much volume. You can run off into a saucepan or grant, then gently pour this back on the grain bed, repeating until there aren't any noticeable particles in the outflow. Or you can pump the outflow back onto the grain bed in the same manner. Manual or automated, it pretty much works the same.

Your sparging equipment depends on your method. Batch sparging is easy on any system; simply add water, drain, and repeat. Continuous sparging isn't much harder, although you have to balance inflow and outflow to keep the water level on the grain bed relatively consistent. If you don't have a complete system where the liquid transfers are relatively automated, you may find it easier to batch sparge. For continuous sparging, I don't like spray-type systems that aerate the water; I prefer to keep the water level about an inch above the grain bed and gently add water there. If you aren't adding water directly to the grain, it doesn't really matter how it gets there.

Boiling Wort
The requirements for your boil kettle are fairly simple. You need to be able to hold the complete preboil volume, which can be as much as 3 gallons (11.4 liters) more than your target volume, including allowing for expansion while boiling and the froth that is created before the hot break. I find that a half-barrel keg is just enough for a vigorous 10-gallon (37.9-liter) batch. Obviously, the boil kettle must be direct-fired.

On simpler systems, you might be able to get away with using the boil kettle as your hot liquor tank, as long as you're able to store some of the boiling water during the sparge. It makes the job more difficult, and you have to move sizeable amounts of boiling water around, so think hard before choosing this alternative. You may find it simpler to use a smaller hot liquor tank and boil the water in batches; this way you could possibly use an older pot (perhaps your old kettle, or a pot "borrowed" from your kitchen).

Chilling and Separating Wort
The subject of chilling is covered extensively in the Mastering Techniques chapter, so I'll just quickly review the choices and the impact on equipment

selection. The two basic approaches for chilling are to use a counterflow chiller or an immersion chiller. With each of these, you also have the option of adding a recirculating system. You may also have a pre-chiller for your feed water, or a heat exchanger (or simple ice batch) for your recirculating system. You also have the option of incorporating a hopback when using a counterflow chiller or when using an immersion chiller with the recirculating option.

Your decision points are how fast you want the wort chilled, where the cold break will wind up, whether you want to add late hops during the process, and how the wort is separated from the trub. If you want the wort chilled as quickly as possible, then use either chiller with a recirculating option, and pre-chill the feed water and chill the recirculated wort. If you want to allow the wort to naturally clear and settle and then chill as it goes to the fermenter, you should choose the counterflow chiller. I used this method for years with great results; it also allows late hops to be added at knockout.

I don't see much advantage to using an immersion chiller without recirculating. It's slower than a counterflow chiller and tends to be bulkier to store. A hopback is a good idea, if you don't have a reliable way to filter the wort on the way to the fermenter. The hopback can assist in this approach, but it will always add a late hop character. Remember that hot wort has to hit the hops in the hopback to get the best hop character. On my system, the false bottom using the whole boil hops acts as a similar filter; I can add whatever hops I want—they don't have to be added at the end. When I want the effect of a hopback, I just add the hops directly to the kettle and immediately begin recirculating and chilling.

Whether or not you pre-chill the feed water and chill the recirculating water depends on how cold you want the beer entering the fermenter. If I'm making a lager, I'll usually use this approach, so I can get it colder sooner. Otherwise, I'd have to take my fermenter and chill it in my refrigerator before pitching. If I can cool the beer to pitching temperature, I can get the yeast started immediately. If I'm making an ale, I normally don't worry about pre-chilling my feed water unless I'm brewing while it's very hot outside. Check the temperature of your feed water before using it; if it's higher than your pitching temperature, pre-chill it by running it through an ice bath or heat exchanger.

If you use a counterflow chiller, the cold break will wind up in the fermenter. If you use an immersion chiller, or if you use a counterflow chiller with the recirculating option, the cold break will wind up in the boil kettle. Careful racking, or running through whole hops as a filter, will remove the break material from the wort. If you find significant trub in the fermenter, you can always treat it as a settling tank—just let it rest for an hour or two, then rack the clear beer into another fermenter. If you choose this option, defer pitching the yeast until the wort is in the final fermenter.

My system has a false bottom in the boil kettle, which means I need to use some amount of whole hops to help filter the wort. If I use pellets, I typically have to put them in a tight-mesh bag so they don't clog the system. It's the one part of my system I'm not totally happy about. I would like to use more pellet hops, since they offer a wider range of hop varieties and store better.

Other solutions exist for separating hops and break material from your wort. I've tried a variety of curved pickup tubes, screens, filters, and similar solutions without much luck. I can't seem to keep the fine particles or whole hops from eventually clogging the filters. There must be a two-stage solution to this problem that involves a coarse filter keeping larger material away from the outlet and a finer filter used later, or a way to rack from the top of the kettle rather than the bottom. I don't want to rack from my kettle manually, though. Even when bagging pellet hops and using a whirlpool to create a cone of material in the center of the kettle, I still find it difficult to draw off the wort without picking up particles. Maybe I'm fighting the design of my system when I'm trying other approaches; when I use it as designed, it works great.

Fermenting and Conditioning

Most homebrewers ferment in carboys, but other choices exist, such as cylindro-conical fermenters and open plastic buckets. I've used all of them but generally prefer carboys, since they are easiest to clean and I can see what's going on without opening it. There is a choice of volume for most systems; I tend to brew 5.5-gallon (20.8-liter), batches, so I wind up with at least 5 gallons (19 liters) of finished beer. To comfortably contain the fermentation, I use 6.5-gallon (24.6-liter) carboys fitted with carboy handles to make them easier to lift.

I like the concept of cylindro-conical fermenters, since you can easily get rid of trub, rack off the beer, and catch the yeast for repitching. However, they are difficult to move and require more effort to clean. Since I brew some distance from where I ferment, I would still have to use carboys to capture the wort from the brew kettle. They are available in a variety of sizes and can be purchased with heating and chilling options. I still haven't figured out the best setup for one of these, but I do own one, so I'll keep working on it, perhaps as a dedicated lager system.

Plastic buckets with lids are nice if you know you are going to top-crop yeast, or if you expect significant blowoff (such as from Wyeast 3068 or 3787 yeast). I tend to use plastic buckets for making fruit meads, since I have to get into them several times during fermentation. Don't write these off as beginner tools; they still have value for advanced brewers and may also allow you to experiment with open fermentation used in traditional English styles, or with variations in fermenter geometry and head pressure as a way to manipulate esters.

There are several types of airlocks; all work. Pick the ones you like, and don't let them run dry. My one airlock-related tip is to get "universal stoppers" instead of numbered stoppers; they can't be pushed into the carboy, and they fit a wider range of openings. Quite handy.

You can aerate or oxygenate your wort using a variety of tools. When I use oxygen, I like to use a sintered stainless steel diffusion stone on an oxygen tank with a regulator and a filter. I bought the whole thing as a kit, except the oxygen tank, which comes from my local hardware store. When I use air, I like to use a mix-stir on a drill. This is designed to de-gas wine, but it works great on beer and mead. I work up a big vortex and whip air into it. I've heard of people using aquarium filters to add air to their wort. Personally, if I'm going to the trouble of setting up, I'm going to use oxygen and get better results.

I know several brewers who have incorporated an aeration system inline with filling the fermenter. Running off from the kettle, the chilled wort passes through a system that forces it through small openings, causing it to spray and pick up air. These approaches are quite simple and work well. My only concern is controlling the amount of foam produced, since the carboy is filling at the same time the air is added. When aerating or oxygenating after the carboy is filled, you can see when to stop or reduce the rate. I guess the same could be done with the inline system by regulating the flow.

Equipment related to making starters is covered in the discussion of yeast in the next chapter. My recommendation is to get a stir plate and an Erlenmeyer flask. You can make starters in growlers and plastic bottles, but the advantages of a stir plate are too big to ignore. I get much more predictable results since I started using one.

I have different zones in the house set up for fermentation, and I adjust my brewing schedule to take advantage of ambient temperatures. Unfortunately, I don't have a basement, so I have several dedicated refrigerators (even a walk-in) to simulate these environments. I set my walk-in at lager fermentation temperature (48-50° F, 9-10° C) and also use it as a cold cellaring location. I store beer ready for consumption here, unless I'm trying to protect it for a long time. I have a chest freezer with a temperature control set at lagering temperature (34° F, 1° C). I normally ferment when house temperatures are in the 60s (16-20° C), knowing I can find spots a few degrees warmer if necessary.

I use other gear during and after fermentation, such as a wine thief for sampling, a hydrometer and measuring jar for gravity readings, an infrared thermometer for temperature readings, a pH meter for pH readings, a blowoff tube and catch jar for vigorous fermentations, a siphoning tube for transfers, and a CO_2 tank for purging containers and blanketing beer after transfers. I use brushes and a carboy spray wand for cleaning. I clean with PBW and sanitize with either StarSan or One-Step.

When I do a secondary fermentation or conditioning step, I use the same carboys used during primary fermentation. I normally transfer to a keg for lagering, mostly because it's easier to load kegs into my lagering freezer than it is carboys. I fit my lagering keg with an adjustable pressure relief valve to keep the pressure from getting too high.

Packaging
You have choices to make in clarification, carbonation, and storage. There are several ways to clarify your beer that don't involve extra equipment (except normal racking gear). If you want to get more involved, you can get a plate filter. These work with a keg system; you fit it inline and push the beer through it into a target keg. I have a plate filter system but only like to use it for very pale beers where clarity is at a premium, and only if fining hasn't produced the desired results. Filtering does waste some beer, and filter pads are expensive.

Beer can be packaged in bottles or kegs. Minimal equipment is needed for bottling. A bottling bucket, racking cane, siphon tube, and bottle filler will get the bottles filled. A capper will seal the bottles; you have a choice of handheld wing cappers and bench cappers. I have both and prefer to use the bench capper when there are more bottles to process. It's helpful to have this gear even if you don't regularly bottle; you may need to use it if you bottle from kegs for competitions or gifts.

Kegging takes more equipment, mostly enough kegs to hold all your beer. You have a choice of fittings; ball-locks are most common. Standardize on one system, so you don't have to maintain multiple parts. Beer and gas fittings are needed, along with hoses and clamps for connecting to your CO_2 tank. Dispensing equipment includes a CO_2 tank, beer line, clamps, and taps of various types. Some specialized equipment is needed to clean and repair kegs, typically long, thin brushes, replacement gaskets and O-rings, poppet valves, relief valves, and tools for removing keg posts.

Transferring beer from kegs can be accomplished with beer-to-beer keg jumpers (this also works for cleaning kegs), by running it through a filtering system, or by using a counter-pressure bottle filler or BeerGun. Various lengths of beer line and gas line can make the job easier, since you may be adopting the system to different needs over time. Kegging is a highly personalized subject. With enough basic parts, you can build different devices to do whatever you want. I find it useful to keep an ample supply of various keg parts (O-rings, washers, poppets, fittings, etc.) around for replacing failed components or for building a new solution (like hooking up to someone else's dispensing system).

Learning Your System

Building your system is one thing, but knowing how to use it to make beer is another. It takes time to learn a system or to adapt to it after you have made changes. You often won't make beer as good as you previously did until you learn how your new system responds, so don't be discouraged—this is a normal part of the learning process.

Think of systems in abstract terms, like black boxes with inputs and outputs. You don't necessarily have to understand the inner workings of each of the parts of your system if you have a good feel for how it responds. That is, if you can predict outputs given certain inputs, then you have developed a feel for your system. This is the systems approach for managing complexity; it allows you to learn the system a piece at a time. As you gain more experience, you can begin to learn why each piece of equipment or each process produces those outputs, but at the start you're just looking for predictable outcomes.

If you think of your brewing system as a collection of black boxes, linked together by their inputs and outputs, then you have an understanding of the relationship of the components to each other. You begin to develop an appreciation for how changes you make in one step affect how later steps function. Understanding both the relationship between system components and how each individual component responds is necessary for mastering your system.

So what are some of the key things you should know about your system? Basically, I think it's important to understand the range of anything that can be adjusted and how those changes affect the outcome of each step. How do you make adjustments, and how do you measure the effect of those changes? Each measurement you take (even if just a visual assessment) provides a measure of feedback that controls how you adjust your process. So understanding when your change has the correct effect is just as important as knowing how to make the change. You have to learn to recognize when your process is right and when it's time to stop fiddling.

Some examples of process control points to learn about your system, as a way of characterizing how it functions include:

- How accurate are your thermometers and other instruments (like pH meters)? Are you confident in them; when were they last calibrated? How fast do they respond? When do you take measurements, and how long do you have to wait before you get a meaningful measurement? Instant-read thermometers can respond much faster than traditional thermometers; test them and see how much contact time you need before you can rely on the reading. If you pick a number while an instrument is still changing, then you are grabbing unreliable data. Let readings stabilize before recording them. I find that my thermometers respond much faster than my pH meter.

- How much temperature do you lose when moving brewing water between the hot liquor tank and the mash tun? If you are trying to hit a certain mash-in temperature, the difference is important, since that becomes your strike temperature goal. On my system, this difference is about 15° F (8° C).

- When your mash is resting and you are getting a consistent temperature reading, how stable is that temperature over time? How much will your mash cool in one hour? Depending on the ambient temperature (I brew outdoors), I can see heat loss of 8 to 10° F (4-6° C) or more per hour if I am using an uninsulated tun. If I use a "mash cozy" (a homemade insulated blanket for my mash tun), I can reduce that to 1 to 2° F (1° C) per hour.[1]

- When step mashing, how do you increase the temperatures? If you are doing it by direct fire, how much will the temperature continue to rise after you cut off the heat? This likely depends on your method (recirculating, stirring) and the responsiveness of your thermometers. Learn when you need to cut off your heat to hit the target temperature.

- How long do you have to do certain steps until conditions stabilize? For instance, how long do you have to stir the mash (or what techniques do you need to use) in order to get a consistent temperature throughout it? If you haven't tried this before, get a thermometer with a long probe and move it around your mash tun. Take readings at different depths and locations. See how much variability there is. Are there steps you can take (such as preheating the mash tun, using rice hulls, using a thinner mash, etc.) to reduce this variability?

- How do you measure your volumes? One of the first challenges when moving to larger systems and doing all-grain brewing is hitting your target gravities and volumes. Your mash program may work perfectly as planned, but if you don't hit the target volume, the finished beer may have a completely different character. Determine how you can accurately measure the volume in the brew kettle. This affects when you stop running off and when you stop boiling. I have a measuring stick that is marked based on known volumes added to my kettle, always measured from a known reference point.

- What is your evaporation rate? This can depend on other factors, such as how hard a boil you are conducting and the local weather conditions, but take an average reading for "normal" conditions to use as your baseline.

---

[1] I made a mash cozy out of a fiberglass water heater blanket sandwiched between sheets of reflective duct insulation, all bound together with duct tape. It fits tightly over my mash tun, slides into place, and has some heat resistance. It won't win any style awards, but it does the job.

This helps you determine your initial boil volume to hit a target volume based on boil length. Yes, you can measure the final volume, but if you reduce the boil time, you may not get the same effects (hop utilization, DMS reduction, break formation, etc.).

- How much loss do you have from final boil volume to initial fermenter volume, and from initial fermenter volume to final finished beer volume? Again, this can depend on many other factors, but for an average beer, how much trub do you leave behind? You may not get the maximum volume if you are trying to get the clearest possible beer. Many of my batch sizes are odd volumes, because I'm always trying to wind up with at least five gallons of finished beer. Your recipes should be based on the final boil volume, not the final finished beer volume. Scale your recipes appropriately to get the finished beer volume you desire.

- How do you measure your mash thickness? What water-to-grist ratio are you trying to achieve? On some systems (such as mine), you cannot simply measure the water added to the mash tun, since there is considerable water under the false bottom. Your measurement should be based on the amount of water in direct contact with the grain, not the total volume used. On my system, I measure the amount of water it takes to reach the top of the false bottom and deduct that from my strike water calculations when determining mash thickness. Regardless of how you measure mash thickness, learn what the thicknesses look like. More often than not, I add water until I achieve the desired consistency rather than a specific volume. Note that this can affect how you hit your target mash temperature, so don't take this less precise approach unless you can easily adjust the temperature. After you get a good feel for your system, this part of the process really does become second nature.

- In general, how many pounds of grain are needed to hit different gravity targets in the final wort? Yes, you can calculate your system efficiency (and you should, if for no other reason than to have a value to use in brewing software calculations), but it also helps to have an intuitive feel for how many pounds of grain are needed to hit different gravities on your system. As you adjust your techniques, measure the effect on efficiency. You may not always want to extract the maximum number of gravity points from your beer; this can have an impact on malt flavor and quality. However, there are other steps that can increase your efficiency without sacrificing quality (such as performing a mash-out, or cutting your grain bed before lautering).

- How do you adjust the mash runoff? How do you adjust the sparge (if not batch sparging)? What runoff rate do you target to meet your objectives? Are you trying to complete the process quickly, are you looking to maximize extract, or is there some other goal? Discover the desired rate that best meets your goals, and determine how to adjust your system to achieve that rate.

- How do you recirculate? How long do you typically have to do it to achieve clarity? Are there any special steps you must take? Do you use this as part of your mash-out process? What flow rate is needed?

- Do you need to take any special steps to separate hops and hot break from the boil? Do you need to let the beer rest, whirlpool it, chill it, or do any other steps? On my system, I have to use some whole hops to provide a filter bed; otherwise, I have to take additional steps. So the equipment choices in your system can affect ingredient selection and process control.

- How do you chill? How does your feed water temperature affect the final temperature of the wort? If you are using a counterflow chiller, how fast can you run off to get the desired amount of chilling? When do you need to pre-chill the water?

- What kinds of techniques are possible on your system, and how difficult are they to perform? What additional equipment (e.g., decoction pot) do you need to perform these techniques? Do you need to reconfigure your system to perform them? How much additional time and effort do you need to allot when planning these steps? If you are making multiple sequential batches, how much can you pipeline your steps? Is there a possibility to do advance work or overlap steps? This affects how you plan your brew day.

Some of these examples are system- and equipment-dependent; they may not make sense on all systems. However, they give you an idea of the types of control points and measurements you may need to understand to properly control your system. As you gain more experience, continue to look for the meaningful aspects of your system—you need to identify those key steps that affect the outcome of your beer. Don't assume that all control points are of equal importance; they're not. Focus your efforts initially on those that make a big difference, then later, worry about fine-tuning the rest.

Optimizing Your Brewing

Once you have learned your system, what steps can you take to improve your brewing? Many people stop once they have mastered their system, figuring there is nothing else to learn. This is a mistake, since the difference between a competent brewer and an expert brewer is often measured in how efficiently and effectively they perform the same tasks. If you can improve your output and results simply by better planning and focus, then you have truly mastered brewing.

I call this goal the zen of brewing: You can achieve a deep, meaningful understanding of the entire process as a whole through direct intuitive insight. If you can completely grasp the brewing process as practiced on your particular system, you can in effect become one with your system and control it with effortless grace. This, in my opinion, is what separates the top-tier brewers from everyone else; they simply seem to always know what to do and are not wasting time or effort to get the results they want. It's not so much about learning more techniques, but rather internalizing the techniques and processes so that thoughts and desires are more directly translated into actions and outcomes. For those who have learned a second language, it's like the epiphany that happens when you stop translating in your head and start thinking and speaking directly in the other language.

Some of this mastery comes through simple repetition and understanding of the processes and techniques we've previously discussed, while executed on your particular system. However, other parts involve changing the way you think and plan your brewing, and how you approach tasks. Can you use other clues to understand when a process control point is properly managed, or must you always directly measure it? Where does precise measurement make a difference, and where can you estimate and approximate? We'll examine these topics as we think about internalizing our techniques and optimizing our processes.

Planning Your Brew Calendar

The most obvious reason for planning your brewing calendar is to have a beer available by a certain date, taking into account how long the particular style needs to condition and be ready to serve. Some might take this a step further and consider not just when a beer is drinkable, but when a beer actually is at its peak flavor. This is the essence of planning your calendar for competitions, a topic that will be covered in more depth in Chapter 9. However, there are other practical reasons for arranging the order in which you make your beer.

You may wish to **reuse yeast** from one batch to the next. If you have a list of recipes or beer styles that you want to make during a brewing season, you can arrange them in a way that allows you to repitch the yeast. Be sure to allow sufficient time for the beer to ferment fully and allow for the time needed to rack the beer and clean the yeast before repitching. Racking to a secondary is always an option if the beer needs additional conditioning.

Planning your batches around **equipment availability** is another consideration. Having available fermenters is probably the biggest concern, but you may also be constrained by available kegs or other parts of your packaging process. If certain pieces of equipment need to be repaired, you may be able to make some styles and not others.

Certain **ingredients** are only available during specific times of the year. Seasonal yeast strains are the most obvious ingredient subject to limited availability, although this can be somewhat mitigated if you bank those strains yourself. Those wishing to take advantage of the new hop harvest may factor hop availability into the schedule; the extreme form of this scheduling is when brewers make so-called wet hop beers with freshly harvested hops. Another form of ingredient availability to consider is when your local supplier is out of a particular ingredient and you have to order it by mail. You may restructure your brewing schedule around when expected ingredients will arrive (the same may also be true when ordering new equipment).

Using **opened ingredients** may also drive your brewing schedule. I have certainly gone through phases where I make several successive beers featuring a single sack of malt. Taking this approach allows you to use the grain at its freshest, and also to get more experience with using the ingredient under different conditions. Using an opened bag of whole hops is another example of this constraint, particularly if you don't have a good way of resealing opened hop bags.

These are not very difficult or contrived examples, yet consider the impact on your brewing schedule if you don't account for these issues. You can reduce wasted time by using some advanced planning and avoiding these hassles.

Planning Your Brew Day

Much in the same way your brewing calendar can be optimized, so can your brew day. I think of this approach like a chef; you do the prep work before you start cooking. The cooking term is *mise en place,* or having all that you need to cook ready and waiting. All ingredients are measured and available, all equipment is properly cleaned and set up, and all instructions and information are ready.

Every brewer brews differently; you adopt your own techniques and processes and apply them to your system. But you can still use common planning and preparation techniques to optimize the brew day. It starts with breaking down all the steps. Think about their order, what equipment you need to set up, what ingredients you need, and how much time they take. You may be able to interleave prep tasks with brewing tasks and shorten your overall day. Likewise, you may be able to do some advance setup the night before you brew, enabling you to get started quickly.

Think about what consumes the most time during the brew day. Is it heating the strike water? Setting up the burners and kettles? Measuring and milling the grain? Mashing? If you are able to start the longest task first, you will often shorten the brew day. If you can take preliminary steps to start the longest task or tasks quickly, you can also finish sooner. However, there is a more rigorous way to tackle the planning problem.

In project management, there is the concept of the *critical path*, which is the sequence of dependent tasks that must be completed to get the job done on time. It helps to identify the minimum time needed to complete a complex project involving multiple tasks. Any delay in a task on the critical path (the "weakest link") will cause the entire project to take longer to complete. There may be any number of other tasks not on the critical path that you need to get finished to complete the project, but they don't have to be done on a tight schedule. Some tasks are dependent, in that you must complete several separate tasks before moving on to the next phase. Your brewing day can be broken down in the same manner.

Fortunately, this isn't a complicated process, and it isn't one that you'll likely have to do over and over. Once you figure out a good sequence for your brewing process, you can repeat it every time you brew. If you add optional steps, you can look at the brewing plan and see where they might impact your schedule. If you have a problem with one of the steps, you can also see what other activities will be affected.

You don't really have to go into all this detail, but if you find you often are forgetting to do certain tasks (like adding the Irish moss) then you might want to at least go through the thought process for planning the day. Checklists certainly do help you remember not to skip certain tasks. You could prepare a spreadsheet or document containing an ordered list of your common brewing steps, and print it out every time you brew. Check off the tasks you need to do for this batch, and keep it handy during the brew session.

If you aren't a planning type, at least try to think several steps ahead. Organize your brewing equipment so you have what you need in the same area. Consider purchasing extra equipment if you routinely borrow items from the kitchen. If you keep the equipment together, if you do forget something, you won't have to go far to retrieve it. Have extra consumables in reserve in case you run out; for example, always make sure you have an extra propane tank in case it runs dry in the middle of a batch. If you buy or make RO water for brewing, have an extra container available.

Pay attention during your brewing sessions and take notes of things to improve in the future. What can you do to minimize the steps? What can you do to minimize waste? For instance, are you always dumping out extra brewing water? Do you find yourself heating water repeatedly? Do you frequently add items to correct previous mistakes? All of these can be minimized with some planning and attention to detail. If these problems arise because you are always thinking of something you should have done but didn't, then you need a better plan for brewing. If you brew infrequently, you might forget some key steps; having your common plan written down is a good investment.

Optimizing your brew day isn't just about sequencing the tasks properly. You can also spend some time prioritizing them. Where do you need to focus your energy and attention? Not every step is of equal importance. I have seen brewers focus a disproportionate amount of their time on steps that ultimately have little consequence on the outcome of the beer. If you understand what matters the most, you can make sure those steps are covered correctly.

An example might help explain this point. Brewers are told that sanitation is critical to success. So they sanitize everything and worry about introducing bacteria at every step. But when you're on the hot side of brewing, it really doesn't matter as much. You don't have to sanitize your mash paddle, since the wort is going to be boiled. So if you are taking that step, it's simply wasted effort. Worse yet, there is an opportunity cost associated with those missteps; the time you spent worrying about something that didn't matter is *time you didn't spend on something that was important.*

You can avoid this wasted effort with a better understanding of the end-to-end process of brewing, and what decisions drive the quality of the final beer. If you take the time to identify these key process control points in brewing, you can better focus your attention and effort at those critical times. I'd rather see a brewer focus on achieving a correct mash pH than obsessing over spreadsheets trying to engineer a water profile, for instance.

If you can optimize your brew day, you might be surprised at what you can do with the extra time. You may find it easier to schedule brewing if you can get it done in a half day rather than a full day. You might be able to make two or three batches of beer in only a little more time than you previously spent on one beer. If you did invest the time to do the critical path planning, you can easily extend that model to see how it would change if you added a second or third batch. Don't do them sequentially if you can start one batch while the next one is in process.

Finally, remember that brewing is often a series of small course corrections. Just because you have a master plan doesn't mean that it has to run like clockwork. There are always issues that pop up when you brew, but if you have a good plan, you don't have to panic when something goes wrong. You can quickly assess the impact and make the small changes necessary to get back on track. Remember that people won't be seeing or judging your process when they taste your beer;

it's all about the finished product. What you do to make it easier on yourself is simply a way for you to get more enjoyment out of your hobby.

Approximating and Estimating

The last section talked about the importance of identifying the critical portions of your process and focusing your attention and energy on those key tasks. This concept can be extended further when thinking about measurements.

In many parts of the brewing process, taking a measurement is critical. But a well-reasoned estimate based on practical experience can often substitute for a direct measurement using a mechanical or electrical instrument. Knowing when you can estimate instead of making a direct measurement is tied into the previous discussion about understanding what is absolutely critical versus what can have a larger margin of error and still be successful.

Estimating can be considered a form of measurement, but you are using your senses as the instrument. You can tell when your mash is done by looking at the changes (cloudy water becoming dark and clear, starchy taste becoming sweet, etc.) and knowing how long it has taken. You can estimate the amount of grain you need for a recipe based on past usage and knowledge of your system. For example, if I know that 10 pounds (4.5 kilograms) of grain can make 5 gallons (19 liters) of approximately 1.054 beer on my system, then I can estimate the amount of total grain I need to make a 1.040 beer. You don't always have to make exact measurements and calculations to be successful; you can *approximate*.

Your ability to make accurate readings without actually measuring is a skill developed through experience and repetition. You might notice chefs rarely measure ingredients while cooking. They know the measurements by sight or feel, and also know when they can correct any mistakes later. Brewers can develop a similar ability for much of their work. If you don't have to take repeated measurements, then you can brew faster. It makes sense to take measurements to confirm your estimates when you are still learning these skills, but once you have mastered them, it doesn't. Exceptions exist, of course. Even top chefs will measure when baking; there isn't a way to correct measurement errors later, and the precise ratios are critical. Brewing is much more like cooking than baking; you can develop the skills that will allow you to not take as many direct measurements yet still make great beer.

Accuracy vs. Precision

A concept that often confuses people when discussing measurements is the difference between accuracy and precision. These two terms are often used interchangeably, but they mean completely different things. *Accuracy* is how close a measured value is to the actual value. *Precision* is the exactness in how a value is specified, usually in the number of significant digits (decimal places). In an ideal world, you'd want a measurement to be both accurate and precise.

Unfortunately, many people mistake precision for accuracy. For example, if you have a thermometer that repeatedly measures boiling water at sea level at 208.43692° F then you have a very precise but inaccurate reading. Your thermometer works well but needs to be *calibrated* (adjusted so that it reads accurately). However, many people would see five decimal places and automatically assume that the value must be very reliable since it is expressed that way. Big mistake. Using an instrument that measures precisely is worthless unless you know that it is calibrated to display accurate results.

Measurements and estimates both model a physical value—a physical entity has a certain value (for example, your mash has a temperature). Taking a measurement gives you a reading of that value; estimating gives you an approximation of that value. But those aren't the actual values. Models aren't always accurate; you have to test them. Instruments used for measurement need to be calibrated, but their accuracy will always have a tolerance (e.g., temperature accurate to within +/- 0.1 degrees Fahrenheit). Estimates have a similar tolerance, but it's based on your judgment and experience. Not all instruments will read with the same accuracy, and not all estimates will be valid. You need to understand the sources of error and accuracy of any instrument you use, whether it is a tool or your own senses.

When you do take readings using instruments, you also need to understand where and how you are measuring. For instance, when you read your mash temperature, how do you know the temperature is the same throughout the mash? Try an experiment: use a long-probe, instant-read thermometer and move it around your mash to different depths and different distances from the center. Do you get consistent readings? How much variation do you have? Do the readings change if you have a thicker mash versus a more dilute mash?

Now consider how enzymes work. Does it really make that much of a difference if your mash is 152 or 154° F (67 or 68° C)? Enzymes don't magically stop working at certain temperatures; they decline slowly. So the differences in temperature are minor when it comes to mash results. But when you think about differences in readings throughout your mash tun, you realize that you may not have as much control over mash temperature as you thought you did. Should you worry about a singular reading being off by a degree or two, or should you worry about getting vastly different readings throughout your mash tun? If you are going to focus your energy on precise temperature control, make sure you first address the accuracy. Get consistent readings, then worry about minute differences.

If you aren't going to address the differences in mash temperature throughout your tun, then you probably shouldn't waste time heating or chilling to change the mash temperature a few degrees. It's a matter of scale. In this case, it's better to go with average temperatures and understand that over time, the temperatures will level out. If you understand the relative scale and importance of issues or problems you have, then you won't waste as much time trying to solve what ultimately won't affect the outcome very much.

The goal of this section is to open your eyes to the sources of error in brewing and measuring, and to make you think about the relative importance of what you choose to do. You can develop skills that allow you to estimate and approximate in areas where precision isn't critical, which allows you to focus your attention on those points of the process where it is. Good brewers learn to trust their palate and their senses, and to let their experience guide their actions. Mastery of your system doesn't mean that you know how to make constant corrections; it's more about the wisdom of knowing when to leave everything alone because it's working correctly instead of trying to force it into another state. Remember that sometimes the correct action is simply to do nothing.

mastering ingredients

Make the most of yourself, for that is all there is of you.
–Ralph Waldo Emerson

Just as a chef must understand the products he works with in order to get the best results, a brewer needs to have a solid understanding of the brewing ingredients (malt, adjuncts, hops, yeast, water) to be able to control the profile of the finished beer. This chapter isn't going to be an exhaustive review of all ingredients; ingredient suppliers are always adding new products, so a detailed list would get dated rather quickly. I'm going to focus on how you categorize, characterize, differentiate, and select each of these types of ingredients.

The goal is for you to be able to choose ingredients that allow you to brew what you want, to be able to understand cause and effect and how ingredient choices affect the finished beer, and to be able to evaluate new products as they are released. This is the essence of learning and mastering; you should be able to branch out and add to your repertoire once you have mastered working with a basic set of ingredients.

For each of the types of ingredients I'm discussing, I provide some background on the key points you need to know to properly work with them. I'll also share the selections I've made, and how I approach using these ingredients. Keep in mind that my choices are my own, and your choices will likely be different.

Assessing Ingredients

When it comes to understanding and remembering the taste and aroma of foods, there is no substitute for actually experiencing them. You can read as many descriptions as you want about certain foods, but if you haven't tasted them, you're only guessing at what they're like. When trying to pick the right ingredients to achieve a certain target beer profile, it's very hard to imagine the end product without first-hand knowledge of their character.

Below are some techniques I use when trying to learn the flavor and aroma profiles of new ingredients. The goal should be to characterize (describe) the profiles and to differentiate them from other similar ingredients. If you can go further and identify possible style matches for the ingredients, that's even better. These types of experiments are good educational experiences for all brewers. If you want to do such an experiment, strongly consider sharing the experience with fellow club members or local brewers. Experiments like these have been very popular at National Homebrew Conferences, local homebrew club meetings, and in BJCP judge training classes. If you can get more experienced palates to help you characterize the ingredients, you will get more useful information from the exercise.

When doing these types of sensory experiments, remember only to change one variable at a time. If performing a yeast experiment, use the same hopped wort. When conducting a hops experiment, ferment them with the same yeast. Use the same water profile and fermentation conditions.

Malt. To learn the flavor contribution from malt, first taste and chew it. This will give a general impression. However, there's no substitute for actually brewing with it. I've made single-malt beers to learn their flavor and aroma contributions. Keep the hops on the low side and don't use a yeast with an aggressive flavor profile. Once when I made a Vienna lager with 100 percent Durst Vienna malt, I overshot my gravity target (1.062 instead of 1.050, probably by boiling it down too far) so I called it a *maibock* instead. To try this recipe, do a single decoction, use 22 IBUs of Sterling hops in the boil, and Wyeast 2206 yeast. I've also made various pale ales with Crisp Maris Otter, Dingeman pale ale malt, and Briess two-row.

For crystal and roast malts, steep them as if making an extract beer (soak them in 150-170° F (66-77° C) water for 30 minutes), then strain. Cool and taste the liquid. You can also ferment this with a neutral yeast to determine the residual flavor profile. Roasted malts can also be cold steeped (see the Mastering Techniques chapter for more information) to determine their character.

Sugars and other sugary fermentables. Taste them raw. Taste them as a diluted syrup. Ferment a small sample with a clean yeast and see what residual flavors remain. Gently mix or swirl the raw ingredients into a sample of a dry, neutral-tasting beer (a commercial beer is fine). This process is like back-sweetening a mead. It will make a sweeter beer, but you should be able to taste the sugar character in a beer without having to ferment it. The best thing about this experiment is that you can do it directly in a sampling cup. When using a dry sugar, mix it with equal parts water in a saucepan over heat to create a simple syrup before mixing it into the beer. It will dissolve easier that way; ask any bartender.

Starchy fermentables. It's hard to tell what some grains will ultimately taste like in beer without mashing them. However, most starchy adjuncts are also food products, so you can get a general idea of their profile by eating the food in as natural a state as possible. Most of the grains can be cooked by simmering in water; if you use flaked brewing products, you can just cook some of those directly. You can also cook polenta, rice, oatmeal, cracked wheat, and other grains the same way. Simmer with twice their volume in water until tender, typically 15 to 20 minutes.

Hops. Crush the hops between your fingers or in the palm of your (clean) hand. Smell them. Steep the hops in boiling water for 2 minutes, then remove the hops and chill the samples. Characterize the aroma profile. The flavor profile is harder to determine this way since the hops aren't treated the same way as in the boil.

If I want to check on the flavor of a hop in a beer, I usually use it as a first wort hop when brewing a test batch. That always gives me the most flavor. For aroma, I throw it in at knockout and then chill quickly. I usually combine these in the same beer by making a single-varietal hop beer.

For single-hop beer, try using the 22 Bines recipe I picked up while Sierra Nevada Beer Camp: Use a simple grain bill; 90 percent of the grist was a split between two-row and Pilsner malt, with the remaining 10 percent Munich. Try something like an India pale ale in the 1.065 OG range, or scale it down as an

American pale ale in the 1.050 range. Ferment with a neutral yeast, like Sierra Nevada's WY1056/WLP001. Hop the IPA to 50 IBUs and the APA to 35 IBUs. Use a 1-ounce flavor addition at 15 minutes, and a 1-ounce aroma addition at 2 minutes for the APA, and increase the aroma addition to 2 ounces for the IPA, optionally dry hopping it with 1-2 ounces. I would evaluate the beer before and after dry hopping to see how the character changes.

Evaluate the beer's bitterness; try to determine if it's a clean or a harsh bitterness. Characterize the flavor and aroma; what components do you sense and in what intensity? Are any of them unpleasant?

Yeast. Split a batch and ferment the parts with different yeasts. You can do this with a homebrew club or other group. I've gone to at least three of these presentations at National Homebrew Conferences, and they are some of the most informative sessions I've ever attended. You can split one batch of beer into many different containers for fermentation; you can use glass growlers or plastic soda bottles as fermenters. Use the same wort and ferment under the same conditions, for best results. If you're doing a simple A/B comparison between a known yeast and a new yeast, then brew a double batch of one of your existing recipes and pitch each yeast into one of the batches.

Malt

Malt in brewing terms specifically refers to germinated and kilned barley. The process by which the malt is handled during kilning, the temperatures used, and moisture conditions affect the final flavor profile and performance of the malt. Malt provides the primary sugar source in wort once its starches have been converted in the mash.

Malt can be identified and described with several terms. The major classification is based on the *type of grain*: two-row barley, six-row barley, or another malted grain (wheat, oats, rye). The next classification is the *type of malt*, such as two-row brewer's malt, Pilsner, pale ale, Vienna, etc. This is essentially the role the malt will play in your recipe. The next (optional) classification is the *variety* of the grain, such as Maris Otter, Golden Promise, Harrington, or Metcalfe; this is like breed of dog. The next identification is the *maltster*, such as Crisp, Simpsons, Weyermann, or Briess; this is who malted the grain. You also should know the *country or region of origin* of the malt—where it was grown—such as the United States, United Kingdom, Germany, Canada, Belgium, or Moravia. Finally, you should know the *color* of the malt, usually measured in Lovibond (°L) or EBC, an indication of how highly it was kilned.

The variety of the malt may not always be specified. The malt you buy could very well be a blend of several varieties, or the predominant variety might not be considered interesting enough to publicize. Varieties tend to be specified if they are considered particularly desirable, or would command a premium price when compared to common malt. You should expect to pay more for Maris Otter malt than pale ale malt (similar to expecting to pay more for a Cabernet Sauvignon than a red table wine). Some other U.K. varieties that are currently available are Pipkin, Halcyon, Optic, Chariot, and Pearl. North American two-row varieties of note are Harrington, Copeland, and Metcalfe.

The availability of malt varieties can change if growers decide they want to sow a different crop. New strains are developed all the time, and those with superior attributes will quickly take over production. When I first started brewing, Klages was the most common two-row variety, and now it can't be found. Be willing to try substitutes if your favorite variety is replaced.

Modification, Diastatic Power, and Protein Levels

In the discussion on mashing techniques, I treated all malts as more or less the same, but that's a crude approximation. Different types of malt have different *diastatic power* (DP), *modification,* and *protein levels.* This information is commonly listed on the malt analysis sheet, the maltster's website, or the website of the seller, although not always in a directly usable form. These factors can affect your recipe formulation and brewing process.

The diastatic power is the enzymatic power of the malt, or the ability of the grain to convert itself and other starches. It is measured in either degrees Lintner (°L or sometimes °Lintner, so as not to be confused with degrees Lovibond for color) or in Windisch-Kolbach units, WK—you may see either depending on the country of origin of the malt). The conversion formula is WK = (L x 3.5) – 16.

The DP of malt is always listed on the malt analysis sheet. Generally, 35-40 Lintner (106-124 WK) is needed for malt to be able to self-convert (i.e., you can use 100 percent of the malt in the grist and be able to get full extract from the grain without any additional enzymes). Munich malt can self-convert, although it might take longer than normal mashes. Munich has a DP of about 40-50 L, compared to six-row, which might be 160 L or higher.

The lower the DP, the longer the malt takes to convert. Mash longer and test for conversion, or blend the malt with another grain with a higher DP. Consider a decoction mash, since the malt will pass through saccharification temperatures more often, giving more time for α-amylase to work. If you use a higher enzyme malt (large DP) than is typical for a known recipe, you may need to raise the mash temperature slightly to get similar results (and vice versa).

Modification is basically the degree to which malt is "mealy" or fully soluble and ready for saccharification. The degree of modification is sometimes described as the ratio of the length of the acrospire to the length of the barley kernel in germinated barley, expressed as a percentage; this is only a proxy, however, for the actual modification. It is the nature of the starch in the endosperm that matters.

The malt analysis sheet again can provide clues to this information. The Grind Difference (% FG/CG) is a measure of modification on malt analysis sheets. (FG and GC refer to fine grind and coarse grind, methods of measuring extract.) Well-modified malt is 1 percent FG/CG or less, while protein rests are likely needed for undermodified malts (1.8-2 percent and higher).

Greg Noonan wrote extensively on understanding malt analysis sheets; look at his work if you intend to read the data sheets. However, understand that in today's brewing, most malt you buy will be highly modified and suitable for a single-infusion mash regime. Some malt is specifically marketed as undermodified, and thus intended for decoction mashing. But those are quite rare. The maltster has done much of the work that traditionally was done by the brewer.

If you brew with some malts and find that your beers aren't clearing properly, then you may need to add a short protein rest to your mash schedule. I find that a short rest at 131° F (55° C) improves the clarity of my beers when I use continental Pilsner malts (Durst, Dingeman, Weyermann, Best), for instance. I've also had problems with Munton's Maris Otter clearing, which is odd since Crisp Maris Otter always clears for me. Malts can vary from lot to lot, so check the malt analysis sheet. However, if you find that a certain malt from a specific maltster always acts a certain way, take that into account when planning your brewing schedule.

In summary, the malt analysis sheet or information from the maltster's website can give you key information about the malt. The diastatic power (DP) lets you know whether the malt can convert itself, and thus offers clues as to how much to use in your recipes. The modification tells you whether or not to use a more intensive mashing schedule or whether to do a single-step mash. High protein levels suggest that a protein rest is needed or that adjuncts should be used. These factors alone won't tell you how the beer will taste, but they do levy constraints that must be considered.

Characterizing Malt

While there are many kinds of malt that brewers might use, I find it easier to think of them in larger groups that share common attributes. I break malts into four categories: base malts, specialty malts, crystal malts, and roasted malts. They are either separated because of the process used to create them or because they are used differently in beer.

Base malts are any malts that contain sufficient enzymes to self-convert in the mash, and that you would use in up to 100 percent of the grist. The types of malt I include in this group are two-row malt, Pilsner (Pils) malt, pale ale malt, Vienna malt, Munich malt, and *rauchmalz* (smoked malt), as well as the pale types of other malted cereal grains (wheat, rye, oats).

Specialty malts are any malts that are primarily used in smaller percentages to add specific flavors to the finished beer; they are often just higher-kilned versions of common base malts. I sometimes call them *character malts* or *flavor malts,* since they are often responsible for the primary flavor character of the beer. I include such malts as aromatic/melanoidin, biscuit/Victory, Special Roast, honey malt, amber malt, and brown malt in this category. These malts are typically mashed along with the base malts to convert their sugars, but many can just be steeped to extract flavor.

Crystal malts are stewed during kilning, so their starches convert to sugars before they are kilned to their final color. These malts do not need to be mashed since their sugars are already converted. The sugars just need to be liquefied and rinsed into the wort. A steep in 150-170° F (66-77° C) water usually accomplishes this goal; this can be part of the mash, done during mashout or vorlauf, or even in the boil. Any malt that is called crystal or caramel falls into this group; many European malts in this class are called cara(something). Special "B" is a very dark crystal malt; one that adds a unique raisinlike character to beer. There are crystal versions of wheat and rye malt, as well.

Roasted malts are usually processed in a drum roaster to develop a much darker color and sharper flavor. These malts do not need to be mashed and can be treated like crystal malts. Common malts in this category include chocolate malt, Kiln Coffee, black patent malt, and various Carafa malts from Weyermann. Roasted barley is also included in this category, although it isn't technically a malt, it's an unmalted grain. As with crystal malt, there are also various roasted wheat and rye malts.

There are also many huskless roasted malts, which have less acidity, less tannin, less harshness, and provide less of a burnt/roasted flavor. Weyermann makes the Carafa Special malts in this way, and Belgian debittered black malt is similar. These malts are key to certain styles (black IPA, *schwarzbier*, or any style that needs to have a dark color without too much roasted or burnt flavors). Weyermann Sinamar is concentrated liquid extract made from Carafa Special II malt. It can be added at any time from the boil to packaging. It allows you add the color and flavor of roasted (but not bitter) malt and is a great way to add some color and flavor of roast to an existing beer.

Selecting Malt

When selecting a type of malt to use, you need to consider its flavor profile and color as part of your recipe formulation, and you also have to consider its impact on your brewing. How does it respond to mashing? Does it impact your efficiency? Does it create beers with good clarity? Are there any problems milling it? Do you notice any issues with beers made from it not being stable? How stable is the raw grain in storage? These are all questions that can impact your selection of a type of malt, a specific version of the malt, or a maltster, as well as the brewing processes and techniques you use.

As you taste different malts, think about their flavor contribution. Are they doughy, grainy, crackery, cookielike, bready, bread crustlike, biscuity, malty-rich, toasty, roasty, or burnt? Do they have any dried or dark fruit character (raisins, plums, cherries)? How sweet are they? How rich are they? Do they have multiple layered flavors? Can you be more specific about some of the flavors, like does roasty taste like chocolate, coffee, or something else? Does the malt remind you of any foods?

You can read descriptions of malts, but it's best to taste them for yourself. Taste can be somewhat subjective, so make sure you agree with a description before adopting it. Once you understand the flavor profile of your ingredients, you can determine how well those ingredients can be used to formulate recipes for specific beer styles. Compare the descriptions in the style guidelines with your own observations about the ingredient flavors.

Pay careful attention to the color specifications (°L or EBC) of the malt you are buying. Different maltsters might kiln their malts to different levels. Chocolate malt is notorious for covering a very wide range, from 200 °L (pale chocolate) to 500 °L. You can't get a different color without also getting a different flavor. Crystal malts from different maltsters might have different values. Check the specifications and buy the color and flavor you need. If you've used brewing software to calculate the color, make sure the grain database is using the same color as the malt you bought.

The goal should be to develop an understanding of a workable set of malts that allow you to brew a wide range of styles. Keep notes as to which malts and maltsters you prefer. If you have problems with storage, stability, milling, clarity, or efficiency, make special note of it. Try to isolate the problem, and avoid malts that you don't like or don't work well on your system. You don't have to understand every malt, but you want to be able to make reliable selections of ingredients to get the end product you desire.

Preparing Malt

Typically, all a brewer must do to prepare malt for brewing is to crush it. However, before you do that, do a little quality control checking. Take a look at your malt, and look for signs of insects (weevils and beetles, usually); they might come out as flies, or just leave a telltale fluffiness or dusty webs in the grain. A few here and there won't cause problems except for perhaps a lower extract from your malt. More than a few, and you should dump the malt. If you just bought it, return it. If whoever sold it to you won't take it back, don't buy from them again. If you've had it for a while, review your storage practices.

Malt should be stored dry, since many insects won't thrive in a low-moisture environment. Storing cool will also help keep any insects from being too active. I also like to keep as much air out of my grain as possible. Most grain sacks are lined with a thick plastic; leave that in place. Squeeze excess air out and twist the liner closed tightly, and then keep it closed with a rubber band or twine. If the liner is attached to the sack, then twist the whole thing closed and tie it well.

Taste the malt to make sure it still has the right flavor profile, and hasn't gotten stale or damp. Neither will make good beer. If you don't know the correct flavor profile, start tasting your malt when you first get it. Understand the taste of your ingredients so you can tell if something has gone wrong before you've started.

When crushing grain, your goal is break the starch into tiny pieces while leaving the husks as intact as possible. The best efficiency could be gained if the starch was turned entirely into flour, and the husks were not shredded at all. That's hard to do on a home system, so you have to make do with what you can. Adjust the mill so that it is crushing the starches in the endosperm without pulverizing the husks. Take a close look at the output of the mill after you make an adjustment; if you aren't happy, keep adjusting and sampling.

While at Sierra Nevada Beer Camp, I saw an innovative method for dealing with the problem of how to get the best crush without shredding the husks: *wet milling.* Just before the grist is milled, it is sprayed with brewing liquor at 140° F (60° C)—this is the steep water for dough-in. The water makes the grain husks more pliable, so they don't get shredded as readily. The brewer can set the two-roller mill fairly tight to get a great crush, yet the husks stay mostly intact. This results in better runoffs and higher beer quality. The total water for the mash (at mash conversion temperature) is sprayed in while grain is being milled, so the mill is actually starting the mash. This whole process takes place under nitrogen. Scott Jennings, who is Sierra Nevada's pilot system brewmaster, recommended that homebrewers could simulate this using an airbrush attachment on an air compressor to spray the grains lightly in a shallow pan, turning once, and repeating, then immediately milling. It's not the same process (what I've described is more accurately called *malt conditioning* in brewing literature), but it can help with the crush. Just don't make it too wet, or the grain will stick in the rollers—bad news.

So What Do I Do?

For base malts, I generally try to select malts from the same country or region as the beer style I'm making. I strongly believe that using indigenous ingredients makes authentic products. I also think British, Belgian, and German malts have more flavor and character than American or Canadian malts.

I like using the American and Canadian malts (two-row brewer's malt, usually) for styles that have a neutral or grainy malt profile. When I need a pale ale malt, I typically pick English or Belgian, depending on how much of a bready, biscuit flavor I want (the U.K. malts have more of this). For Pils malt, I typically go with German or Belgian sources; sometimes the Belgian types have a slightly estery quality, so I pick German malts when I want it to be totally clean. Pils adds some sweetness and a more elegant, rounded flavor than two-row.

I often mix base malts, like pale and Pils, two-row and Pils, Vienna and Maris Otter, two-row and Maris Otter. You can do this to dilute strong flavors in malt that may be inappropriate for some styles, to add malty complexity or increase richness. If you come up with a custom blend you like, it might become part of the house character of your beers.

When choosing crystal malts, understand that crystal 40 is not the same as half crystal 20 and half crystal 60. Color is one thing, but flavor is another. Using more types of crystal malt can add layers of complexity and depth of color, but can also taste muddy if too many are used. Unless I'm looking for one specific flavor (like the caramel candy flavor from crystal 40), I typically use multiple crystal malts for complexity. In wheat beers, I'll tend to use the crystal and roasted versions of wheat as well.

Using unusual malts is interesting, like Belgian crystals in American beers (Joe Formanek first suggested I use Belgian crystal malts in an American amber ale), or Belgian pale/Pils malt instead of American/German. Exchanging American, English, German, and Belgian malts for something untraditional for a style may add complexity (but consider the flavors being added or changed; this could also be something that could move you out of style).

I know brewers that like to add signature malts to the grist: honey malt, biscuit/Victory malt, Special Roast, German extra pale, aromatic, rye, home toasted, smoked, dark Munich, brown malt, amber malt, etc. I don't have any malts that I use in all styles, but I do like the intense richness of dark Munich malt and the rich biscuit flavor of amber malt. Explore character malts; they can be distinctive in larger quantities but can add an interesting complexity in smaller quantities.

Check out flavors of different roasted malts. Huskless versions are good for color, but you need to use more to get the same flavor levels. I don't like harshness in beer, so I often use the Carafa Special or debittered Belgian black malts. However, these won't give you the same flavors. Blending different roasted malts (including traditional with huskless) can give you a more complex or layered flavor. I tend to control harshness more through grain handling techniques and water chemistry than I do with grain selection, although for certain styles (*schwarzbier*, black IPA) I'll be very careful with anything that has a burnt or harsh flavor.

For specialty malts, check to see if they are derived from two-row or six-row; two-row has higher-quality flavor. I'll often use English or Belgian crystal-type malts over American if I see the American crystal malts are based on six-row. Taste the malts and see if the difference matters. I do always use American crystal 40 when I want a pure caramel flavor, however.

Don't overlook using very dark crystal malts, such as crystal 120 and Special "B," and very light chocolates (pale chocolate). Malts in the 100 to 200 °L range can produce some fairly interesting flavors. I think of these malts as giving me more heavily caramelized sugar flavors, dark fruit, and nuttiness. However, these flavors can also be quite intense, so use them more as accents than as primary flavors.

Malt really does vary widely by the maltster. Get to know the flavor profiles of the malts you typically use. You can substitute, but you might get different results—pay closer attention when you are substituting. Check the specs for crystal and roast malts; the color can be different, which will impact the expected flavor profile. Some malts come in different grades or intensities (Weyermann in particular, with its CaraMunich and Carafa malts), so make sure you know which one you need; they have different colors and flavors.

If a recipe calls for smoked malt, I only use Weyermann *rauchmalz* and never use peat-smoked malt. On rare occasions I might use at most an ounce of peat-smoked malt in a Scottish style, but I think it tastes like phenolic dirt. I remember an old posting on Homebrew Digest, in which someone said they used a pound of peat-smoked malt and that it made their beer taste like "an open grave."

Adjuncts

Adjuncts are the additional sources of sugar in beer aside from that derived from malt. They are usually categorized into sugary adjuncts (sugar, honey, molasses, treacle, maple syrup, etc.) and unmalted starchy adjuncts (oats, rye, wheat, corn/maize, rice, barley, etc.). Sugary adjuncts can be added directly to the boil or afterward. Starchy adjuncts need to be mashed along with other grains to provide sugars for fermentation but don't have active enzymes of their own. Some of these grains can also be malted; in that case, they are considered malt, not adjuncts.

Historically, starchy adjuncts such as corn and rice were used to dilute the protein content of six-row malt when brewing, to improve clarity, to lighten the flavor, and (probably most importantly) to reduce the cost of raw ingredients. This isn't an issue for most homebrewers, since few of us use six-row base malts, except in historical recipes. So I'm going to ignore the historical role of starchy adjuncts and focus on their modern use in adjusting the beer's overall flavor profile, wort fermentability, residual sweetness, and body.

Plain sugars are normally used simply to increase gravity, decrease body, and increase attenuation. Belgian *tripels* and double IPAs are good examples; use up to 20 percent sugar in a *tripel* and 10 percent sugar in an IPA to get a drier finish. Other sugars and sugary adjuncts are selected mostly for their flavors. Fermentability can vary, so adding these sugar sources might not result in a higher attenuation. They will, of course, increase gravity. Raw sugars will tend to increase fermentability and can contribute flavor. Honey varies; sometimes I've used it and it thins the body, other times it doesn't. It probably depends on the honey variety and the amount used. It can give a rounder flavor, which may suggest a bigger body to the palate. Try it and see what you think. Molasses, maple syrup, and treacle add a strong flavor (blackstrap molasses especially so), and can take a while to age out.

How starchy adjuncts are handled depends on their form. The key point when assessing these adjuncts is to understand whether the starch has been pregelatinized or not. Starch in grain is a natural storage device; it is designed to keep water out. Malting makes the starch more accessible to water. However, in unmalted grains, the starch granules must be burst in order to hydrate and be made accessible to enzymes. Starchy adjuncts have no enzymes of their own, so the diastatic power of the other malts in the grist must be strong enough to convert themselves as well as the adjuncts. For this reason, using adjuncts with six-row is a good idea, but using them with Munich malt is not.

Most adjuncts are available in flaked form, similar to breakfast oats. These grains are processed using heated rollers that crush and burst the starch granules. Flaked grains can therefore be used directly in the mash without milling. This is the easiest form of adjunct to use. Some grains are torrefied, which is a form of processing that also bursts the starch granules. I've only worked with torrefied wheat; it had a taste like Grape-Nuts cereal. Torrefied wheat can be milled and added to the mash.

Unmalted grain can be used in more of a raw, natural form, like steel-cut oats, corn grits, cracked wheat, and the like. These forms are said to have a stronger flavor but require additional handling. These grains should be milled into small grits or a coarse polentalike flour, then cereal mashed. A cereal mash can be done in a saucepan or small pot on a stovetop. Simply mill about 10 percent of your base malt, mix with the milled grits, cover with warm water (2-3 quarts per pound, 4-6 liters per kilogram), slowly heat to 158° F (70° C), stirring continuously, and cook for 15 minutes. Bring to a boil, and boil gently for another 15 minutes, stirring. Then add this to your main mash, where the now-available starch can be fully converted.

A cereal mash is about as time-consuming as a decoction. The reason you add the base malt to the cereal mash is to provide enzymes to help break down the starches. Most starches gelatinize by 158° F (170° C), so the starches are being made available. So why not just cook it like polenta? Well, have you ever let cooked polenta sit for 5 or 10 minutes? It becomes a sticky mass. Adding the malted grains helps prevent the starch from becoming like glue, so you can more easily mix it into the main mash. Boiling is done to further burst the starch granules and fully make the starches available. The enzymes in the cereal mash are denatured by now, so the enzymes in the main mash will complete the conversion.

An alternative to using the raw grits or cracked grain is to use the quick-cooked version. Quick grits, quick oats, converted rice, etc., are all pre-steamed, which makes the starches more readily available. These have more flavor than the flaked forms but less flavor than the raw grains. They can be added directly to the mash.

So What Do I Do?

If using a starchy adjunct, I almost always use the flaked versions. I don't want to do a cereal mash, so I just mash the flaked grains along with my other malts. I have used torrefied wheat on occasion (it does have a unique toasty flavor), but the flaked grains are 'easier to handle and more available. I'm not often looking for a large flavor addition, so that's why I don't use a cereal mash.

I like to use corn as an adjunct in beers requiring a little extra sweetness or a rounder flavor than I'd get from malt alone. Aside from the obvious styles (American light lagers, cream ale, classic American Pilsener), I use corn in some English bitters, mild, old ale, Flanders red, Irish red, and blonde ale. I might use a half-pound to a pound for character, up to 20 to 30 percent in beers with a prominent corn character.

I've never used rice syrup or flaked rice. Rice doesn't seem to have much of a flavor to me, so I tend to use white sugar, instead. In beers others have made that contain rice, I don't taste it. But since I don't have any first-hand experience with this ingredient, I don't want to say much more.

I've tasted most raw sugars and use the ones that have a suitable profile for the beer I'm making. I found piloncillo to be a little smoky and harsh, so use that only in small quantities. Jaggery is interesting; toffeelike. I've used various raw sugars (turbinado, Demerara, muscovado, which are light to dark in that order) with good success, especially in Belgian and English styles. I might use a half-pound to 2 pounds (227-907 grams) of brown sugar in a 5-gallon (19-liter) recipe. Seeking out international markets is a good way to find unusual sugars.

I avoid brown sugar that is just molasses added to cane sugar. If I wanted that, I'd add molasses and cane sugar myself. Read the label on the sugar container to see how it was produced; evaporated syrup is the least processed.

For plain sugar, I use white sugar from beets. I live in Ohio, and beet sugar is made in Michigan, so it's available. I don't think it tastes very different from cane sugar, but it's a local product so I use it. I want to believe it's closer to what

Belgians use, since their sugar is derived from beets, but that's just a mental game. I'll use it to increase the fermentability and attenuation of beer or to raise the gravity. I've gone as high as 20 percent sugar in a *tripel*.

I use a half-pound to 2 pounds (227-907 grams) of honey in some styles. I like it in blonde ale, American pale ale, and IPA, especially orange blossom honey. I use a half-pound when I want a background accent and more when I want the honey to be noticeable. Darker honeys (like buckwheat) can add a distinctive flavor to darker beers. Wildflower and clover are more generically floral. Don't waste expensive varietal honeys as an accent flavor in beer; make mead with them, instead.

A pound or two (454-907 grams) of Belgian candi sugar is what I use in most Belgian styles, but I only use the darker versions. If a recipe calls for pale candi sugar, I just use beet sugar, instead. I now tend to use the liquid Belgian syrups rather than the rock candy version of candi sugar.

Lyle's Golden Syrup and treacle are ingredients that I've used, often in British styles like mild, old ale, winter warmers, and such, or in some Belgian ales (Golden Syrup only). I use half a can to a can in a 5-gallon (19-liter) batch. I've used these for priming on occasion (as I also have with honey).

Recipe Using Treacle and Torrefied Wheat

I used dark treacle when I tried to clone *Old Peculier* a long time ago. I didn't taste these side-by-side, but it did make an excellent cask ale for the winter season.

Old Stranger Cask Ale—Old Ale

Makes 5.5 gallons (20.8 liters)

10 lbs. (4.5 kg) Crisp Maris Otter malt
1 lb. (454 g) Crisp crystal 80° L malt
¼ lb. (113 g) roasted barley
¾ lb. (340 g) CaraPils malt
¾ lb. (340 g) CaraMunich malt
1 lb. (454 g) torrefied wheat
1 can (454 g) dark treacle
1.5 oz. (42 g) Fuggles whole hops, 5.3% alpha acid, at 60 min.
0.5 oz. (14 g) Sterling whole hops, 6.2% alpha acid, at 10 min.

Wyeast 1098 British ale yeast

Use RO water with 1 tsp. chalk. Mash at 151° F (66° C) for 2 hours. Collect 8.5 gallons (32.2 liters) of wort. Boil 90 min. Ferment at 72° F (22° C). Prime with brown sugar and molasses and serve from cask.

OG: 1.062

FG: 1.016

24 IBU

6% ABV

Oats can add body and flavor in recipes. A quarter-pound can add a little body. A pound is quite chewy; I've used that in imperial stouts to great effect. In an oatmeal stout, I'll go 10 to 20 percent for flavor. Sometimes I toast the oats for added complexity; this is a tip I got from *Radical Brewing*.

I like to use molasses in winter warmers and Christmas beers. Blackstrap molasses I use sparingly (1-4 tablespoons/15-60 milliliters for a 5-gallon/19-liter batch); they are really strong.

Recipe Using Blackstrap Molasses

I used blackstrap molasses in the first beer that won a best-of-show for me, a Christmas ale. This is an all-grain version of that recipe, which was inspired by a recipe in my first recipe book, *The Homebrewer's Recipe Guide*.

Holiday Prowler—Christmas Ale

9.5 lbs. (4.3 kg) Crisp Maris Otter

¾ lb. (340 g) Scotmalt crystal 40° L

¼ lb. (113 g) Crisp chocolate malt

1½ lbs. (680 g) clover honey

½ 454-gram can Lyle's Golden Syrup

¼ cup blackstrap molasses

1 oz. (28 g) Goldings whole hops, 6.1% alpha acid, at 60 min.

1 oz. (28 g) Fuggles whole hops, 4.3% alpha acid, at 5 min.

WLP002

Spices: 4 cinnamon sticks, 1 nutmeg, 1 vanilla bean, 7 allspice, 1½ tsp. whole cloves, 8 coriander seeds, peels from 2 nectarines

Mash grains at 158° F (70° C). 90-minute boil. Steep spices (chopped up) in a tight mesh bag at knockout for 10 minutes, remove, then chill wort rapidly. Ferment at 68° F (20° C). Prime with muscovado sugar and cask condition.

OG: 1058

FG: 1014

19 IBUs

5.8% ABV

Hops

Hops are the dried strobiles (cones) of the female *Humulus lupulus* climbing perennial vine. They provide bittering, flavor, aroma, and antibacterial properties to beer. Lupulin glands in hops contain bitter resins and aromatic essential oils. The alpha acids[1] in the resins contribute bitterness to beer when boiled and isomerized into iso-alpha acids. They are measured in the percentage weight of alpha acids (% AA) compared to the total weight of the hop. The final concentration of isomerized alpha acids in beer is measured in International Bitterness Units (IBUs), a direct indication of the total bitterness. The essential oils contain a large number of volatile aromatic compounds that are responsible for the distinctive character of the different hop varieties.

Common forms of hops available to homebrewers are whole hops and pellet hops, and occasionally half-ounce hop plugs. Whole hops are easy to strain out, have the best fresh hop aroma, and are very good for dry hopping. Unfortunately, they also soak up the most wort, are more easily oxidized, and are less stable. Hop plugs are more stable than whole hops, but they can be difficult to break apart and aren't widely available. Pellet hops offer the best utilization and are stable, compact, and easy to measure. They tend to disintegrate into a green sludge, are hard to separate from the wort, and aren't as well suited to dry hopping. The form of hops impacts the brewing system,

---

[1] Beta acids also can contribute some bitterness, but at a much lower level than alpha acids. Beta acids don't produce as much bitterness from the boil, since they don't isomerize as well, but they can oxidize and add bitterness during storage. This bitterness tends to be of a harsher quality than that from alpha acids. Most homebrewers ignore the contribution of beta acids to the bitterness level of beer. Avoiding oxidation (including of hops) should be a major goal during brewing, so the impact of beta acids on properly brewed and stored beer should be negligible.

mostly in how the hops are separated, and recipe formulation, both in varietal availability and in utilization.

Storing Hops

Freshness is important, particularly for late hops. Avoiding oxidation is your biggest concern. You have to rely on your senses, looking at the color and smelling the aroma, to tell if your hops are fresh. Oxidized hops lose color, develop darker colors, and generally don't look "bright"—even frozen hops will be bright green if they aren't oxidized. The flavor of stale hops lacks brightness, intensity, and character; they can often develop a pungent off-aroma similar to Parmesan cheese or sweaty socks if not stored properly. I store my hops in a freezer at -10° F (-23° C). Once opened, I prefer to transfer the hops to glass jars purged with CO_2 (nitrogen would work better). I keep my unopened hops in their original packaging if they appear to be packed in thick, oxygen-barrier materials.

In addition to keeping oxygen away from hops during storage, try to avoid anything that will oxidize the hops when using them in the boil, in post-fermentation handling, and in packaging. Hops contain a huge variety of organic compounds; oxidizing them can produce quite undesirable flavors and aromas.

Characterizing Hops

Some traditional brewing texts like to categorize hops as being bittering hops, aroma hops or dual-use hops. This notion might have made sense at some point in the past, but it isn't really true today. Many high-alpha hops have amazing flavor and aroma profiles. When I use the terms *bittering hops, flavor hops,* and *aroma hops,* I mean the hop *additions* used for their bittering, flavor, or aroma contributions, not that certain varieties only fit in those categories. Feel free to experiment; in times of hop shortages, making hop substitutions are often the only way to brew.

The term *noble hops* is used to describe traditional, low-alpha, high-aroma hops from central Europe, specifically Saaz, Hallertauer, Tettnang, and Spalt. They tend to be high in humulene and low in cohumulone and other harsh-tasting components. *Terroir* (soil, climate, and growing conditions that impart a "sense of place" upon an ingredient) is almost as important in hops as it is in wine; these four hop varieties are only considered noble when they are grown in the original regions for which they are named. Regardless of this categorization, these hops are wonderful aroma and flavor hops, particularly for lagers. Many other hops have been developed for their noblelike qualities (E.g., Sterling, Crystal, Santiam, Vanguard); those are also well suited for classic continental lagers or for any beers where a floral and spicy quality is prized.

I mostly categorize hops by their aroma and flavor profile, but also by their region, their bitterness contribution (% AA), and the character of their bitterness. Bitterness can be harsh or clean and is often a matter of personal preference. Magnum, Warrior, and Summit produce a clean bitterness, while Cluster and Chinook are more coarse and harsh. High cohumulone levels are thought to produce a harsher bitterness. Bitterness contribution is a factor for recipe formulation, and in avoiding using too much hop mass in your beer (which can give you grassy and vegetal flavors).

Region. Where the hops were grown influences their character, as the discussion of the impact of *terroir* on noble hops illustrates. Hallertauer hops grown in America will not have the same character as those grown in Hallertau in Bavaria. Fuggles grown in America aren't the same as those from the United Kingdom. Perle, Northern Brewer, Magnum, Saaz, and Goldings can be obtained from multiple countries. In general, the native versions are superior to those grown in a new region. I tend to prefer native hops that are bred to have the characteristic of classic hops, rather than the classic hops grown in another area.

Confusingly, sometimes the name of the hop will be similar even if the hop is a different variety; Pacific Hallertauer is not just Hallertauer grown in New Zealand—it's a cross between Hallertauer and a native hop. Look at the hop packaging to find the country of origin; don't just assume the source based on the name.

Knowing the source of hops and if they are native is important to me since it helps me choose classic varieties for specific beer styles. If I'm in the mood to experiment, I'll gladly go intercontinental; however, when making an authentic Bohemian Pilsener, U.S. Saaz just won't do.

Profile. I tend to think of hops by the major flavors and aromas they provide, as well as their intensity. This is similar to how hop character is evaluated by beer judges, so I naturally think about that relationship. Some of the major categories I attribute to hops include citrusy, spicy, floral, earthy, herbal, fruity, and piney. Raw hops tend to have a grassy character, which can also show up in beer. If the hop intensity is light, sometimes I can only get those general aromatic categories. However, if the hops are more intense, then I can often get more detailed in what I pick up.

- The *citrusy* character is most commonly associated with American hops, but it can be found in those from other regions as well. Some of the citrus fruit characteristics found in hops include grapefruit, lemon, lime, orange, and tangerine. The character can seem like the fresh fruit, the zest, or other fruit products (I detect orange marmalade in some English hops.). Tropical fruit (pineapple, papaya, mango, guava, passionfruit), stone fruit (apricot, peach, plum, cherry) or berries (black currant) can also be found in hops.

- *Floral* is a characteristic well known in noble hops and some English hops (especially Goldings). The pleasant smell of fresh and dried flowers is an enticing character in beer. I also perceive it as a rounded brightness that may not always be as distinguishable as a citrusy character, but one that definitely triggers "hops" in your mind.

- *Spicy* is a desirable characteristic of many European hops. It's not the same as spiciness that comes from yeast, which can take on clove and pepper notes. This is more of a mysterious, exotic note that often adds complexity to other aromatics.

- *Herbal* is not as common as spicy but can be a little stronger. It can take on mint, thyme, or rosemary qualities in some hop varieties.

- *Earthy* is a quality of some English hops (particularly Fuggles). It's not really phenolic, but I can see some similarities. It's also not muddy or dirty, more like a forest-after-a-rainstorm aroma.

- *Piney* can be considered like a fresh evergreen bough, a more general woody character. American hops often have this character, either alone or in conjunction with citrusy. Often associated with a "Pacific Northwest" character.

- There are also other sulfur-based aromatics that hops can sometimes provide, often from hop varieties that aren't considered desirable as aroma hops, or sometimes as a background character of a hop with more desirable primary characteristics. These sulfur notes are pungent, catty, onionlike, or like crushed tomato leaves.

Several hops are known for having a complex aroma and flavor with multiple characteristics evident (noble hops are often floral and spicy to me, many American hops are citrusy and piney, etc.). When thinking about which hops to use, consider all the perceptible characteristics, not just the most dominant ones. Consider the intensity and balance of each, and then think about how those flavors and aromas will blend in with the other components of your beer.

Selecting Hops

So what drives the choice of hop varieties for these specific purposes? Personally, I like to use hop varieties historically associated with the region where the beer style originated. I'm not rigid about these choices, but that's my first inclination. I often use noble hops as a component of aroma in almost any style. I might also work American hops into English or Belgian styles, since that mirrors experimentation craft brewers are currently doing.

When selecting hops for bittering, think about the total IBU contribution the style requires and the associated vegetal mass of the hops that must be introduced. It's easy to pick higher alpha varieties for this purpose. I like to use clean, neutral bittering hops such as Warrior, Magnum, or Horizon, unless I'm looking for a specific residual hop flavor contribution. In bolder American beers, I might look at Columbus or Chinook. I prefer Challenger in stronger English beers. In Belgian beers, I'm a fan of Saaz and Styrian Goldings. However, virtually any hop can be used, as residual flavor and aroma qualities are typically low. I try to avoid using excessive quantities of bittering hops (more than 3-4 ounces/85-113 grams in a 5-gallon/19-liter batch, boiled 60 minutes or more) to avoid developing excessively grassy, vegetal, or leafy flavors and to reduce wort loss due to absorption.

Although there isn't a unanimous opinion on this, most tend to believe that selecting hop varieties with a low cohumulone level (less than 25-30 percent) helps produce a less harsh beer. The hop suppliers should provide this data; if unavailable, HopUnion has a very good hop data book available on its website (*www.hopunion.com*). To minimize harshness further, using water low in carbonates and not too high in sulfates will help.

Select flavor and aroma hops based on the beer style, as you might expect. While these additions will supply some IBUs, I tend to think of them more in terms of ounces of hops to get the right level of flavor and aroma. In a 5-gallon (19-liter) batch, flavor and aroma additions of a half-ounce (14 grams) or less will tend to give light contributions. I might use a quarter-ounce (7 grams) of hops for something background. An ounce to a half-ounce (14-28 grams) will give something fairly noticeable, while an ounce to 2 ounces (28-57 grams) will give a strong character. More than 2 ounces (57 grams) gets into the aggressive ranges.

Some varieties providing a big hop aroma and flavor are Cascade (floral, citrus), Centennial (bright, fruity), Amarillo (apricots, peaches), Simcoe (grapefruit, pineapple, pine), Citra (grapefruit, pineapple, mango, pine), East Kent Goldings (floral, lemony), Sorachi Ace (lemony), Summit (orange, tangerine, grapefruit), Styrian Goldings (orange marmalade), and any floral, spicy noble hop (Hallertauer, Tettnang, Spalt, Saaz) or noble-derived modern variety (Sterling, Crystal, Santiam, Vanguard).

So What Do I Do?

Using hops in beer is like using spices in cooking; what you pick depends partly on the cuisine you're cooking and partly on your mood. You might have favorite choices that give you a "comfort food" feel, but sometimes you might be in an experimental mood. Hops are a great way to express yourself in your beer. As with other ingredients, I have certain "go-to" varieties but also try to evaluate new varieties when I get the chance. Sometimes I win hops as a competition prize (or even a door prize); that gives me a reason to give them a go.

Think of hops in terms of flavor families and general characteristics, and choose accordingly. Since my system needs some amount of whole hops, I'm somewhat constrained in my choices. So I definitely factor availability into my selections. I've given some of my favorite varieties in the last section, where I discuss getting a big hop character. Flavor notes are what to consider when thinking about how hops will fit in with the rest of the recipe.

I think of things like "citrusy American hop," "noble hop," "floral English hop," "clean bittering hop" when I go to make my selections at the store. If I'm looking for a signature character, I'll obviously pick that hop. But many hops are interchangeable, and I don't often get hung up on a single varietal unless it is absolutely critical for that style.

I like Cascade and Centennial as a combination, as well as Amarillo and Simcoe. I like Styrian Goldings when I can find them, and am happy to use them in both English and Belgian styles. Many German hops work well in Belgian beers, but I see more and more uses of Amarillo in Belgian styles (*La Rullés Tripel* uses them, for instance).

Try not to use more than four hop varieties in a single beer. Complexity works to a point, and then it starts getting muddy and indistinct. I'm not counting bittering hops that don't have a noticeable character; I'm just talking about finishing hops.

For high-alpha bittering, I like Magnum for a clean bitterness and Tomahawk otherwise. Challenger is my favorite for English beers, but they're somewhat hard to find. For moderate bitterness, I'll use whatever I have; it doesn't much matter. More often than not, I'll just use the same types of hops I'm using for late additions, so the character will be more compatible.

I like Hallertauer and Tettnang for noble hops and am quite happy with American versions like Crystal and Sterling. Czech Saaz has a very distinctive note that Phil Sides Jr. once called "fresh sea breeze"—a great description. I use it sparingly, since it jumps out so easily. It's another hop that I like to use in Belgian styles.

I don't dry hop much anymore, although I do when I make IPAs and American barley wines. I much prefer hops added at knockout or in the whirlpool.

I love the flavor from first wort hopping, so I use that technique a lot. I try to use low cohumulone varieties where possible. The hop flavor from first wort hopping can be huge, so try not to overdo it. I use a smaller amount of hops for first wort hopping than for a normal flavor addition.

I really don't like harshness from hops, so I tend to use low cohumulone varieties for late hopping. I tend to use the all-late-hopping technique more frequently due to the superior flavor and lower harshness. I also limit the total ounces of hops used to reduce vegetal and grassy flavors, so it's a tradeoff when using the all-late-hopping technique.

If given new hops, I'll test them out in a single hop batch and use first wort hopping and whirlpool hopping to maximize the hop flavor and aroma. I tend not to use all-late hopping, since I want to know if the hops will be harsh when used for traditional bittering. I'll compare the beer with the raw hops and a simple tea made of the hops to see how true they are to their raw character.

I store all my hops in the freezer, either in their original unopened oxygen-barrier bags or packed in glass with CO_2 blown on top of them. I've got 10-year-old whole hops that are still bright green stored this way. I typically measure my hops on a digital scale.

Yeast

Brewer's yeast is a single-celled fungus responsible for anaerobically metabolizing (i.e., fermenting) sugar in wort into alcohol, carbon dioxide, and various flavor compounds. There are two main species of yeast used by brewers, *Saccharomyces cerevisiae* (ale yeast) and *Saccharomyces pastorianus* (lager yeast). There are other species in the *Saccharomyces* (literally "sugar fungus") genus, but those aren't typically used in brewing (although *S. bayanus* is used in winemaking). Other genera of yeast are sometimes used in brewing, most notably *Brettanomyces*, which like *Saccharomyces* is in the *Saccharomycetaceae* family.

The classification of yeast has changed over the years. Lager yeast were formerly known as *S. carlsbergensis* and later as *S. uvarum*. *Saccharomyces cerevisiae* is also used in breadmaking and winemaking. The strains of yeast that brewers use aren't recognized as distinct in the formal taxonomy; they are like breeds of dogs or cats. They are the same species but have different traits—traits that are very important to brewers.

By U.S. law, wort becomes beer the moment when yeast is added. This supports the old saying that "brewers make wort, but yeast make beer." Even though yeast haven't consumed any sugars yet, and there is no alcohol present, the liquid is known as beer once it contains yeast. Regardless of the legal definition, brewers still have work to do during fermentation to ensure that the beer turns out properly.

Key yeast-related activities that a brewer must perform include choosing a proper yeast strain for the recipe being brewed, preparing the yeast for fermentation, and managing and monitoring the fermentation process. This is in addition to all the work done in wort preparation, which can be thought of as the cooking process in which the yeast are the diners, the wort is the food, and you are the chef.

Choosing a Yeast Strain

The yeast strain controls much of the final profile of a beer and is one of the more important choices a brewer makes. I select yeast primarily based on flavor profile, but secondarily on potential for off-flavor production, flocculation, temperature range, alcohol tolerance, attenuation, and stability.

For most yeasts, I'm not going to be pushing alcohol tolerance or temperature range, since I tend to ferment in "normal" ranges. I avoid making beers at times of the year with incompatible temperature ranges and rarely make a beer so big that it won't ferment completely without help. Rather than picking a yeast strain by alcohol tolerance, I'll just pitch more yeast and make sure it has enough nutrients and oxygen.

I don't think attenuation is that important, since I mostly control attenuation through wort fermentability, not yeast selection. When making a dry beer style, chances are I'll be picking a highly attenuating yeast, anyway, since I'm matching the yeast to the style first. If you pitch a sufficient quantity of healthy, active yeast, most yeast strains will ferment your wort completely.

Flocculation is a minor consideration, since I can always use finings. However, there are a few other things to consider. I might prefer a powdery yeast when looking for higher attenuation, or I intend to lager for a long time. I typically pick a highly flocculent yeast when making a cask ale, or when I want a naturally bright beer without additional handling (maybe I intend to transport the keg somewhere to serve it and want it to be ready quickly).

Stability affects the ability to repitch multiple generations of the same yeast. I normally don't repitch more than four or five times, so that's not typically an issue for me. So that leaves the flavors a yeast strain produces as my main focus.

I think first about the style of beer I'm making. Obviously, I'll match an ale strain with an ale and a lager strain with a lager. Then I'll start looking at strains that are associated with breweries or styles from the same country as the style. When making a style that has a commercial example that I enjoy, I might try to use the same strain as that brewery. Fuller's (WY1968), Sierra Nevada (WY1056), and Ayinger (WLP833) are examples of breweries with well-known yeast strains.

If I'm developing a beer to style or to my own specifications, I first think about general characteristics that yeast can influence. Is the beer going to be malty or hoppy? Will it be sweet or dry? Does it have a clean, neutral yeast profile, or is there some residual yeast character. If so, what kind of yeast-derived flavors and aromas (esters, phenols, higher alcohols, etc.)? How intense are they, and are they associated with any particular fruits (apple, pear, banana, citrus, dried fruit, stone fruit, etc.), spices, or other descriptors?

If the yeast profile I'm envisioning reminds me of a commercial example or style, I'll try to select my yeast based on that association. Otherwise, I'll choose first based on the strongest components in the profile. I'll use my tasting notes from previous batches more frequently than I will descriptions from yeast companies. I find those descriptions to be overly broad and hard to envision. Matching based on original source brewery is a much better option, in my opinion, but you have to rely on possibly unconfirmed data.

Remember that the flavor profile of a specific yeast strain is also dependent on the fermentation temperature and other fermentation conditions. You can often change a yeast profile significantly with a large change in temperature. If you're experimenting this way, this is a good time to check the recommended temperature range for the yeast strain. Going outside the norm will likely result in off-flavors or a poor fermentation.

When finalizing my selection, I check for "show-stoppers" in that strain. I'm mostly looking to avoid problems, so I'll screen for potential off-flavors and general finickiness. There are certain flavors I don't want in my beer (excessive sulfur, diacetyl, etc.). If a yeast strain is known to produce large quantities of those flavors, I'll avoid it. Some yeast are known for large nutrient or oxygen requirements; Ringwood yeast is one. I'll try to avoid those yeasts that don't have much tolerance for fermenting outside their narrow preferred conditions.

Try to learn your favorite strains in detail. Split batches for comparison and adjust the fermentation conditions. Try your favorite strains in different styles. Try unusual things, like making a robust porter with lager yeast, or fermenting lager yeast warmer to accentuate fruity characteristics. If you're experimenting, it's a good idea to keep a control; that is, ferment one of the beers in a known good way, so that you know the data is valid. If your control beer matches previous batches, then you're likely seeing the true character of the yeast.

Preparing the Yeast

There are two main ways I use yeast. Either I'm working with fresh yeast, or I'm reusing yeast from an existing batch. If I'm going to pitch new yeast, I will almost always make a starter in order to get the fermentation starting quickly. If I'm reusing yeast from an existing batch, I will typically wash the yeast so that it performs better during the subsequent fermentation. Both processes are fairly simple.

Using New Yeast: Making a Starter

Most yeast suppliers package their liquid yeast in "pitchable" packages (e.g., the White Labs tube, or the Wyeast XL pack). These are directly usable in average-strength homebrews (5-gallon batches of 1.048 wort) when they are fresh and well stored (refrigerated). However, I usually like to make a starter so that the yeast are actively fermenting when pitched; this results in a quicker start to fermentation and less chance of off-flavors developing. For larger batches (1.060+), it's important to make a starter to let the yeast multiply, so that you are pitching at the proper rate for the size or gravity of the beer (or use more of the pitchable packages, but that can get pretty expensive).

I used to make starters simply by following the directions on the Wyeast package—boiling some dry malt extract, cooling it, pitching the yeast, and letting it sit around until ready to use. I now take a more rigorous approach, which is more like what professional breweries use when they are stepping up their yeast. I saw the technique at Sierra Nevada, but most of what I do came from conversations with Jamil Zainasheff.

I use a 1-liter Erlenmeyer flask and a stir plate; I got both from Northern Brewer, but they are available from many suppliers. I use extra pale dry malt extract (DME) as my sugar source. I also tend to use some Wyeast yeast nutrient as well (I use GO-FERM whenever I use dry yeast, but that's typically only when I make mead).

To make a 1-liter starter, I boil 3 ounces (85 grams) DME and ¼ teaspoon yeast nutrient in 1 quart of water in a saucepan for 15 minutes, and then cool in an ice bath, stirring. This is similar to how cooks make soups and stocks quickly. Once cooled to 72° F (22° C), I'll transfer it to the sanitized flask, add the sanitized magnetic stir bar, and pitch the yeast. I'll cover the top lightly with aluminum foil; it doesn't need to be tight. Then I'll put the flask on the stir plate and adjust it until I see noticeable circulating motion.

If I did everything right, a day in advance is usually sufficient for the yeast to ferment the starter. But I don't really like pitching the full starter when I only want the yeast; the spent wort doesn't usually taste very good, and I don't like diluting my wort. So I'll normally make my starter two or three days in advance. After one day, I'll turn off the stir plate and let the yeast settle. Then I'll carefully decant the liquid and leave the yeast slurry for pitching.

At this point, I can either pitch the yeast directly into the wort, or step up the starter to give the yeast more growth. If I'm going to pitch the yeast directly, I want it to be close to the temperature of the wort (within 10° F, 6° C) so the yeast don't get stunned by the transfer. If I'm going to step up the yeast, I'll repeat the starter process again. If I'm making a higher-gravity beer, I'll boost the DME in the starter to 4 ounces. I don't want the starter gravity to get too high, since high-gravity fermentations are stressful on the yeast; the OG shouldn't be more than 1.060 or so.

When using dry yeast, I won't make a starter but typically use more than one yeast packet. For a normal-strength beer (1.050), I'll use two packets and add another packet for every 25 gravity points. I rehydrate my dry yeast in 1-pint (437-milliliter) 104° F (40° C) filtered water with 1 teaspoon GO-FERM for every yeast packet. After 15 minutes, I'll stir the yeast into solution and pitch it into my beer.

Repitching Yeast: Washing Yeast
Whenever I repitch yeast, I like to make sure I'm getting a fresh, clean, healthy sample. There are occasions when I've been able to score some yeast from a brewpub. That's my favorite method, since it's so easy. The brewmaster will open the valve on the bottom of the cylindro-conical fermenter and wait until a thick, clean yeast slurry is coming out, and then fill a sanitized container (I use Nalgene bottles) with nothing but yeasty goodness.

If I can't get yeast from a brewpub, I'll often reuse yeast from a previous batch of my own. In that case, I always taste the beer that most recently was fermented with that yeast to ensure it is producing good-tasting beer. Assuming that passes, I'll only repitch when the yeast has been handled properly—that is, I haven't subjected it to the unnecessary stress of high temperatures or a long period of bulk conditioning. In those cases, I'll get fresh yeast, instead.

I don't like to repitch directly onto the yeast cake of a previous batch, because it can contain trub, dead yeast, hop particles, and other things I don't want in my carboy. So after I transfer the beer (either to a secondary or to a keg), I rack or pour off the remaining liquid, leaving the solid yeast on the bottom. I'll add some sterile water (preboiled and chilled) onto the yeast and shake it up, so I can pour. I'll then pour the yeast into a tall, 2-liter Nalgene bottle. I top it up with water but not completely. Then I shake the bottle to thoroughly mix up the yeast.

While waiting for the yeast to settle, I can then clean the carboy for reuse. As the yeast start to settle, take note of all the heavy stuff with darker particles that falls out quickly. You don't want that. Then wait a bit and see if a light frothy layer forms on top; you don't want that either. You want the middle layer, where the yeast has a kind of sheen and looks creamy. Pour off and discard the watery layer on the top, save the creamy part in the middle, and throw out the dregs. That creamy part is what you can repitch. Use it soon, or store it cool if you have to use it the next day.

Obviously, you'll want to maintain sanitary conditions during these transfers. Note that yeast that is repitched can be deficient in nutrients, particularly zinc. To compensate, I like to add either ½ teaspoon of Wyeast Yeast Nutrient or one Servomyces capsule to the next batch of beer. I often do the yeast rinsing and carboy prep during the boil, so I'll be ready to go after chilling the beer.

Managing Fermentation

Fermentation is one of the key control points for brewing, and one where you must exert indirect control. You aren't telling the yeast what to do; you're creating the conditions for the yeast to do what they do naturally. So in this case, you have to "think like yeast" and try to understand what they want. If you own cats, this will probably be second nature to you.

Books have been written on managing fermentation, so I'll just focus on the few main practical focal points for homebrewers. I believe the key to fermentation is providing sufficient oxygen, providing sufficient yeast nutrients, pitching a large, healthy starter, and properly controlling temperature. I have been curious about the impact of fermenter geometry on fermentation for years but have not seen much written about it in the brewing literature. I think it could be another factor worth investigating.

Your goals for fermentation management are to see a rapid onset of fermentation, a complete reduction of fermentable carbohydrates (full attenuation), proper levels of flavor and aroma compounds (including reduction of intermediates), and the expected flocculation and sedimentation of yeast. This is how yeast behaves when it has been provided the proper environment for fermentation, and when the fermentation is managed appropriately. If your fermentations aren't coming out this way, then some investigation is warranted.

Oxygenation. There is some contradiction in theory and practice on the subject of oxygenation versus aeration. While at Sierra Nevada Beer Camp, I learned you can get desired oxygen levels using filtered air. Yet I've also read that only pure oxygen can get you sufficient levels. The way I look at it is that if I'm going to use a sintered diffuser hooked up to some kind of system, I might as well use oxygen to drive it. I get the green bottles of oxygen at a local hardware store, and run it on full for 1 minute through an inline filter into a sintered stainless steel diffuser.

If I can't do that for some reason, I fall back to the same method I use when I'm making mead. I use a mix-stir aerator attached to a cordless drill and whip air into it until the foam is up to the top of the carboy (I normally use 6.5-gallon/24.6-liter carboys for 5.25-gallon/19.9-liter batches). I think this is much superior to shaking the carboy in results and safety.

Manipulating the oxygenation rate and timing can affect the fermentation. Oxygen can be introduced after pitching as well to support yeast growth further. I don't generally do this since I'm concerned about developing off-flavors (oxygen introduced by the Yorkshire Squares recirculation method is responsible for noticeable diacetyl in Samuel Smith beers), but I've heard of the practice. If you do decide to add oxygen after pitching, do it before the wort is halfway to its attenuation target. Using less oxygen or skipping it entirely can lead to higher ester development.

Nutrients. Avoiding excessive adjuncts and conducting a proper mash will normally provide all the nutrients yeast need. However, if you aren't measuring nutrient levels directly, using some commercial yeast nutrient is cheap insurance to guard against sluggish fermentations. I use Wyeast yeast nutrient, ½ teaspoon per 5-gallon (19-liter) batch. Others exist, but that's what I've always used with good result. If you do use a different nutrient source, check whether it contains zinc—that's the only mineral needed for fermentation that's deficient in barley.

I generally add the nutrients near the end of the boil, but they can also be added later. When making mead, I use staggered nutrient additions, and that helps the fermentation by providing nutrients when the yeast need them. I would like to experiment with adding nutrients to beer in staggered additions to see if that affects the fermentation (perhaps adding one-third of the nutrients each day for the first three days of fermentation).

Pitching. Before yeast is pitched, make sure the wort is properly prepared: nutrients added, gravity target hit or adjusted, any settling or trub removal done, oxygenation done, wort at pitching temperature. I like to have my yeast at or slightly below the temperature of the wort to make it as gentle as possible on the yeast.

Pitching rate is certainly important, but to tell you the truth, I don't worry about it too much. I always use fresh yeast, and I almost always make a starter. If I'm making a bigger beer, I'll either step up the yeast, buy more yeast to use, or make a lower-gravity batch first and reuse the yeast.

I can think of two conditions where someone might want to manipulate the pitch rate to try to achieve a certain outcome. Underpitching can create more esters, so some people deliberately underpitch when making wheat beers. I'm not a fan of underpitching, since I don't want a slow start or a sluggish fermentation. Overpitching in a hoppy beer can reduce the bitterness, since the yeast can take up some of the bitterness from the beer.

Temperature control. I normally get the wort to the proper pitching temperature during the initial chilling process. If I need a colder pitching temperature, I'll use ice to chill the water leading to my chiller, or I'll chill the recirculation loop. I'd rather have a fast chill than a slow chill from placing it in a cool location; a better break will result.

I have several different temperature zones available for fermentation. I have a room-temperature spot, a walk-in set to 50° F (10° C) that I can use for lager fermentations, and a lagering fridge set to 35° F (2° C). If I need to lower the temperature of a fermenter in the room-temperature location, I tend to use a water bath. I put the carboy in a large plastic tub and add 2-liter bottles of ice water. I change the ice twice a day. This provides a large thermal mass and will keep the temperature of the fermenting beer from rising too much.

If I'm looking for less of a temperature decrease, I'll either set a fan to blow on the carboy, or use the same approach but put a wet T-shirt over the carboy. That's a little messy, so I usually do that in a shower enclosure. If I need a warmer temperature, I'll move the carboy to a warmer room or use a Brew Belt.

When controlling the fermentation temperature, I use the temperature of the beer itself and not the surrounding space. I use an infrared thermometer from the kitchen to take the temperature, or one of those orange carboy caps fitted with a thermowell and a long thermometer.

Most of my fermentations are handled the same way; I start cool and let them rise. A rising temperature during fermentation tends to give you better attenuation and diacetyl reduction. Constraining fermentation temperatures can cause some yeast strains (Belgian strains, in particular) to slow down or stop prematurely. If you are planning on a rising temperature during fermentation, that's all the more reason to start fermenting at a cooler temperature and to have a large, active, healthy yeast pitch.

Fermenter geometry. This is a topic not well understood, but from what I've been able to determine, shallower fermenters tend to generate more esters. I think open versus closed fermenters might also be a factor, so it could also be due to a different underlying cause such as physical pressure on the yeast. I've been exploring this mostly with Belgian styles, trying to understand how Belgians can ferment as warm as they do and still get beers with good fermentation character. It could be due to the shallower or open fermenters not driving the temperature of the fermenting beer as high as what you would experience if using a taller fermenter (like a carboy). I'm looking at using large food-grade plastic pans from restaurant supply houses as possible fermenters. It's something I continue to explore, but I mention it because I think it is another factor that will eventually be better understood and give brewers more control over their fermentations.

So What Do I Do?

Working with a smaller set of yeast lets you learn them better, so you can get reproducible results and know how each yeast responds to different fermentation conditions. Your goal is to be able to pick a yeast and know how to work with it to get the desired outcome. I have a set of yeasts that I use most frequently, but I'm not afraid to experiment with other strains. If I make a split 10-gallon batch, I'll almost always take that opportunity to use one known yeast and one new yeast.

I try to avoid lager yeasts that produce a lot of sulfur (WLP820 Oktoberfest yeast is one that I tried and didn't like). I shy away from ale yeasts that tend to produce fusels or diacetyl (hello, Ringwood). I try to avoid phenols in most yeast. Picking Belgian strains is an interesting exercise and is mostly based on personal taste. I personally don't like the banana/solvent character of WY1214 when fermented warm, so I try to avoid it. One of these days I do want to try it fermented around 60 to 62° F (16-17° C) just to see if it's better.

For English ales, I really like WLP002/WY1968 for most styles. I like WY1318 London III for maltier or darker styles (mild, porter, old ale). For drier beers or IPAs, I'll go with WY1028. The WLP002 yeast is the Fuller's strain and is a great yeast for cask ales, since it's so flocculant. Just be careful to not let the fermentation temperature drop below 65° F (18° C), or the yeast will drop out regardless of attenuation. I generally ferment most English beers around 68° F (20° C).

For lagers, I like the WLP833 bock yeast in almost any style, WY2206 for neutral beers or those with a higher attenuation, and WY2124 for malty beers. I usually ferment my lagers at 48 to 50° F (9-10° C), and lager them between 32 and 35° F (0-2° C). If I have to go warm on lagers, I'll use the San Francisco lager strain WLP810 (my secret weapon for Baltic porters), unless I want to have more esters produced, as in a *Bière de Garde*; for that, I'll use whatever German lager strain I have on hand.

For Belgians, I like WY3787 for Trappist-type beers, and WY1762 for variation. WY3522 is OK, especially if you want to go warm. The Orval yeast (WLP510 Bastogne ale) is a new favorite that I'm trying in a lot of different styles. On my last trip to Belgium, I stopped at a number of small breweries that were making a wide range of beers using Orval yeast. My favorite was *La*

Rullés Tripel, but that was enough to tell me that this yeast is a general-purpose Belgian workhorse strain.

WY3787 is an interesting yeast; it's from Westmalle but Westvleteren uses it, too. According to *Brew Like a Monk*, the two breweries use very different fermentation temperatures. I haven't explored the range of temperature variations, but I do tend to start cool (65° F, 18° C) and let it rise to wherever it wants to go. I've seen the strain struggle if you try to constrain the fermentation temperature. I've also had to let beers sit on this yeast longer (with occasional rousing) to get full attenuation.

For American ales, I like WY1272 American II or the WLP060 American Blend unless I want an absolutely neutral character, then it's WY1056/WLP001. I like the little extra fruitiness from those strains, but I don't like to go warm. I stay in the 65 to 68° F (18-20° C) range, typically.

I use WY1728/WLP028 for Scottish, WY2565/WLP029 for *Kölsch*, WLP004 for Irish reds or stouts, WLP515 for Belgian pale ale, and other very style-specific yeasts (particularly if I can associate the yeast strain with the brewery). For *hefeweizens*, WY3068 is my clear favorite, but I've also liked WLP380 Hefe IV and WLP3638 for darker versions. I ferment most of those on the cool side, below 65° F (18° C).

Water
Water makes up most of beer, but it is one of the most misunderstood of all brewing topics. For the most part, there are only a few critical things you have to do with your water. Yet I see so many brewers obsessing over spreadsheets and gram scales at the expense of mastering the fundamentals of brewing. Please, if you only take away one thing from this book, stop messing around with your water so much! Water adjustment is an advanced topic and should be one of the last things a brewer should worry about.

If you are a relatively new all-grain brewer, just remember three things to check about your water: (1) does it taste or smell bad? (2) does it have any chlorine in it? (3) does it have a high level of carbonates? If you answered "yes" to any of those questions, then you have to do something about your water. Otherwise, just try to use your water as is, and see what kind of beer you can make.

If you are a moderately advanced all-grain brewer, you should understand the calcium level of your water and its pH. You should get a water analysis from your water supplier, or send your water out for analysis. You should own a good pH meter and keep it calibrated. You should feel comfortable trying to replicate water profiles from famous brewing cities, if that suits your fancy.

If you're an advanced all-grain brewer, you can take more precise and frequent measurements and try to introduce tighter process controls, but you shouldn't feel that you have to mess around with your water so much that the beer quality suffers. If you have more measurements, then you can pinpoint those processes that need to be tweaked, rather than guessing. But if you're making great beer, don't think you have to do anything more advanced than what I'm advising for the moderately advanced brewer.

Water Sources and Classic Profiles, A Cautionary Tale

Homebrewers have often looked at published water profiles for cities known for brewing certain styles of beer (English pale ales in Burton, stouts in Dublin, Pilsener in Plzeň (Pilsen), *dunkel* in Munich, Dortmunder in Dortmund, etc.) and tried to replicate them when brewing those styles. I've done that as well and think it is an appropriate method when you're trying to replicate a historical style. But you have to understand the nature of your data.

Regional water supplies influenced the development of world beer styles, since some beer styles would work better with certain types of water. However, brewers eventually learned to adjust their water (for example, that's why bitters can be made in London, which has moderately carbonate water). So, you can't always associate a regional water profile with a beer. How do we know what breweries used? Did they use public water? Was their water treated? Has the water changed over time? Is a municipal report from today of any use when trying to replicate the conditions that existed when a style was first formulated?

Understand that breweries can have different sources of water (municipal source, private wells, springs, etc.). Their water supply is variable and can change dramatically between seasons. Some water reports contained data that is averaged over multiple samplings, even between seasons. Other reports aren't necessarily sampled from the same supplies used by the breweries. Note that many published samples of water profiles are simply wrong; many are inconsistent—you couldn't have ion concentrations like that without having unreasonably high pH levels.

For these reasons, it's hard to chase "classic water profiles" except maybe to favor certain minerals for specific styles (sulfates for Burton water, for example). What you are interested in is the profile of water *as used* by the breweries when making those classic styles—does anyone claim to have that historic information?

So my advice is not to worry too much about replicating water profiles; it's much more important to get the mash pH right. Then you can worry about adjusting flavor ions in the water to suit certain styles. That's a much more modern way of thinking about water, and one less likely to have you ruin your beer because you didn't understand the impact of all your water adjustments.

Water Basics

The key aspects of water that matter to brewers are pH, hardness, alkalinity, residual alkalinity, and "flavor" ion profile. The mineral content of water impacts all of these. I'm not a chemist, so much of what I know about the technical side of water in brewing can be traced to discussions I've had with A. J. deLange over the last decade, and more recently with Martin Brungard and Colin Kaminski, as well as writings of Kai Troester.

pH is a measure of the acidity of water; it is related to the hydrogen ion concentration. pH is a scale between 0 and 14, with 7 indicating a neutral balance of hydrogen (H+) and hydroxide (OH-) ions at 25° C (77° F). Municipal water sources in the United States tend to be in the range of 6.5 to 8.5 and have varying mineral profiles.

The literal definition of the term pH is somewhat in doubt; some have described it as potential hydrogen or power of hydrogen. Others say it's a shorthand and approximation for the chemical notation p[H+] or negative logarithm of the concentration of hydrogen ions (protons) in solution. It was first described at Carlsberg in Denmark in the early 1900s and subsequently adopted by chemists. The usage is not in doubt, even if the original term is somewhat of a mystery.

pH varies with temperature; room-temperature samples tend to measure about 0.3 pH higher than the same sample at mash temperature. Be careful how you compare measurements; adapt a common system, typically measuring at warm room temperature (25° C, 77° F), using a pH meter with Automatic Temperature Compensation (ATC), or by keeping a temperature compensation table handy.

pH influences a number of factors in brewing, including enzymatic activity, mash efficiency, protein coagulation and precipitation, viscosity, foam stability, haze stability, fermentability, attenuation, color, clarity, and taste of the wort and beer. Final pH affects the taste and digestability of the beer, the bitterness perception, as well as its susceptibility to spoilage organisms.

Mash pH should generally be in the 5.1 to 5.8 range, with best results seemingly in the 5.2 to 5.5 range. Runoff from the mash shouldn't rise above pH 5.8 to avoid tannin extraction; this is often done by acidifying sparge water with phosphoric acid to the 5.2 to 5.8 range.

Water hardness is a measure of calcium (Ca^{+2}) and magnesium (Mg^{+2}) ions in the water. It doesn't say anything about the anions (chloride, sulfate, carbonate) present. Hardness is an indication of how difficult (hard) it is to get lather from soap, not a very useful concept for brewing. But calcium is important, so that's why brewers use it as a measurement.

Hardness is often characterized as *temporary* or *permanent*. Temporary hardness will drop out when boiled, with calcium carbonate precipitating. This lowers the final calcium available for brewing. Permanent hardness is based on sulfates and chlorides and won't precipitate calcium when boiled. It makes a difference depending on how you treat your water before you use it, and how much calcium you expect to be available for the mash and in the final beer.

Hardness alone doesn't tell you much about how suitable your water is for brewing, except to provide some insight as to whether calcium will be available or not. Having around 50 ppm of calcium is generally accepted as desirable for brewing, particularly in the mash.

Alkalinity of water is a measure of its pH buffering capacity, or how much it resists change of pH. It is a measure of carbonates (CO_3^{-2}), bicarbonates (HCO_3^-) and hydroxide (OH^-) in the water, and is defined by how much strong acid is necessary to move a sample to a predetermined pH. At normal water supply pH, most of the alkalinity is present as bicarbonate.

Residual alkalinity is a measure of the alkalinity remaining in solution after phosphates in the malt react with calcium and magnesium in the water, precipitating out insoluble salts and lowering the pH. This residual alkalinity will continue to buffer the solution against pH change. This measure was first described by German brewing scientist Paul Kolbach in 1953.

Residual alkalinity is useful for comparing water profiles from different cities and seeing how it might have impacted brewing methods, but too much has been made of its significance in everyday brewing today. It is not critical to determining beer color, mash pH, or other functions. Misinterpretation and misapplication of Kolbach's original research has led many a brewer to overadjust their water, often resulting in a drink that tastes more like Alka-Seltzer than beer.

The goal of understanding brewing liquor pH, alkalinity, and residual alkalinity is to try to get your mash pH into the proper range so mash enzymes can function properly. If your mashes are getting into the proper range, then you shouldn't be focusing on water adjustment so much. This is a separate issue from worrying about sparge chemistry and tannin extraction. Worry first about your mash pH. Then think about not ruining it by extracting tannins. Take one step at a time.

Ions in brewing. Calcium and magnesium affect hardness. Carbonates and bicarbonates affect alkalinity. Together they affect pH and mash chemistry, so always think about them together. Sodium, chloride, and sulfate are more important for flavor, and are often called *stylistic ions* or *flavor ions*.

Calcium is the most important ion for brewing. It is an important co-factor for mash enzyme activity, helps in protein coagulation (hot and cold break, for clarity), and is beneficial for yeast, among several other advantages. The mash should have at least 50 ppm of calcium, and concentrations up to about 200 ppm are not detrimental.

Magnesium accentuates flavor and sourness at lower concentrations but can be astringent and bitter at higher doses. It can also affect mash pH but is less effective than calcium.

Sodium (Na^{+2}) can accentuate flavor in lower doses, but can be salty, sour, harsh, and toxic to yeast in higher concentrations.

Chloride (Cl⁻) accentuates fullness and sweetness in beer and can accentuate malty beer styles. It improves beer stability and clarity but can be harsh in higher concentrations.

Sulfate (SO_4^{-2}) accentuates dryness in beer and bitterness in hops but can taste sulfury, harsh, and bitter in higher concentrations. Sulfate and noble hops don't mix particularly well, so avoid using it too much in continental lagers.

Bicarbonate (HCO_3^-) is the primary alkalinity source in brewing (and drinking) water. Carbonate (CO_3^{-2}) salts disassociate in water to form bicarbonates at brewing pH levels. Malt phosphates can reduce alkalinity, as can the acidity in roasted and highly kilned grains, or in acids. Calcium carbonate is nearly insoluble in water of pH 7 and higher. Adding it to an acidic solution (such as the sweet wort in the boil) will keep it in solution.

Assessing Your Water

Before you start adjusting your water, you should understand what you have. I think of this assessment phase as a triage process, where you decide if your water is good as-is, whether it needs to be adjusted or blended, or whether it is unusable and must be replaced.

The first step you should take is simply to smell and taste your water. Does it taste good? Does it taste clean? Is it free of any off-aromas? If it smells or tastes of chlorine, how is it after you've run it through a charcoal filter? You don't need a full system to do this test, just run it through a Brita filter. That will remove chlorine, heavy metals, as well as some of the calcium. A Brita filter replaces calcium and other positively charged cations with hydrogen and uses an activated charcoal filter to remove chlorine. If this water tastes good, chances are that you can get a charcoal filtration system to treat your brewing water.

Next you want to evaluate your ion levels and pH, which are related. If you are on a municipal water system, you can request a free analysis from your water supplier. It won't often be formatted in a way that is meaningful to a brewer and will likely contain a lot of extraneous data. But it should contain some of the basic information you need, including the pH level, the alkalinity, the hardness, and the concentration of most ions useful in brewing.

If you are on well water, or if your municipal water report doesn't have the information you need, your best option is to send your water to Ward Labs (*www.wardlab.com*) and request a Household Complete Mineral Test. It's not very expensive, and it gives you a good listing of minerals important to brewing. You can request other tests from them on an à la carte schedule. They are quite reliable and probably the best choice for homebrewers who don't have the ability to do their own analysis.

Armed with this data, you can determine the suitability of your own water supply for brewing. Many brewing software programs allow you to enter your water profile, which is useful for storing this information.

If your water is only slightly high in some of the desirable ion levels but has low carbonates, it may work best for you to dilute it with RO, distilled, or deionized (DI) water. It's straight algebra to calculate the target ion levels; you are keeping the same ions, but increasing the volume, so the concentration will be reduced.

If your water will take too much effort to fix (typically because it has a high carbonate level, a high pH, substantial iron content, contaminants present, is salty-tasting, or otherwise is not tasty), then it may be easier for you just to start with a neutral water profile from a reverse osmosis (RO) system and add back any salts you want for the style of beer you are making. That's what I do, since my water has excessive carbonates, high pH, and significant total dissolved solids (yes, it tastes "minerally"). I also might add some yeast nutrient to add some trace elements for yeast health.

Your primary goal should be to have a reliable, predictable water supply. It gets tiring to always have to test and adjust your water before you brew. If you have a reliable source, then you can easily calculate whatever batch-specific adjustments you need. One of the benefits I have from using RO water is that I don't have to recalculate the adjustments I make for pH and available calcium.

Note that RO water isn't the same as distilled or deionized water. It can still have some minerals in it, depending on how recently the RO membrane was cleaned and the system was serviced. You can generally consider RO water to be roughly neutral in ion content, but if you want to be certain, send it off for analysis or measure it yourself. My pH meter also measures total dissolved solids (TDS). So I do a quick check on each batch of RO water I buy to see if I can assume it has no minerals. If I get a positive reading, I assume the TDS is from calcium carbonate based on my water supply.

Remember that water sources can change throughout the year, and the water profile can change considerably from season to season. You may wish to run an analysis for each season to get a good idea of what you have. If you read a water report and see wide ranges reported, try to figure out if that's due to seasonal differences. Call the water department and ask them how it varies over time.

If you don't analyze your water every time you brew, know that you are making an approximation. If you don't know your baseline water supply at the moment you are brewing, then why are you using a spreadsheet to calculate salt additions to the third decimal point? You are confusing precision with accuracy. Your result will be unknown, so all that extra effort is for naught. Am I suggesting getting a full analysis every time you brew? No, not at all. But I am suggesting that you don't have to focus on precision with your measurements if you don't know precisely what you started with.

Adjusting Your Water for Brewing

When adjusting my water for brewing, I tend to think about three distinct phases: chlorine removal, ion adjustment, and pH adjustment. I think about the impacts water has on brewing, particularly on the mash pH chemistry and the finished flavor profile. All other issues are secondary to me.

If you have chlorine in your water, you need to remove it, or you risk developing medicinal-tasting, chlorophenolic flavors in your finished beer. If your water is otherwise good, simply running it through a charcoal filter is likely to be sufficient. Many breweries brew successful beer doing only this step. Boiling or carbon filtering can remove chlorine, but chloramines must be filtered out or precipitated using Campden tablets.

When using your home water supply, you must bypass any water softeners. These work on the principle of ion exchange, substituting sodium (which you don't want) for calcium and magnesium (which you do want). They can be used as a pretreatment before running your water through a reverse osmosis system, however, since the RO process will strip out virtually all minerals. Softening very hard water can extend the life of RO membranes.

If you adjust the ion content of your water, be aware of everything you are adding. You aren't just adding elemental calcium, for instance. You're adding a salt, which contains calcium and some other anion (sulfate, chloride, carbonate, etc.). Keep in mind the effect of each of the ions you are adding on the flavor profile, mash and boil processes, and the pH.

The mash has a way of settling to a proper pH on its own. Don't think you have to force it. If you want to be paranoid about anything, just be sure you have at least 50 ppm of calcium in the mash, and that your sparge water is below pH 5.8. In general, alkalinity is not desired, so if you water has a lot of it, consider using RO, distilled, or deionized water, whichever is easiest for you to find.

General advice for water adjustment:

- If your water meets general parameters for brewing, water adjustment is one of the last tweaks you want to apply in your brewing. Definitely learn the other methods first.

- It's easy to overadjust water, so try to mess with your water as little as possible. I hate tasting overadjusted beers; they often taste like Alka-Seltzer to me.

- You don't need to adjust your ion content to achieve a certain color for your beer; color is not a factor in water adjustment.

- If your mashes are settling in the pH 5.2 to 5.5 range, then don't worry about adjusting alkalinity or pH. If you aren't getting husk astringency or other problems from the sparge, you probably don't need to adjust sparge water pH.

- In general, moderate hardness is good. Try to provide at least 50 ppm of calcium for the mash. Calcium chloride is the most neutral source. Calcium sulfate can enhance hoppiness but can also add dryness. These both add hardness without increasing alkalinity. Avoid using calcium carbonate unless you need to raise the pH.

- Add minerals to the mash to influence the pH only (or to provide calcium). Everything else is pretty much superfluous. Focus on mash chemistry first. Everything else is for the finished flavor profile and can always be added to the brew kettle.

- If you are concerned about astringency, keep your sparge water below pH 6 but not significantly lower than the pH of your mash. Adjust sparge water with phosphoric acid, if necessary. The mash is largely a phosphate buffer, so adding more phosphate at close to the pH of the system, while it will have an effect, should cause a minimal shift. Certainly if both mash and sparge water are at pH below 5.5, the pH won't go above that value.

- Your water should not have iron, but can have trace elements (zinc, copper) that are used by yeast. Commercial yeast nutrient mixes can supply these if they are not present in your water supply.

- If alkalinity of your water is low, you can add phosphoric acid to your brewing liquor and use that for both mashing and sparging without any negative consequences.

- If the alkalinity of your water is high and it's hard (temporary hardness), you should remove the carbonate hardness, dilute your water, or use RO water. In general, alkalinity and carbonates are undesirable in beer and should be avoided.

- If the mineral profile is an important part of the style profile (e.g., Dortmunder export), then the sparge water should have the same mineral profile as the strike water.

- Avoid high sulfates in beers with noble hops, as they can lead to increased harshness.

Methods of Water Adjustment:
Chlorine removal. There are two types of chlorine that may be in your water, chlorine and chloramines. Active carbon filtering will remove chlorine, as will boiling. If boiling, you need to boil the water before you use it, since chlorophenolics can be formed as soon as the chlorine contacts the malt. Chloramines are more persistent (boiling won't remove them), but Campden tablets can neutralize them. The general rule of thumb for using Campden tablets is to use one tablet (potassium metabisulfite, about 695 milligrams) to neutralize the chloramines in 20 gallons (75.7 liters) of brewing liquor. Boiling can be used to remove chlorine and temporary hardness at the same time; however, it is energy intensive and time consuming. Commercial RO systems often have an activated charcoal filter inline to remove chlorine, as well.

Hardness adjustment. Increasing hardness can be done by adding gypsum (calcium sulfate), calcium chloride, or Epsom salts (magnesium sulfate). Which salt(s) you select depends on what stylistic ions you want along with your calcium or magnesium. Hardness can be (mostly) removed with reverse osmosis or reduced by blending with RO or distilled water.

Alkalinity adjustment. Increase alkalinity by adding chalk (calcium carbonate), although it isn't very soluble and is generally used only in the mash. Decrease by boiling (reduced temporary hardness), adding phosphoric acid (you can add others, but you don't want to because of flavor additions or danger in handling), or using acidulated malt (if Reinheitsgebot matters to you). The alkalinity will reduce in the mash naturally due to reactions with malt husks.

In general, hardness is good but alkalinity is bad. Alkalinity can be neutralized; it's what's left over (the residual alkalinity) that is undesirable from a flavor standpoint. Adding acid or calcium/magnesium salts (increasing hardness) reduces residual alkalinity. Adding carbonates increases residual alkalinity. Just be aware that you are affecting more of your water chemistry than residual alkalinity when you make these additions—it's these unintended side-effects that tend to ruin the flavor of beer.

pH adjustment. Salts will affect the pH in the mash, but not when added to water. If you want to lower the pH of brewing liquor, use phosphoric acid. Other acids can be used, but phosphoric is the most flavor-neutral when used in brewing. You rarely want to raise the pH in brewing; if you do, you can often achieve this by blending with your unadjusted water, since the pH of water is naturally higher than what is used in brewing. In the rare cases when pH needs to be adjusted upwards, a potassium hydroxide solution can be used, but this isn't typically commercially available; you'll need a chemistry friend to prepare it for you. Calcium carbonate and potassium carbonate can be used to raise the pH of beer but only if actually dissolved. Calcium carbonate is notoriously insoluble, particularly at nonacidic pH levels. These salts can also leave behind undesirable flavors; I don't use this method.

Mineral profile adjustment. Use gypsum, calcium chloride, Epsom salts, or chalk depending on what final stylistic ions you want. You can add these salts to the mash, sparge, or boil. Add salts to the mash when you want calcium to be available or need to control the pH. Add salts to the boil for flavor impact. Most salts provide calcium; you just want to think about what other baggage you're bringing along for the ride.

Some of the salts used in the mash will not carry over to the kettle, and sparging can also dilute the salts. If you're looking for a certain flavor profile or to match the water of a specific city, consider adding kettle salts. You do want to be sure you have some calcium in the boil, as it helps with break formation and with yeast health.

If you're concerned with the need to add calcium carbonate to buffer the acidity of dark grains during the mash, ask yourself why you need to mash your dark grains. Can't you just mash your paler grains and add the dark grains at mash-out? You're interested in the mash pH, so why mash something that isn't adding much fermentable sugar anyway? Most dark grains are simply added for flavor and color, so why let them ruin your mash chemistry and drive unwanted salt additions?

The chloride-to-sulfate ratio is something that some British brewers feel is important. Generally, they favor sulfate in hoppy beers and chloride in malty beers. For balanced beers, use an even ratio. If you want to follow this approach and are looking for a place to start, try a sulfate:chloride ratio of 2:1 for bitter beers, 1:2 for milds, and 1:3 for stouts and porters. I use something similar when I'm brewing, but I'm not as rigid about it. Think not only about the ratio but about the total amount of salts added.

In the *Handbook of Brewing* (2009), Esslinger says "for sensory reasons, the ratio of noncarbonate to carbonate hardness should be 3:1."[2] So he's saying that calcium chloride or calcium sulfate should be used more than calcium carbonate (or carbonates in the water). Personally, I don't generally add any carbonate to my water, but I might experiment with this advice in the future to see if it makes a noticeable difference in the flavor profile.

As practical advice for homebrewers using RO water, in a nominal 5-gallon (19-liter) batch, I find the following volume-based additions are a good starting point and a rough approximation useful for most brewing situation:

- 1 tsp. (5 ml) $CaCl_2$ to malty beers

- 1 tsp. (5 ml) $CaSO_4$ to hoppy beers

- 2 tsp. (10 ml) $CaCO_3$ to dark beers (if mashing the dark grains).

[2] Hans Michael Esslinger, *Handbook of Brewing: Processes, Technology, Markets*, Weinheim, Germany: Wiley-VCH, 2009.

If a beer is both malty and hoppy, then use both calcium chloride and calcium sulfate in whatever ratio you think matches the flavor profile of the finished beer when comparing malty to hoppy. Just keep the overall addition at about 1 teaspoon (4.2 grams).

If you are measuring using teaspoons instead of gram scales, then you can use the following approximations when trying to hit a certain ion concentration:

- $CaSO_4$ adds about 59 ppm Ca and 141 ppm SO_4 per tsp. (in 5 gallons)

- $CaCO_3$ adds about 38 ppm Ca and 57 ppm CO_3 per tsp. (in 5 gallons)

- $CaCl_2$ adds about 61 ppm Ca and 107 ppm Cl_2 per tsp. (in 5 gallons).

Note that the volume of salts varies depending on how finely they are ground and how much water they have picked up from the air. Measuring weight is much more accurate, but if you're just looking to be in the ballpark, then measuring by volume is fine. I measure by volume, because I want to be assured of having some of these ions, and the exact concentration doesn't matter to me.

Example of Professional Water Treatment

While attending the Sierra Nevada Beer Camp, I was able to ask professional brewers some direct questions about how they handle their water. I was also able to see what process controls they felt were most important. Their approach matches well with my own thoughts, so I'll describe what I saw as an example.

It was very interesting that Sierra Nevada treats *all* its brewing water (liquor) with phosphoric acid to a pH of 5.5—not just the sparge water, but the strike water and any other liquor used in the brewery, hot or cold. The brewers find it easier to do it once and then use a known good water supply rather than adjusting it at multiple points in the process. Pretreating brewing liquor to adjust the pH did not have a negative effect on the mash. All our batches had a mash pH between 5.1 and 5.3, which is what Sierra Nevada targets.

The brewers measure pH at usage temperature, which is important since (like specific gravity) pH changes with temperature. The pH of a sample at room temperature is as much as 0.3 to 0.4 higher than the same sample at mash temperature. Home instruments might not work in higher mash temperature ranges, so knowing the adjustment is handy.

Sierra Nevada uses gypsum (calcium sulfate, $CaSO_4$) and calcium chloride ($CaCl_2$) to achieve the necessary mineral profile for the beers. Hop-focused beers get more calcium sulfate. Salts are added in both the mash and the kettle. Calcium in the mash helps with the conversion, but the kettle salts are to achieve a specific flavor profile, to compensate for the dilution of sparging, and to make sure sufficient calcium is available for the yeast—most of it is lost during lautering. Homebrewers should be aware that you don't have to put all the salts in the mash, and that not all salts in the mash carry over to the kettle.

So What Do I Do?

My tap water is horrible for brewing—high alkalinity and carbonates, and my house has a water softener—so rather than spend time and energy trying to fix all those things, I just buy reverse osmosis water at a local supermarket and adjust it for my use. I test for total dissolved solids to see whether I need to measure my strike water for pH adjustment. I treat my mash water with phosphoric acid to lower the pH to around 5.5. I add brewing salts (calcium sulfate or calcium chloride, depending on the style) to the mash. I check my mash pH with a decent pH meter. And I sometimes add salts to the boil. That's how I make most of my beer.

The amount of salts I add are mostly based on the underlying beer style and whether it's a malty or hoppy beer. If I'm trying to make a historical beer, I might try to emulate a city's water profile, but usually I don't, because I don't trust the raw data. I tend to add my dark and crystal malts only after mash-out during the vorlauf (or I cold-steep them and add them to the boil), so I don't worry about the impact of dark grain on my mash pH. Since I use RO water, I don't have to worry about fiddling with it very much, just adding enough calcium for a proper mash and then "seasoning to taste" for the final beer.

At kegging, I check the pH of my final beer to make sure it's 4.5 or less and adjust it downward with phosphoric acid if it isn't (which is rare). Stylistic ions can also be adjusted at this point if the flavor profile isn't right (again, rare). But mostly I try to avoid messing with water too much.

Soft water works very well for me, and I can turn it into just about any brewing water I want. But more often than not, I make beer with soft water because I like the taste. Try it; you might be surprised at how much you like the beer made this way. Even with something like a Burton ale; loading it with gypsum might taste more "authentic," but making it with soft water might make it taste "better." Keep an open mind and trust your palate. This is a real-world example of how I took what was available and adjusted my processes, ingredients, and methods to match.

Brewing is both an art and a science. Don't overemphasize the science part. I've seen and heard a lot of people spend way too much time on water adjustment. It can get you in the ballpark, but remember that you are dealing with rough approximations, no matter how many decimal places you use. Let your palate be the final judge. If your beer doesn't taste right, make the adjustments that will correct it regardless of what a spreadsheet might tell you to do. You're the brewmaster; act like it.

applying your knowledge

Always listen to experts. They'll tell you what
can't be done and why. Then do it.
–Robert Heinlein, American science fiction writer

Once you have successfully mastered the basic techniques of brewing, understand your commonly used ingredients, and know how your brewing system responds, you are ready to solo. The rest of this book is devoted to lessons on mastering brewing by developing your own style, approaches, and methods.

The subjects in this part of the book aren't necessarily linear; you can learn them in most any order. In fact, I encourage you to jump around and read the topics in whichever order most suits your interest. When giving advice to others, I try to adjust my conversation to skip over what is already known and to focus on the new material. I can't really do that in this book, because the background and learning style of each reader will be different.

It's probably more useful to make sure you have a background on beer styles and evaluating beer before trying to formulate recipes, so you may want to take those chapters in order. Competition brewing tends to build on all the other lessons in the book, so that may be best saved for last.

Chapter 5 contains three major topics. It discusses the background knowledge necessary to understand and work with beer styles, it contains tips on developing a good palate for sensory evaluation, and it provides lessons on how to critically assess or judge your own beer. These skills are foundational, since they help you understand what your beer should be and allows you to determine if it has met your goal.

Chapter 6 is a detailed discussion about recipe formulation, including how to be creative and develop new styles. It includes practical lessons on how I go about building a recipe and uses several of my recipes as examples. I cover different scenarios based on what kind of recipe you're trying to make and how much information you have, including how to converge on your target during successive iterations of your recipe.

Chapter 7 is about troubleshooting common problems with your beer, both technical and stylistic. The focus is on faults that advanced brewers might encounter, not the typical new brewer issues. Much of the stylistic troubleshooting advice centers on identifying and diagnosing the process- or ingredient-related root causes for the problems you detect. Most advanced brewers can fix problems if they simply know where to look.

Chapter 8 covers topics related to post-fermentation handling of your beer, including how you might want to adjust it to match expectations. The topic of blending beer is covered in detail. The goal for the chapter is to explore the range of controls you have for tweaking your beer up to the point of consumption and learning how to fine-tune and adjust your beer to be exactly what you want.

Chapter 9 discusses the special issues associated with brewing for competition or for any occasion when your beer absolutely has to be at its best. You don't have to enter competitions to get practical, useful advice from this discussion.

CHAPTER 5
evaluating your own beer

How much easier it is to be critical than to be correct.
-Benjamin Disraeli, 19th century British prime minister

What background and skills are necessary for you to be able to evaluate, describe, and appropriately understand your beer in context—that is, moving beyond knowing your beer is just something that you like, to understanding how it fits in the world of beer, and how others see it? To do this properly, you should have knowledge of beer styles, have a critical palate, and be able to assess your own beers in an unbiased manner.

Beer styles provide a way for producers and consumers to communicate about what to expect in a beer. Palate development allows you to recognize and differentiate the many different tastes in beer. Critical assessment techniques provide the framework for analyzing your beer. My background as a successful brewer, the principal author of the Beer Judge Certification Program Style Guidelines, and the most experienced BJCP judge makes me as good a candidate as any to discuss these topics.

Brewers often enter their beer in competitions not to win awards but to get good feedback from judges. You can save a lot of money and time if you develop these skills yourself. Your goal should be to not have to rely on others but rather to use your own abilities. This is actually one of my advantages in competitive brewing; I don't need to enter my beers in competition to get feedback.

Think of the topics in this chapter as sort of a mini-BJCP judge training boot camp. Once you have mastered these skills, you are well suited to judge beer in a BJCP-sanctioned competition. Perhaps you will consider taking the BJCP exam, if you haven't already done so.

Many brewers focus on the technical side of brewing without paying as much attention to the artistic side. Tasting beer is a subjective skill and one that is often hedonistic. So it's more important to make a beer that is palatable than one that is technically correct; your goal is to make something that tastes good, not something that matches a certain number. You aren't judged on mash efficiency, after all; you're judged on flavor. If you are able to use your own palate and sensory skills to assess your own beers, then you will see the payoff every time you drink your beer.

Understanding Beer Styles

Beer styles are part of a structured method for categorizing and describing beer. They are intended to be a convenient shorthand for discussing beer, and to allow all who taste the beer to be able to describe it using a common framework and language. A beer style is simply a structured definition of a certain type of beer that may have originated in a certain country, region, or city, or be known by its color, strength, ingredients, process, or flavor profile. It's the quick response given when someone asks you, "What kind of beer is this?"

Beer style descriptions are typically organized into a comprehensive set of *style guidelines,* which can add another layer of structure by categorizing the styles into related groupings. The most common set of guidelines for homebrewers is the BJCP Style Guidelines, which are used in most homebrew competitions. The Brewers Association publishes guidelines for commercial competitions it sponsors, and several beer-rating websites (such as Beer Advocate) maintain their own guidelines. Beer writers often have their own categories; in fact, most modern style guidelines are based on the early writings of Michael Jackson and Fred Eckhardt.

In subsequent discussions, I'm using the BJCP Style Guidelines as my frame of reference, since they are the most widely used beer guidelines for homebrewers. Those guidelines don't describe every beer style made in the world but do include those most entered in homebrew competitions. The guidelines are based on currently acknowledged, world-class commercial examples, historical references to styles no longer brewed, and writings of noted beer researchers and journalists.

The Purpose of Beer Styles

Most style guidelines are created with a purpose in mind. The guidelines of the BJCP and the Brewers Association are designed to assist competitions by providing a frame of reference for brewers and judges, and by grouping together similar beer styles for judging purposes. Without beer styles, competitions would be nearly impossible to conduct. Judging would simply become a hedonistic event, where judges would pick beers according to their own personal preferences. The outcome would be totally arbitrary and would depend on the background and whims of those who judge the beers—not a desirable situation.

Style guidelines from consumer-oriented organizations are meant to provide an easy way to discuss beer and to compare similar commercial examples. Beer writers group beer so they can tell a story, usually discussing how styles were developed and how they are currently made. Whichever set of guidelines are chosen as a reference, be sure you understand why they were created and try to use them for their intended purpose. Problems arise when this advice is not followed.

For some professional brewers (and even homebrewers), even mentioning the subject of beer styles is like waving a red flag in front of a bull. Some beer enthusiasts support the idea of beer styles but strongly disagree with particular style descriptions or sets of guidelines. These strong responses are generally either based on a misunderstanding of the purpose of the guidelines, on observations of them being used incorrectly, or on a dislike of the person or group making the guidelines. These contentious issues are what led me to call beer styles a misunderstood necessity.

Some professional brewers look at the style guidelines as limiting, as if they are telling them how and what to brew. Nothing could be further from the truth; style guidelines are an attempt to categorize what brewers are brewing or what has historically been brewed. The guidelines take in the range of world-class examples and the characteristics that make these beers taste so good. Most individual beer styles have quite a wide range and allow for significant brewer creativity.

Guidelines naturally evolve over time as consumer's tastes and commercial examples change. New styles emerge (look at double IPAs and black IPAs as recent innovations), while others tend to fade away and be forgotten. Some brewers continually push the envelope and try to create new and unique beers. Those are best judged on their own individualistic merits as Specialty Beers, the catch-all category in the style guidelines where creativity is king.

Even if the notion of style guidelines is not something you accept, understand that most craft beer aficionados will use beer styles to communicate. If you ask a bartender in a good pub, "Do you have any IPAs?" you should expect him to tell you about his hoppiest beers. If you go to a beer store and ask, "Can you recommend a stout?" then you should expect to be led to the dark beers. If you go to Belgium and ask for a *tripel*, you should ask if they got your order right if they hand you a glass of brown beer. Styles exist, even if people just think of them as "type of beer."

Understanding BJCP Terms

The BJCP Style Guidelines use some specific terms with specialized meanings that might not be immediately obvious; the most important terms are *Category, Subcategory,* and *Style.* When thinking of beer, mead, and cider styles, the *subcategory* is the most important label—subcategory means essentially the same thing as style and identifies the major characteristic of one type of beer, mead, or cider.

The larger style categories are arbitrary groupings of beers, meads, or ciders, usually with similar character or historical ties. However, some subcategories are not necessarily related to others within the same category. If there is ever any confusion about inferring some attribute by how a beer is categorized, always defer to the specific descriptions for each subcategory.

The purpose of the structure within the BJCP Style Guidelines is to group styles of beer, mead, and cider for competition purposes—*do not attempt to derive additional meaning from these category groupings.* For example, look at the BJCP categories for Light Hybrid Beer, Amber Hybrid Beer, and Sour Ale, where seemingly unrelated beers are grouped according to sensory impact. They don't all have historical or regional ties, yet they are judged together so as to minimize variation in palate impact that judges would experience.

The 'Narrowness' of Styles

Some styles are quite well known, others are historical notions, while still others are artificial creations for the purpose of categorizing relatively unique beers or for grouping similar beers for judging purposes. That said, there is a notion of narrowness of style that applies to the variation between commercial examples within a style. Some styles are based on a small number of examples (e.g., California Common), while others may have explicit requirements (e.g., Kölsch)—those are narrow styles. Other styles embrace multiple stylistic variations (e.g., Foreign Style Stout, Old Ale), and hence are broader. Some styles allow a great degree of creativity on the part of the brewer, and therefore are wide open (e.g., Mild, Belgian Dark Strong Ale). All of these factors contribute to styles being handled differently.

The nature of the research into the styles is another factor. Some styles have many commercial examples; these styles are relatively easy to describe. Some styles are historical, have few sources, or are not widely available; these styles may be less fully described. Styles also tend to evolve, and descriptions may describe variations over time. In some cases (e.g., English IPA), the styles describe beers the way they used to be made more than the way they are currently made. This allows the historic heritage of a style to be preserved and the beer to be brewed by homebrewers, even if most commercial brewers no longer make it that way. Styles may be rediscovered (e.g., Porter, *Witbier*) and be revived in their historical context. It is a judgment call on the part of the BJCP to decide how best to handle a style. Beers tend to be described in the way that they were when they were the most authentic and popular.

The Style Space

I like to think about the style space a beer occupies—that is, which styles of beer are closest to the style you are discussing, and which variables are different. For example, an American Pale Ale fits between a Blonde Ale and an American IPA in hoppiness and strength. Back off on the hops (and maybe the strength) and you have a Blonde Ale. Increase the strength (and maybe the hops) and you have an IPA. Tweak the malt-hop balance to favor the malt a bit more, and you have either an American Amber Ale or an American Brown Ale (add more crystal malt for an amber, add some chocolate malt for a brown). Play around with the varieties of malt, hops, and yeast while keeping the strength and balance the same, and you have an English or Belgian Pale Ale.

The style space also comes in handy if you're interested in making a specialty beer. The gap between styles is fertile ground for identifying "out-of-style" beers that could be described by their own style. Black IPAs are an example of a gap in the styles. There are dark pale ales but not dark IPAs. American Stouts are dark, strong, and hoppy, but the roast character, body, and balance are different. If you can change a few variables and make a new style, then you have something you can enter as a specialty beer. There are black IPAs but no black pale ales; decrease the gravity of a black IPA and you have another style.

If you're judging beer (even your own beer), it helps to know the nearest neighbors in the style space. If you think a beer is out of style, then maybe it's a better fit in an adjacent style. Each different characteristic in beer (gravity, bitterness, color, flavor, body, etc.) is a potential vector in the n-dimensional style space. If you determine your own beer hits an adjacent style better before entering it in a competition, you may wind up with a higher score, since you'll be judged against a different style description that may be a better match. If you're judging in a competition, you may be able to give the brewer better advice on how his or her beer tastes if you can refer to another style by name.

Some people have attempted to map the style space graphically (I sometimes see charts like this when a brewpub is trying to explain its lineup). Such an exercise is difficult, because beers typically have more dimensions than are shown on the graph. You can show a few attributes, like color and strength, but those don't fully model the profile of the beers. They only show you a small part of the actual difference between the styles. Those limited models may be helpful if you are only concerned about the balance between two of the variables (for instance, graphing bitterness versus gravity shows the relative hop intensity of a beer).

A better way to illustrate the style space is to focus on one style and then show only its nearest neighboring styles. This type of chart could show the attributes which, when changed, result in the adjacent styles. That's much easier to understand and use in the general case, but it doesn't show you the full landscape of beer. You would have to compare multiple charts (or use spider graphs) to get that type of information.

How to Read and Apply the Styles

As someone with a keen interest in improving the BJCP Style Guidelines, I've observed countless times how the descriptions are used in practice. Most people generally understand how to use them properly, but I've also seen many get confused and wind up with poor results. I'd like to cover the practical use of the style guidelines and identifying what is important to know when brewing beer, entering competitions, and judging beer.

Here are my lessons learned in how to properly read and apply the guidelines:

- Don't overfocus on a single phrase in the style description. You may be giving it more importance than it is due. For example, if a *hefeweizen* is described as "may have a tart character," don't think you have to add lemons or acid malt in order to generate this impression. It's a natural component that can come out in some beers; don't force it.

- Pay attention to the order and intensity of the descriptors; this will give you an idea of the overall profile. Try to map out primary, secondary, and background components. Your idea is to capture the balance; if you change the priority and intensity of the style components, then you are describing a different beer.

- Understand what is required versus optional in a style. For example, old ales and barley wines may have an oxidized character; don't penalize beers if they don't. IPAs require a hoppy aroma; if it is missing, then it's not right.

- Avoid the halo effect of a single commercial example defining the entire style for you. For example, not all American pale ales will taste like *Sierra Nevada Pale Ale*. That doesn't mean they aren't good examples. Styles aren't meant to be a clone beer exercise.

- Understand the range of the style (how narrow or how broad it is, as described in the "narrowness" discussion). This defines how much creativity a brewer can apply and still be within style. Don't make a style more narrow or broad than it is; think about the overall style space.

- Avoid looking at the details without looking at the overall impression. The various attributes of beer styles have some range to them (for example, the allowable bitterness or hop flavor). It's possible to choose values for each of these attributes that seem to fit the style definition yet create a beer that doesn't fit the style at all. When in doubt, the overall impression and balance trump the individual style attributes. The beer as a whole has to make sense for the style.

These factors help you understand what is important for the style. As you can tell, I'm trying to get you to envision the *essence of the style*, the overall impression and balance of the components present, to know what must be present for the style to be valid and what separates it from other styles. That is how a style is defined; by the big picture.

Developing Your Palate

To evaluate a beer properly, you have to develop your palate and be able to critically distinguish flavors. Aroma plays a strong part in flavor recognition, since the tongue can recognize five basic tastes (sweet, sour, salty, bitter, and umami), but the nose can recognize literally thousands of scents. The perception of flavor depends on the basic tastes, the olfactory (aromas and smells) responses, and the physical sensations in the oral cavity (the mouthfeel). When I discuss developing your palate for beer tasting, I'm concerned with building skills in all three of these areas.

Your goals should be to understand what contributes to being able to taste beer critically, to learn techniques for tasting and smelling beer, and to learn how to practice the skills necessary to develop a discriminating palate and to master tasting. Your tastes change and your palate evolves over the course of a lifetime. You lose taste buds as you age, but you learn to distinguish and appreciate more flavors and aromas as you experience them and commit them to memory. Sensory experiences are very closely tied to memories and often provide the most vivid learning episodes.

The Tongue Map

Before we talk about tasting, we first have to clear up a huge misconception about taste: the *tongue map*. (You know the one; it shows the tongue as tasting sweetness at the tip, bitterness at the back, and sour/salty at the sides.) It's completely wrong; the map was based on a misinterpretation of earlier research and has been almost impossible to purge from beer and brewing literature. Just like cooking enthusiasts who say, "searing meat seals in juices" (it doesn't), people still think the zone-oriented tongue map is accurate.

The article "Making Sense of Taste" states:

In reality, all qualities of taste can be elicited from all the regions of the tongue that contain taste buds. There is no evidence that any kind of spatial segregation of sensitivities contributes to the neural representation of taste quality, although there are some slight differences in sensitivity across the tongue and palate.[1]

This means that flavor receptors exist throughout the tongue, and all tastes can be sensed in all areas. There are localized regions of higher sensitivity to certain tastes, but that does not imply that other areas do not sense those tastes. The maps also leave out the fifth basic taste, umami or savoriness (the taste of glutamate, an amino acid found in meats, fish, and legumes, and a flavor enhancer in MSG—monosodium glutamate). The bottom line is that to taste something properly, you should involve your whole mouth, tongue, and palate.

There are four kinds of projections called *papillae* on the tongue; three of these structures have taste buds (specialized taste cells in the mouth). Taste buds are also present on the soft palate. The front half of the tongue, the lips, the insides of cheeks, and the soft palate are sensitive to all flavors. The sides of the tongue (at the back) are slightly more sensitive to sourness. The very back of the tongue is a little more sensitive to bitterness and umami. The center of the tongue is slightly less sensitive to flavors.

Understanding Balance

The concept of *balance* in beer seems very simple on the surface, but it turns out to be quite challenging. Balance refers to the interaction and harmony between two or more of the beer's constituents in the overall flavor profile. The topic is somewhat complex, because determining balance is somewhat arbitrary—it may differ dramatically depending on the subjectivity of the taster, the type of beer, or the tasting conditions.

More specifically, beer balance is the synergy of all the components that formulate an enjoyable tasting experience: aroma, flavor (taste, malt and hop flavors, esters, phenols), bitterness, alcohol, acidity, residual sweetness, and mouthfeel (body, carbonation). In a balanced beer, individual components

---

[1] David V. Smith and Robert F. Margolskee, "Making Sense of Taste," *Scientific American* 284: 3 (March 2001), 32-39.

support and enhance each other, and the resulting combination is appropriate for the particular style of beer.

The use of words like *synergy, balance,* and *harmony* shouldn't imply that all flavors are of equal intensity. That is much too simplistic (and generally wrong). It means that the components complement each other in a pleasant way. Balance is extremely style-specific; a balanced IPA will be way more bitter than a balanced cream ale, for instance. Confusingly, "balance" can also mean equal intensity if speaking only of two components in relation to each other without regard to the underlying style; the usage depends on the context.

By far, the most straightforward balance to discuss in beer styles is between maltiness and bitterness. Without bitterness, the maltiness would seem cloyingly sweet. Without maltiness, bitterness would seem harsh and unpleasant. The ratio of bittering units to gravity units (BU:GU) is a rough approximation of balance in a beer, with bitter styles generally having a ratio of 0.6 or higher. Malty beers are generally 0.45 or lower. Evenly balanced beers are usually between 0.45 and 0.6. This formula works best when the beer styles being compared have similar final gravities.

Sweetness and body also balance bitterness, so if a beer has a higher final gravity and more residual sweetness, the apparent bitterness will not seem as high as the same number of IBUs in a dry beer. Sweetness has much more of an impact balancing bitterness than does body, however. Alcohol can sometimes provide a sharp bitterness, as can roasted grains. These aren't measured in IBUs but can affect the maltiness-bitterness balance in some styles.

The ester profile can affect the balance, since fruity esters can enhance apparent sweetness. Sourness in a beer balances sweetness, so a sour beer will seem more bitter (and often thinner in body). Phenols and tannins can be astringent and bitter, and both also enhance the apparent bitterness. None of these are taken into account in standard measurements of gravity or bitterness, yet each can impact the balance.

So how can we reconcile all these disparate characteristics? For starters, avoid relying too heavily on the BU:GU ratio—it's an approximation at best and influenced by all the factors listed. Next, try using your palate and detecting these individual components. If you are able to detect warming alcohol, you can conclude that some of the bitterness may be coming not from hops but from that same alcohol. Likewise with dark roasted grains, phenols, tannins, and other bitter substances—you can taste their flavor or mouthfeel in addition to their bitterness.

The "scrubbing bubbles" of high carbonation can cut through malty sweetness, providing balance and making the apparent sweetness seem lower. Carbonation can also add a prickly acidity that can make a beer's body seem lighter. Likewise, a flat beer will often seem thin, even though it may have a full body.

Finally, remember that serving temperature can play a role in balance. A cold serving temperature numbs the tongue and suppresses malt flavor, and makes the beer seem more bitter, since the bitterness components (hops, tannins) are not affected. Lower temperatures make beer seem a bit less acidic. Higher serving temperatures will make alcohol more apparent. So sometimes balance can be achieved simply by manipulating the serving temperature.

Aroma Techniques

To assess the aromatics of the beer, swirl the glass and tilt it toward you. Inhale deep in the glass—the lower side of the glass near the surface of the beer. Be careful, you're judging aroma, not nosefeel. Use a deep inhalation lasting a few seconds, which should get heavy aromatics. Then consider what you've smelled. Swirl again, stop swirling, then tilt and smell again—this time towards the upper side of the glass (farthest from the beer). This will get lighter aromatics. Repeat again, smelling in the middle of the glass using a series of short, quick sniffs. Finally, keep the glass level and smell a few inches above the glass. Each of these sniffing techniques may give you a different impression.

It's easy to overwhelm your sense of smell with repeated sniffs of the same substance. To help alleviate this sensory overload, cleanse your olfactory bulb between each set of sniffs. I like to just turn my head and take a few sniffs of my shirt sleeve—it's a totally different aroma, and helps reset your nose to sense new aromas. It works with almost any different aroma, as long as the cleansing aroma isn't too strong. I've been offered coffee beans for this purpose at some beer competitions but found them way too strong. You want to reset your olfactory bulb, not fry it.

You are looking to pick up as many different aromas as you can find. You will definitely want to assess the malt character. How strong or intense is it? Is it sweet? Does it have a noticeable and identifiable malt character? Is it bready, caramelly, richly malty, toasty, or something else? Can you give those specific aromatics a name? Malt is to beer as grapes are to wine; you need to describe the character of the primary ingredient and relate it to any expectations you may have been given by how the beer was described.

Next look for the **hop** character. Do you detect any? If so, how intense is it? Is it grassy, harsh, or clean? Can you give the aromatics a name, such as citrusy, earthy, floral, herbal, piney, spicy, or woody? How is the hop intensity as compared to the malt intensity; how are they balanced?

Now assess the **fermentation** character. Did the yeast add any interesting aromatics (fruity esters, spicy phenols, etc.)? Is there alcohol noted? Are there any fermentation faults? If a certain type of yeast was mentioned or is implied by the style (*hefeweizen*, for instance), does it have the characteristic aroma? Alcohol can definitely be sensed in stronger beers. If it is sharp and aggressive to the point where it overwhelms other components, it is a negative.

Refer to the chapter on Troubleshooting for a list of common beer characteristics; many of them are detectable by aroma. Do they persist or do they blow off quickly? Characterize the overall fermentation character: is it clean, fresh, dirty, yeasty, sulfury, or something else?

Were there any **special ingredients** (fruits, spices, herbs, smoked malt, etc.) used in this beer? If so, do you detect their presence? If a special ingredient is fermentable (e.g., fruit), then the character might not have the same impression as the fresh ingredient. For example, wine does not smell like grapes, it smells like fermented grapes. Don't expect fruit in a beer to always smell like the raw fruit. The amount of residual sugar in the beer can affect the impression of fruit, since fruity aromatics are often found with sweetness in fresh fruit. Declared special ingredients should be noticeable but balanced, and in harmony with other ingredients.

Noticeable **acidity** is not typical in most beer styles but is a feature of some such as *lambic*. It can often be sensed in the aroma. Acidity that comes from fruit or yeast can often be sensed more readily in the aroma, since the presence of balancing malt in the flavor can sometimes mask it. Carbonation often will play up the nose, since the bubbles help volatilize aromatics.

Was there any **special processing** (e.g., oak aging) used in this beer? If so, do you note the character? Oaking will often impart a woody, toasty, vanilla character. Other special handling techniques will produce aromas as well. Icing (or "eising," as in *eisbock*) will concentrate aromatics, for instance.

Finally, you'll want to consider the overall **balance**, harmony, and pleasantness of the beer. Do the ingredients complement each other? Are they in balance given the style and declared special ingredients of the beer? What is your overall impression of the quality of the beer? Is it well made from good ingredients? Does it have any off-odors? Is this something that you are now eager to taste?

Tasting Techniques

Tasting a beer involves exploring the full range of flavors (malt, sweetness, bitterness, alcohol, esters, phenols, acidity) and mouthfeel character (body, carbonation, warming, creaminess, astringency). Flavor and mouthfeel are normally described in different sections of a beer scoresheet, but they both involve tasting and are discussed together here.

As with aroma techniques, it's important to cleanse your plate between samples. Anything relatively neutral will help; plain bread, matzo, or unsalted crackers work well for this purpose. Avoid strongly flavored artisan bread, salted crackers, and heavily toasted products. Beer and bread share several common flavors, so you don't want to carry over any flavors from the cleansing to the tasting. Use clean water (without a chlorine taste) to rinse your mouth and finish the cleansing of your palate.

To assess the flavor of a beer, there are several techniques that can be used. All involve taking small sips; some beers can be quite strong, so taking gulps is a quick way to shorten your effectiveness as a judge. Take a sip into the front of your mouth, and swish the tip of your tongue through it. Take a sip and move your tongue side-to-side to swish it through your mouth. Take a sip and let it rest on the top of your tongue. Chew your beer; get your entire mouth involved. Take a sip and aerate the beer by breathing over it in your mouth (it will make a slight slurping or gurgling sound). Take a sip and swallow, focusing on the aftertaste. After swallowing, *keep your mouth closed* and exhale slowly through your nose—you may pick up additional aromatics this way. These techniques can be combined. They each involve different areas of your mouth and may give you additional flavor impressions. As you develop your tasting skills, you may decide to use different tasting techniques to look for different flavor or mouthfeel elements.

The first task is to characterize the **malt flavors** and any **residual sweetness**. Do you get a distinct, clean malt flavor, or is it muddy and indistinct? Are there specific malt flavors you taste? Is the flavor distinct and identifiable, or rather generic and grainy? How well does it blend in with the other flavors? How strong or intense is it? How would you describe the malt character: Is it grainy, caramelly, bready, biscuity, cookielike, richly malty, toasty, roasty, burnt, or some other flavor? Use the descriptors discussed in Chapter 4: Mastering Ingredients.

What is the level of sweetness in the finish? Common descriptors include dry, medium-dry, moderately sweet, moderately high sweet, sweet, or cloyingly sweet. Do not confuse sweetness with maltiness—sweetness is only a measure of residual sugar. The perception of sweetness is also affected by the sweetness-to-bitterness balance; the absence of balancing bittering hops can make a beer seem sweet.

Now address the **bitterness and alcohol** level. The bitterness is normally apparent in the finish, although it can rise sharply early in the palate in strongly bittered beers. The point in your palate where the balance flips from being malty to being bitter is a measure of the overall balance of the beer. Very malty beers will start malty and taste malty in the finish and aftertaste. Balanced beers will start malty but finish with an equalizing bitterness. Bitter beers will seem bitter on the tongue and stay bitter into the aftertaste. The intensity of the bitterness should be described (high, medium, low), the character of the bitterness should be noted (is it harsh or clean), and the balance between the bitterness and the maltiness should be characterized.

A useful skill to develop as a brewer is to estimate the bitterness level in a beer. This can be difficult but can be developed, as long as you have known reference samples. Look up the measured IBU levels of commercial beers and taste them. Remember how you perceive the differences. Know that malty sweetness can offset bitterness, so see how the perceived bitterness changes in dry to sweet beers. Personally, I think it is more important to be able to characterize the perceived bitterness level (low, medium, high) than it is to state an IBU level, since it is the perception of bitterness that plays the more important role in the overall balance of the beer.

Alcohol in beer can be noted as a flavor, can add to the perceived bitterness of beer, and can provide a warming (sometimes hot and burning) mouthfeel. Most average-strength beers should not have a noticeable alcohol character, or else it is a flaw. Stronger beers should have a smooth, aged alcohol, not a hot, burning, solventy character. A hot alcohol character is often an indication of a young beer that needs more cellaring. The best strong beers often have a "sneaky" quality to them, in which the alcohol is more often felt than tasted. Note if any alcohol was detected, and if it was a flavor or a mouthfeel. Characterize the alcohol (warming, burning, smooth, aged), and mention if it adds to the perceived bitterness. Identify where you detect it (as a taste or an aftertaste).

What about the **hop flavor** and any **fermentation character** (esters, phenols, acidity)? Identify the intensity and the character of each. Try to differentiate the type of hop character, using descriptors from Chapter 4: Mastering Ingredients. If you can identify specific hop varieties, that's great; otherwise, try to describe the perceptual characteristics of each. Be as specific as possible ("grapefruit" is more descriptive than "citrusy," for instance). Try to rank the individual flavors in the order they were perceived, often the most intense coming first. Do these flavors enhance or clash with other flavors in the beer? Do you get them as distinct and readily identifiable flavors, do they all mingle together in tasty union, or do they step on each other in a muddy mess?

The **special ingredients and processes** can add another whole realm of flavors: fruit, spice, oak, etc. Some malts and yeast can produce flavors that mimic those from fruit and spices. However, if there are special ingredients declared, those should be noticeable and generally identifiable but well balanced and harmonious with the other ingredients (relative to the style and intent of the brewer). Try to generally describe the character and strength of each flavor component you detect. See if you can give it a name (e.g., cinnamon) or at least a general description (e.g., spicy), and an intensity (light, moderate, strong). The more descriptive you can be, the more information you are passing along.

Normally, **yeast**-derived flavors are mentioned along with discussions of fruit, spice, or alcohol. However, if there are fermentation **flaws**, those should be noted. See the list of characteristics in Chapter 7: Troubleshooting for more information—most of the faults can be tasted. If no fermentation issues are noted, identify the beer as having a *clean* fermentation.

The **aftertaste** of the beer is the flavor impression you get once you have swallowed it. You can describe the length (short, medium, long, memorable) of the aftertaste, which is the duration it takes for the flavors to dissipate. What kinds of flavors are you getting? Are they different from flavors noted when tasting the beer? Are they pleasant and balanced? Is there anything off?

Note that taste perceptions can be influenced by mouthfeel textures. Alcohol enhances the perception of sweetness, reinforces acidity, can mask odors, and may cause a burning sensation. Astringency may have a rough, gritty character and can mask bitterness and reduce the perception of sweetness. Bitterness is often confused with astringency (bitterness is a taste, astringency is a mouthfeel).

The overall balance of the beer should be described, as discussed in the section on Balance earlier in this chapter. Balance is relative to the specific style of beer; it does not mean that flavors are in equal proportions or intensities. Balance describes how well the individual components complement each other in the intended style of the brewer.

When discussing balance, identify if any components are too strong or weak. Does any individual component overshadow the beer, even when taking style into account? Is there any component that is lacking (e.g., not enough alcohol in a barley wine)? Are the special ingredients identifiable yet not overly dominant? The best beers are not one-dimensional; they have interest and character. They do not all have to be complex; dry, delicate, restrained beers can be wonderful. Do not attempt to equate a dry, crisp lager with a sweet, rich old ale in complexity and character; judging them each on balance relative to their intended style is the best way to level the playing field.

Keep the aroma in mind when evaluating the final taste of the beer. Do the flavors you get match what you expected, given the aroma? Do the flavors mirror the aromatics? For example, if you smelled citrusy hops, did you taste them as well? Are there any additional flavors? If so, what are they? Is the beer balanced? Are the tastes present in the proper proportion given the style? These questions often will give you the best idea of the overall impression of the beer.

Mouthfeel describes the nonflavor sensations in your mouth when you taste something. It includes the tactile sensations, the textures, and the feelings associated with drinking. The sparkle of carbonation, the warmth of alcohol, the sharpness of acidity, and the roughness of tannin are all mouthfeel characteristics. The body of the liquid provides weight on your tongue and may coat your mouth. Tingling, numbing, drying, cooling, warming, and coating are all mouthfeel sensations. Beer can be described in textures such as smooth, soft, velvety, rough, hard, or harsh. Flavor, mouthfeel, and aftertaste are best characterized together.

The most straightforward components of mouthfeel are body, carbonation, and alcohol warmth. **Body** is a measure of the relative viscosity of beer (weight of the beer on your tongue) and can range from light/thin to medium to heavy/full. These are the normal ranges for body, but a beer could have lighter or heavier body as a fault. A very light body is described as watery, while a very full body is viscous, thick, or syrupy. As a very general analogy, light body is like skim milk, medium body is like whole milk, and full body is like cream. The perception of body is influenced by alcohol and sweetness levels; stronger and sweeter beers will seem to have a fuller body.

Carbonation describes the level of dissolved carbon dioxide in solution and ranges from low to high. Most styles should not be totally flat, but in some, such as English cask ales, a light level of carbonation is acceptable. High carbonation has a fairly wide range as well, with some Belgian ales and German wheat beers being very highly carbonated. The amount of carbonation can often be sensed by the outward pressure on your cheeks when you hold a full sample of beer in your mouth, by the prickly feeling the bubbles make on your tongue, or by the way in which sweetness and other flavors are quickly wiped away from your palate.

The **alcohol** in a beer can be unnoticeable or range from a pleasantly warming sensation to a hot burn. A smooth, warming quality is a positive character in a stronger beer. Hot, solventy, burning sensations are always a negative. Stronger beers should have noticeable alcohol, but the alcohol should be well blended and balanced with other flavors. Higher alcohol generally is perceived as having increased body, more warmth, and perhaps a bit more bitterness.

The **acidity** in a beer might be noted, particularly if it becomes sharp, puckering, or tingly. Low levels of acidity can be a flavor enhancer if it is in the background. High levels of acidity might affect mouthfeel in a generally negative way.

Tannins and creaminess also affect mouthfeel. Tannins can produce astringent, drying, harsh, and puckering sensations. They can come from hops, dark grains, oaking, or brewing process faults. They are generally undesirable in most styles; note them if you detect any. Creaminess is a velvety, silky, smooth, luscious sensation in the mouth, as from drinking cream. It may be present in some styles, particularly oatmeal and sweet stout. Describe the level you note.

Malty vs. Sweet

One common misunderstanding with many brewers and judges is the difference between sweetness and maltiness. *Sweetness* is simply a measure of the residual sugar in beer, while *maltiness* is the flavor of malt. A beer can be malty without being sweet (many German lagers and Belgian ales fit into this category), and a beer can be sweet without being malty (it could be sugary-sweet, like some mass-market Belgian fruit lambics that are back-sweetened). If you drink wine, the equivalent to maltiness is fruitiness; a wine can be fruity without being sweet, yet many people routinely confuse the two.

It's easier to think of sweetness as the opposite of dryness. It is something sensed in the palate and aftertaste. If you perceive sweetness initially on your palate and it lingers through the aftertaste, this is likely to be actual sweetness. If it seems malty-sweet initially but then finishes dry, then that is how maltiness is perceived. A beer can be both sweet and malty (malty-sweet); English barley wines and old ales are obvious examples.

Sweetness is one of the five basic flavors, but there are many flavors that can be associated with sweetness depending on the source. Sugars developed in malt in the kilning, mashing, and boiling processes will have the flavor of their constituent malt. Munich will have a richer flavor, Vienna a toasty flavor, crystal a caramel flavor, etc. If these sugars remain in the finished beer, then the perception of maltiness and sweetness will both be present. The flavor of cane or beet sugar will taste like common table sugar. Sweetness from honey will have a different flavor and can also have the floral character associated with the nectar from which the honey was made.

The confusion comes from wanting to use "sweet" to describe both the basic flavor and the flavor of the raw ingredient. It helps to be more specific in identifying the type of sweetness as the flavor descriptor (sugary, caramelly, malty, etc.) while reserving "sweet" as a description of the finish (as opposed to "dry"). This is both more accurate and less confusing.

When judging beer, I often use sweet in several contexts but I try to be clear as to what I mean. I might say something like "starts out malty-sweet but finishes dry and refreshing." If a malty beer finishes dry, it enhances drinkability. This is why Germans can drink liters of Oktoberfest, while a similar amount of old ale would be nearly impossible to finish. A sweet beer that finishes sweet will seem heavy and harder to drink; connoisseurs might call it a *sipping beer*. In extreme examples, a sweet beer could be called cloying, tongue-coating, and heavy or thick in body.

Building Your Skills

You don't often get sympathy from people when you explain you're trying to build your skills in beer tasting, but it is actually work that requires practice and concentration. My favorite way to build skills is something I call *cross-training*—that is, to learn about tasting other things besides beer. Take a wine tasting class; I learned more about tasting from a 10-week class given at a local wine shop than I did by almost any other method. You can participate in food tastings, whiskey tastings, and several other venues where your palate can be put to the test.

When I work on *palate training,* I focus on three key areas: learning to identify a specific flavor, learning to recognize a flavor at threshold level, and learning to distinguish the flavor from similar flavors.

When you taste a beer, try to sense and identify the flavor or aroma. Does it remind you of a food or of a raw ingredient in beer? Some roasted malts smell like dark chocolate or coffee, for instance. When combined with sweetness, the chocolate could take on a milk chocolate tone. Use your memories of those aromas and flavors to try to associate the flavors in beer with a descriptive term. Always try to attach words to your perceptions. You might be triggering memories, but unless you can recall the associations, they'll be of limited value in tasting.

Tasting a wide range of fresh foods will help you develop more recent associations. Look for food terms that are used in the style guidelines to describe beer, then go find those foods and smell and taste them. Try the blindfold test. Have a friend feed you various items and see if you can identify them by smell and taste alone. Do this in a group for more fun.

If you can identify a smell or taste, try to detect it in lower intensities. See if you can determine your thresholds and if you have any sensory "blind spots." If you can't smell something, it's likely genetic and there's nothing you can do about it. However, you can know that you have this handicap and rely on the senses of others when you are tasting.

Sometimes you can blend beers to get new flavors, or to dilute existing flavors to test your threshold levels. This can be another way of generating new beers to test. It can also give you practice on beer blending skills (see Chapter 8).

When you can tell smells and flavors apart, try differentiating those that are subtly different. For instance, collect all the citrus fruit you can find. Try to tell them apart using only your senses of smell and taste. Then repeat this experiment with hops that have similar characteristics.

Training and practice involve repetition. You may not be able to build a lasting memory with only one exposure. Try these experiments over and over, alone and with groups. Practice picking apart flavors when you taste a new food. See how many ingredients you can identify. Then do the same thing with beer. Understand the taste of the single ingredients, and see how many you can find when tasting a new beer. Run this mental experiment every time you taste a beer. Go drinking with beer geek friends who won't mind discussing the details of beer with you; spouses often tire of this exercise, so don't be a bore to unwilling accomplices.

A common method of palate training is using doctored beer—spiking samples of beer with chemicals associated with beer components or flaws. This is a great way to test your threshold levels and to test if you have any blind spots. It is very easy to adjust the levels and compare them against common sensory levels that have been tested in the general population. The BJCP provides sensory kits from the Siebel Institute free of charge to groups preparing to take the beer judge exam. Getting in on a study group that has one of these kits is a perfect way to practice your sensory evaluation and to compare your skills with others.

Keep in mind that *doctored beers* have limitations. You aren't actually tasting homebrew or commercial beer that is flawed. You are tasting beer with chemicals added that simulate a flaw. An actual flawed beer will often have other flavors and clues as to the root problem. Don't assume that the flavors you taste in a doctored beer will always be the same in actual beer. Flaws such as diacetyl, DMS, and oxidation can take on many different flavors, for instance. A doctored beer kit will typically only have one of those flavors.

One way you can build your practical skills is by using the *triangle* test, a common technique in sensory analysis. To do this, you need to taste three samples, two of which are identical, and see if you can select the different one and identify why it is different. You can't do this on your own, since the samples must be unknown to you. It's a fun project with a group, so you might want to enlist some beer geek friends and practice together. Take turns preparing the samples so everyone can learn.

Here are some tips to reduce sources of error that could influence the results:

- You should have some palate cleansers available, such as plain crackers and water.

- Samples should be presented uniformly (same cups, same sized pour, same lighting). If color or appearance could be a clue, present the beers in opaque cups. Each sample should look exactly the same, or the testers could be blindfolded.

- Samples should be marked with random three-digit codes, since some people may associate certain numbers with better choices. Use a spreadsheet to generate the numbers (e.g., the RAND function in Excel).

- Don't let different testers talk or provide suggestions to each other. Boothlike partitions are used in professional panels.

- Randomize the position or order of the odd sample. The middle sample is often chosen as the different one. If you present the samples in a triangle shape, then there is no middle sample.

- Only include those tasters who are interested in the project, and stop when they are tired. Motivation plays a role in performance.

Have the tasters record their results on paper as they go along. Collect the data, tabulate the results, and share the outcome with the tasters. Discuss what differences existed, and see who did the best job of identifying the differences.

Commercial breweries often use this technique in their quality-control testing. It allows researchers to determine if there is a significant difference in samples (for instance, in the taste of an older versus a newer beer), or if a new variety of hop can be distinguished from one previously used. As a brewer, you can use this technique for a variety of purposes, but practice using it is a good way to train your palate and measure your results.

Critically Assessing Your Own Beer

When people ask me for the single most important thing they can do to become a better brewer, I usually tell them to learn how to judge beer. Yeah, I get a lot of surprised looks in return—maybe they were expecting a lecture on mash techniques, yeast management, or sanitation. But thinking like an engineer, I know that you can't really control a process without incorporating a feedback loop. Brewing is one such process where a feedback loop provides better results. If you think about the process of producing tasty beer, critical structured tasting ("judging") provides just the right information to make subsequent corrections ("brewing better beer").

Evaluating your own beer is an advanced skill. You have to be a good beer judge—which requires its own special set of skills—but you also have to be able to set aside your biases and knowledge of the beer in order to assess it as another judge would. Getting practice as a judge in the BJCP is invaluable, since it forces you to repeat the basic assessment of a beer over and over again. This repetition allows the evaluation process to become second nature, which makes it easier to block out any advance information you have about the beer.

I'm not going to discuss how to become a BJCP judge or take you through the process of how to judge in competition or how to fill out a BJCP scoresheet. But I do think it's important to be able to use the basic assessment skills a judge employs and to understand how a judge evaluates a beer. This is a skill known as *structured tasting*. It provides some rigor to the simple sensory analysis that palate training employs. These skills can help you greatly if you enter your beers in competition, but they will also help you shorten the feedback loop and make your brewing process more responsive to change.

Evaluation is a systematic, structured assessment of something, or a determination of merit, worth, or significance against a set of standards. Good beer judges will perform an evaluation of every beer they sample, even if it isn't for a competition. This evaluation can be performed silently and as a mental exercise, or it can be written down as notes. Regardless, this is the basic practice needed to develop the skill of assessing beer as a judge.

Before you begin assessing your beer, you need to decide what you are trying to determine. Are you evaluating a new beer for faults or for style fidelity? Are you trying to decide if your beer has finished conditioning and is ready to drink? Are you checking if your beer is ready to send to a competition? Are you picking which keg to bring to a party? Are you taking notes on what you need to improve when brewing the beer again? Are you doing a basic triage where you decide if an old beer is drinkable, should be dumped, or needs some fixing up? All of these are valid questions to ask, and each might cause you to alter your approach to assessment, since some questions are more detailed than others. If you're just trying to decide if you should bring a keg to a party, you don't need to do a full-blown assessment; just taste it and jump to the overall impression. If you're going to be adjusting your recipe to incorporate feedback, you'll want to be as detailed as possible.

Structured Tasting

You don't have to be a BJCP judge to assess a beer properly. The training, study, and practice all help, but I know many excellent judges who have never taken the exam. However, these judges know how to perform structured tastings of beer. That is, they can completely, thoroughly, and accurately describe the major perceptual characteristics (aroma, flavor, appearance, mouthfeel) of a beer. This is most important aspect of judging, and one that many BJCP judges and novices gloss over in their quest to identify faults, discuss beer styles, and hypothesize about potential corrections.

First things first—to judge a beer, you have to understand and be able to articulate what you are tasting! Brewers entering competition, or friends just handing you one of their homebrews, want this information first. If they are advanced brewers (or professionals), chances are this is the only feedback they'll want. Yet this is scary for many new judges, since they don't always have the trained palate or the vocabulary to describe what they are sensing. I recommend that judges in training start with the checklist version of the

BJCP scoresheet, since it lists much more detail about possible sensory characteristics. For the latest BJCP scoresheets, look on the BJCP website (*www.bjcp.org*) under the Competitions section.

When evaluating a beer, follow the same general order as the sections on BJCP scoresheets: Aroma, Appearance, Flavor, and Mouthfeel. These categories guide you through the entire sensory experience of evaluating a beer. Within each category, look at the sensory aspects listed under each section. Ask yourself whether the beer contains that attribute or not, and if so, in what intensity. I like to think about the sensory characteristics in the order I perceive them, rather than how they are listed on the scoresheet. If you were describing the beer to someone, you'd want to list the most intense characteristics first, since those are the dominant flavors and aromas. Use the checklist scoresheet to check your thoroughness—get used to looking for all those flavors and aromas, even if they aren't present.

Use the techniques and methods described earlier in the Developing Your Palate section. Once you can identify if a perceptual component (say, malt or hops) is present and in what intensity, then you can get down to the business of describing it in more detail. This is where the additional adjectives come into play on the scoresheet. For example, is the malt grainy, bready, biscuity, toasty, caramelly, roasty, or just richly malty? Are the hops citrusy, piney, earthy, floral, spicy, or grassy? Can you be more precise? Is the citrus like grapefruit, orange, or lemon?

Think about all that was discussed in the Mastering Ingredients chapter. Remember that beer can be made of many ingredients, and each lends its own character. You can describe a beer with multiple adjectives, if they all apply. An imperial stout will have more than just a roasty malt character—it will be quite a bit more complex. Describe all that you perceive, taking care to identify the quantity (intensity) and quality (detailed description) of each. Identify which characteristics are most dominant, and try to determine the relative balance of each of the components.

Those are the essentials of structured tasting. Repeat the process for each section of the scoresheet, describing what you perceive in the beer. Once you get enough practice using this process, you don't have to use the checklist scoresheet—you can simply take structured tasting notes. I often use a small pocket notebook for this purpose, but any medium that captures your thoughts will work.

As with any new skill, the amount of practice you put in will have a measurable effect on how well you perform. Get into the habit of doing a structured evaluation every time you taste a beer. You don't have to write it down; you can do it mentally, if you remember the process and the steps. This is what I often do if I'm at a bar, or drinking in a social setting. Take a few sips and run through the process. I can do a quick evaluation in less than 30 seconds and then get back to the fun of drinking. A more thorough check will take a few minutes. It's the mental exercise that counts, not how you write it down. If you do this exercise with other beer geeks, you can turn all that talking about beer into practice.

Evaluating for Faults

So far, we've focused mostly on the positive sensory aspects of beers—those attributes that can be considered desirable or features of some styles. There is another class of perceptions that don't belong in beer—these are faults, or potential errors to correct. Faults can be broken into two major groups: technical faults and style faults. Technical faults are generally derived from brewing, fermentation, or storage mistakes, while style faults are often balance-related (too much or too little of a certain attribute—such as esters or bitterness—for the type of beer brewed).

A discussion of common faults in beer is presented in Chapter 7: Troubleshooting, but the method of evaluation can be summarized quickly. When you are evaluating your own beer, you describe what you perceive as a fault, try to identify the root cause, leveraging your knowledge of your process and ingredients, and select plausible solutions for the problem. This will tell you whether you can fix this batch of beer, or whether you must make the corrections in your next batch. See Chapter 7 for a full treatment of this topic.

Evaluating for Style

Sensory training is mostly a function of practice. The more you do it, the better you get. However, there is another dimension to judging that requires more study and knowledge—understanding beer styles and how well a beer matches them. Admittedly, this is more important to some brewers than others. Those who enter competitions will likely be fairly fanatical about beer styles, while many professional brewers act as if they could care less about them.

Beer styles and sensory analysis have been discussed earlier in this chapter. When you know the beer style, you develop a mental picture of what you are tasting, so you can immediately begin looking for the key characteristics of the style. Once the perceptual components of a beer have been described and any technical flaws identified, you can compare the sample beer against a reference standard, like the BJCP Style Guidelines. If you are trying to clone a specific commercial beer, that reference beer itself is the standard. If you're creating a new type of beer, your basic vision for that beer should also suffice as a standard.

Regardless of the reference used, you need to understand the essentials of the style you are brewing or tasting. Style guidelines can contain a wealth of information, but it's easy to get lost in all the detail and miss the big picture. You should be able to describe any beer style in a paragraph, touching on the main required points that define the style and separate it from others. Often this is simply the overall balance of the beer and the major flavor impression. Don't worry about specific style parameters as much; you're trying to hit the key style characteristics.

Think about what best defines the beer style in question, and evaluate your beer against those aspects. You can get many small points correct, but if you miss any of the major defining characteristics, then the beer won't seem right. Again, it's more important to get the impression correct than the measured parameters. An IPA should be a bitter beer, not simply one measuring more than 50 IBUs. The impression of bitterness is affected by the intensity of the malt and other flavors, the amount of body, and the overall attenuation of the beer. When all those factors are considered, the impression needs to be one of bitterness, and that's how the beer will ultimately be judged.

Balance is probably the most important point to get right. But balance is a very misunderstood word, since it somehow implies an absolute balance. In beer judging, balance is always relative to the target style. A balanced IPA is very different than a balanced Scotch ale. A malty beer needs enough bitterness so that it doesn't seem cloyingly sweet, while a hoppy beer needs enough malt so that it doesn't seem harsh. Understanding what constitutes a balanced beer in the specific style is the key to brewing a good example. The rest is mostly choosing the right malt, hop, and yeast varieties to get the right flavor profile.

Gap Analysis

Your goal in critical tasting of your own beer is to identify gaps between what you have and what you want. These differences are what you need to focus on when making changes or adjusting your beer. The first changes you should make are the ones that hit key stylistic elements of the beer—those important attributes that define the style. Worry about the lesser changes later.

I like to record tasting notes along with the recipe, so I can see what changes to make the next time I brew it. If a flavor element is off, I think about the cause and effect of ingredient selection. Should I use a different variety of malt, hops, or yeast? Should I vary the percentage of some element? Knowing which flavors are produced by the different source ingredients is very helpful when making these adjustments. Some of this is learned by trial and error, which is another reason for keeping detailed tasting notes of all your beers. Quiz other brewers when you note a flavor you like, asking them which ingredients produced that outcome.

One technique to use when figuring out what changes to make with a future batch of beer is blending (a topic covered in depth in Chapter 8). If a beer needs more bitterness, I might add a little bit of an IPA or other strongly hopped beer. If that works, I'll note it in the recipe log and try adding more hops in the next batch. This works with just about any flavor component. You can blend on a small scale (in a glass, not a keg) so you can keep trying different proportions. If you find something you like, scale it up. This is a fast way to try different ideas without having to brew a batch again. It's an experiment, and not all experiments work out. That's OK—you're still learning something.

Applying Lessons Learned

When judging your own beer with an eye towards improving your brewing, it's most important that you be objective and honest with yourself. It's often difficult to judge your own work, but you have to set aside those feelings and put yourself in the shoes of a dispassionate judge in a competition, or a consumer at a bar. Judge your beer as you judge other beers.

Practice is an important part of building and maintaining any skill. While self-study is helpful, you also need to periodically check your skills against others, so you know that you have learned them well. In matters of perception, you need to know that you haven't got a perceptual blind spot (for example, not detecting diacetyl) or other bias that may affect your judging. For your tasting notes to be useful to you, you have to be able to trust them.

When performing structured tastings of your beer, take good notes. You will want to record a full evaluation at least once, then make notes on how the beer changes over time or how it tastes under different serving conditions. You are developing a profile of your beer that you will use as a reference. If you make changes, you will want to compare your current version against previous incarnations. Not all changes work out; you need to be able to tell from your notes which version turned out the best.

Use the feedback wisely, whether your own or from others. Be careful about making too many adjustments at once, unless you are very well practiced. You need to be able to gauge the impact of your changes. If you are fine-tuning a beer, you probably should only make one change at a time. If you are quite far away from your target or have multiple problems, feel free to make more changes.

Finally, know why you are brewing. Are you trying to brew better beer for yourself, are you trying to win competitions, or do you simply want to have something you're proud to share with others? Keep in mind that judging and tasting are subjective, and that you won't always please everyone. As long as you are happy with yourself, you are getting the right enjoyment out of brewing.

CHAPTER 6
envisioning your beer

Creativity is allowing yourself to make mistakes.
Art is knowing which ones to keep.
– Scott Adams, *The Dilbert Principle*

My favorite topic when talking about brewing is how to go about developing your own recipes. While I don't mind trying out recipes from others, I really get the most enjoyment out of creating something that I envisioned. Even if I'm just taking another recipe and modifying it, I feel that I'm putting my stamp on it. One of the ways I distinguish good brewers from great brewers is their ability to create recipes; that's one characteristic of someone who has mastered the art. I certainly see an analogy to cooking; top chefs are expected to be creative and build their own recipes—it's one of the things that separates them from simply being competent cooks. This chapter discusses my thoughts and lessons on how to develop these critical skills.

Different minds think in different ways. Whether you're a right-brained or a left-brained type of person, you can still develop good recipe formulation skills. It makes a difference whether it's easier for you to visualize the end goal and leap towards the finish, or whether you take a logical, methodical approach. Think about the difference in style between *Radical Brewing* and *Designing Great Beers*; they both can help you build recipes but go about it in very different ways. If you haven't figured it out, I'm more of a right-brained person by nature, but I do have a very left-brained engineering education. So my examples tend to emphasize conceptualizing the solution, but then I might describe a rigorous way of getting there. Don't let my schizophrenia get in the way of developing your own recipe formulation techniques.

Crafting recipes does take some vision, since you need a creative concept. Your sources of inspiration can come from anywhere. I might be inspired by other beers I've tried, certain flavor pairings, foods I've tasted, or simply a desire to brew a certain style for a specific purpose. If I'm trying to be creative, I do keep in mind the overall style space concept introduced in the last chapter. And I do try to brew to style, even if the style is something I'm creating on the fly. One way of looking at brewing to style is that you know how you want your beer to turn out. The only difference is that the concept came from a set of style guidelines, not your own imagination.

As you develop your recipes and then subsequently brew them, seek consistency in outcome. You want your processes to be consistent and your recipes repeatable; I consider that part of mastering the basics of brewing. If you are changing your recipes to try to move your beer closer to your vision, then you will have to have some consistency while you are experimenting. Otherwise, how can you know if your changes are what drove the differences you note, or whether it is just random chance?

When brewing a recipe again and trying to hone it, start by varying ingredients or processes one at a time. That's the basis of experimentation; you have to be able to compare your experiment with a control (something you know for sure; a reference). As you get more experience, you should be able to change multiple variables at once and still be able to determine the outcome. If you make multiple changes and can't identify the cause of a certain outcome, you can always try the experiment again with fewer changes.

I like the experimental approach, since you are seeing for yourself what works best, learning what the differences are, and can make up your own mind whether something is worth the effort. I call this the *Cook's Illustrated* way of brewing. *Cook's Illustrated* is a cooking magazine that is known for exhaustive testing of recipes by varying ingredients and methods one at a time and testing the outcomes. It's a very time-consuming and labor-intensive approach, but if you absolutely want to find out the specific cause and effect of any individual change, that's the way to go.

When building recipes, don't be afraid to do research. Read brewing texts, articles, and books, do online searches, talk to brewers you know and trust, get ideas, and then decide what you want to do. If you understand your system and are familiar with a core set of ingredients and processes, you should be able to formulate your own recipes. Feel free to learn from the work of others, but always check to see if their recipes are repeatable on your system. I often have to adapt recipes I get from others.

As you gain experience and build confidence, you need to own your recipes. Whether they work or not is totally your responsibility. Your goal should be to develop your skills to the point where you can create new recipes of your own, brew to style, clone beers, create new styles, fuse beer styles, adapt recipes, and really understand how the changes you make will affect the final profile of your beer. You don't have to worry about how other people brew, or whether your recipes work on their systems; take care of yourself first. Once you know your system and methods inside and out, then you can consider how your recipes might translate.

Basic Beer Math

While I often refine recipes using brewing software, I like to be able to do quick back-of-the-envelope approximations. I can use these to answer quick questions or to do a sanity check on another calculation. Here are some of my most commonly used calculations:

- **Calculating final gravity and volume.** First, understand that **the total gravity points in your kettle are a constant,** regardless of the amount of water present. So at the start of the boil, measure your OG and volume. *OG x initial boil volume = total gravity points.* If you boil off water, you will still have the same gravity points. So to get final gravity, divide by final volume. *Total gravity points / final boil volume = FG.* If you want to hit a certain gravity target, calculate what final volume you need and then measure that. It's easier than measuring gravity during the boil. If you want a certain batch size but don't have enough gravity points, add additional fermentables to reach your gravity target.

- **Calculating fermentable additions.** If you want to add additional fermentables, know that most liquid fermentables (liquid malt extract, honey, syrups, etc.) add about *36 gravity points per pound* and most dry fermentables (dry malt extract, sugar, etc.) add about *45 gravity points per pound.* If you need to add to your total gravity points from the first calculation, use these to calculate the weight of your additions.

- **Calculating evaporation rate.** This one is easy. Take the difference between your starting volume and ending volume and divide by the boil length: *(starting volume – ending volume) / boil length = evaporation rate.* This will tell you how much volume you lose per hour. This rate can vary based on a lot of environmental conditions, but you should have a baseline for your system. Use this to estimate your boil length given your actual starting volume and desired ending volume.

- **Calculating your final volume.** Measure how much waste you have on your system (hop mass, trub, kettle waste, etc.). Measure the usable volume of beer you have and compare against the final boil volume. The difference is the waste. Adjust your batch size based on the final boil volume, not the final volume in the fermenter. The waste will vary if you add a lot of whole hops or if you have excessive break.

- **Calculating efficiency.** Figure out how many points your grain would give you if fully converted. Most base grain is around 36 points per pound, crystal and roasts are less (roughly 26 for crystal types and 22 for dark malts). You can look these up in most brewing software. Calculate the theoretical limit of your extract, which is the number of pounds of grain multiplied by the potential extract. Then compare that against your actual extract (total gravity points you get in your kettle). The actual extract divided by the potential extract is your system efficiency in percent.

- **Estimating grain.** After you've made some batches, take a look at your system efficiency and calculate how many points per pound you get from your grain at your efficiency. I find that I get roughly 5.4 points per pound at 75 percent efficiency in a 5-gallon batch. So that means a 1.054 beer should use about 10 pounds of grain. Calculate this rule of thumb for your most common batch size and your system efficiency.

- **Estimating hops.** You can use the hop utilization formulas to estimate IBUs based on alpha acid units (AAUs) of hops, which are the stated alpha acid content of the hops multiplied by the number of ounces of hops. For example, two ounces of 5% AA hops is 10 AAU. In a 5-gallon batch on my system when using whole hops, I find a 60-minute addition adds roughly 3.5 IBUs for each AAU. So those two ounces of 5% AA hops would give me about 35 IBUs if used as bittering hops.

- **Calculating Alcohol by Volume.** This is an easy calculation everyone should know. (OG – FG)/105 = ABW. ABV = 1.25 x ABW.

Recipe Formulation

Even if I don't always think about it consciously, I tend to follow a fairly standardized process when I formulate a recipe. I start with the more general conceptual ideas, then progressively home in on the final recipe. It's not always a linear process; some steps are done in parallel, and iteration is often involved. Before we get into the main discussion, here's a summary of the steps involved:

1. Decide on a target concept.

2. Determine general stylistic parameters.

3. Determine the total fermentables based on the OG target.

4. Determine the total hops based on the IBU target.

5. Let the flavor profile drive the grain bill, hop selection, yeast choice, fermentation method, and water adjustment.

6. Adjust grain bill based on the desired attenuation (based on the FG target).

7. Select a mash method.

8. Select a hopping method.

9. Adjust water if necessary.

10. Account for any special ingredients, processes, or techniques.

I think about the recipe in phases: ingredient selection, wort production (mashing), boiling, fermenting, and conditioning. I'm filling in pieces in all sections as I make choices, but when I'm done, I go back and look at the end-to-end recipe to make sure I've thought about all the choices. Of course, there are always unusual or unique things that should be noted for a specific recipe (e.g., adding spruce—where does that go? adding spices—where and how?).

Decide on a target. What's your general idea? Do you intend to clone a commercial beer, create a beer that is a good match for the BJCP Style

Guidelines (what we call "brewing to style"), modify an existing beer or recipe, fuse different beer styles, create a beer inspired by an idea, concept, or food, or brew something completely random? There are different approaches you might take for each idea, but everything begins with a vision for your beer. You should be able to describe what you're trying to do in a phrase or a sentence, such as "clone *Schneider Aventinus*," "brew a great Belgian *tripel*," or "make an oatmeal stout that tastes like oatmeal raisin cookies."

If you intend to clone a beer, you need to do some research to identify everything you can about it. Visit the brewery's website, look for information in beer enthusiast websites such as *beeradvocate.com* or *ratebeer.com*, read books on the beer style, do Internet searches for any other information, ask questions on Internet beer or brewing forums. Maybe someone has visited the brewery and taken down detailed notes; that's what I do every time I visit a good brewery. You never know when you might want to know the mash temperatures for *Orval*.

When you are cloning a beer, you are looking for the overall parameters of the beer, for starters, but also any information on the ingredients and process. You are filling in clues in a puzzle, and the bits of information are simply pieces of that puzzle. Get enough of them, and the solution starts to fall into place.

If you can't find specific information about a specific beer, see what recipes you can find for the style of beer. This can give you a starting point and let you home in on the final result yourself. This takes longer and is an inherently more iterative process, so you're always looking for shortcuts. Some others might have clone recipes and be willing to share them. Take these with a grain of salt, however, unless you know the brewer can brew and has a decent palate. I've run into way more people who claim to have brewed a clone of a particular beer than ones who have actually done it.

Do a structured tasting of the beer and record your notes. Can you identify any of the ingredients by taste? Even if you can't, you'll want to record a detailed profile of the beer to give you something to compare against when you brew your version. You might also want to do this experiment with other beer friends of yours, particularly if any of them have judging skills or palate training.

If you aren't cloning a beer, then you do many of the same steps, except you are less worried about matching the profile of a specific reference beer. You likely are willing to accept a wider range of results, such as making a great American pale ale, which is different than cloning *Sierra Nevada Pale Ale*. You'll still do research about what ingredients and process are typically used in the style of beer you are making. You can decide to follow those norms, or use your own ideas to get to your desired target profile. Remember, if you enter a beer in a competition, no one knows how you made it; just worry about the final results.

If you are trying to brew to style, read the previous chapter again. Make sure you understand the description of the beer you are making, especially the overall impression and balance. Don't get lost in the weeds trying to tweak very minor points at the expense of overall drinkability.

If you are trying to make a beer like one someone else has made, be sure to ask for the recipe. Most brewers freely share their recipes and are honored that someone would think enough of their work to make their beer. You can decide yourself if you want to try to recreate that beer exactly, or if you want to repurpose it by making your own changes. I'll often try a beer that I think is nearly perfect but could be improved with a small change. If I have the recipe as a starting point, making those little improvements becomes much easier.

However you get there, make sure you have defined the target profile of your finished beer. Then you can start thinking about the rest of the process, such as the components that will give you the desired outcome. Keep in mind that these components aren't just ingredients but can also be processes (brewing, fermenting, etc.). Your goal should be to get a consistent outcome and be able to predict how your beer will taste based on the recipe you put together. How you get there is your business. You don't have to do it traditionally. Try new things; you might invent something.

Determine general stylistic parameters. Nail down your target stylistic parameters for the recipe. You need goals for the original gravity (OG), final gravity (FG), alcohol content (ABV), bitterness level (IBUs), and color. Attenuation, alcohol content, original gravity, and final gravity are all related and play a big part in determining the balance of the beer.

You often can't find all these parameters if you're trying to clone a beer; a brewery website might list the ABV or OG, as well as the bitterness level. You can estimate color by looking at pictures. Some beer or brewing books might list parameters; if you can find them, you're lucky. You can determine FG of commercial beers by direct measurement. Just de-gas the beer (whip it until the bubbles all come out), and measure it using a hydrometer. If you're really hardcore (and have money to burn), you can send the beer away for analysis; search online for beer analysis or laboratory services.

If you are brewing to style, obviously, you'll need to pay attention to the relevant style guidelines. Just keep in mind that you have to do more than hit the numbers to get a beer in style; not all combinations of the range of acceptable numbers will make a beer that fits the style well.

Determine the total fermentables based on the OG target. If you have the target starting gravity set, you can then calculate the total amount of fermentables to use on your system. Your system efficiency will be influenced by the mash and sparge methods you choose, so be prepared to readjust if you change methods from your default choice (typically a sparged infusion mash).

Determine the total hops based on the IBU target. The target IBU level affects the amount of hops you will use. Again, the method of hopping will have an impact on your approach, but try to get in the right range of bittering hops by determining the alpha acid units (AAUs) you will need to hit your IBU target. I always like to write recipes using AAUs for bittering, since the alpha acid content of the hops I use can change. If the recipe is already in AAUs rather than ounces, I can convert directly when I see which hops I have on hand. Remember that AAUs are simply the alpha acid (AA) of the hops multiplied by the ounces used. You still have to specify how many minutes the hops will be boiled.

Let the flavor profile drive the ingredients. This is the hardest part of recipe formulation. Here you are matching ingredient selection (inputs) with desired final flavors (outputs). It helps tremendously if you have a good understanding of the finished flavor profiles of your ingredients and how processes can change them. In this step, you are making your preliminary choices for the grain bill, hops, yeast, fermentation method, and water adjustment, since all of these impact the final flavor profile of your beer.

I usually pick a yeast quickly based on the beer style. Some styles have obvious choices (like *Kölsch*), but other styles might be able to use a wide range of yeast. If I'm trying to clone or emulate a beer from a specific brewery, I'll try to use that brewery's yeast if it is available. There are several Internet sites that discuss the sources of commercial yeast and the equivalencies between yeast suppliers. The one I like to use was originally put together by Kris England and is hosted on Jamil Zainasheff's site: *www.mrmalty.com/yeast.htm*. Yeast suppliers seem quite reluctant to identify the origin of their yeast, but it's the single most important factor I consider when choosing yeast, since I can readily taste the outcome and see if that's what I want.

The fermentation method can be set after the yeast is selected, since the yeast strain will have its own requirements. Most strains produce a widely different flavor profile depending on how they are treated, so choose accordingly. I wish all yeast suppliers would put out charts like White Labs does for its Belgian strains: *www.whitelabs.com/beer/belgianchart.pdf*. This is the type of information you should be seeking to develop on your own if you can't find it elsewhere.

Select a temperature to get the yeast character you want. I typically try to get yeast to ferment as cleanly as possible, so I don't try any tricks to get yeast stressed. I often pitch relatively cool, and generally let the yeast rise in temperature and do what they want. If there is a specific temperature or environmental requirement for yeast, I pick that before moving on to the other ingredients, since I want to know what yeast flavors will be present. For example, I might try to get fruitiness from malt rather than yeast, so I'll want to know if the yeast will be providing that character or not. If I try to get too much fruitiness from the yeast, I worry about getting too many other off-flavors as well.

Next I choose the grain bill. In recipe formulation, I tend to think about grain in terms of percentages, so I can scale the recipe more easily to different batch sizes or different gravity levels. This is also helpful if you are using a resource such as *Designing Great Beers* to pick your ingredients, since the ranges are shown as percentages. I tend to pick grain based on the country of origin of the style first. Generally speaking, I'll use English malt in English beers, German or Belgian malts in European beers, and American malts in American beers. There are obviously exceptions, such as if I want the flavors of English malt to be in an American beer, or if I want the refined maltiness of German malt rather than the grainier American malt in an American beer.

Leverage your knowledge of the malts to select base malts, character malts, crystal malts, and roasted malts. Every beer has base malt, so select the one with the flavor profile you desire. Are you looking for complexity, or do you want only some of the flavor of a grain? Then blend your base malts. It's interesting to make single-malt beers to learn their flavor, but it's also fun to blend various base malts to see what you get. I like blending Crisp (British) Maris Otter with Durst (German) Vienna malt for the base of many malty beers. In German beers, I often use Pilsner malt to cut the richness of Vienna and Munich malt. Some American beers won't really taste right if you don't use a neutral-tasting grain, even if English and German malts are of higher quality. Sometimes they just give you too much flavor.

Use your knowledge of the intensity of flavor you get from quantities or percentages of different grains. You may have to compare your ideas against your brewing logs, other recipes, or references like *Designing Great Beers* to get an idea of how much of each grain to use. If you keep it in percentage terms, you don't have to worry about changes affecting your gravity target; you'll calculate the actual weights once you are complete.

For hopping, I first try to identify the number and quantity of hop additions, then I'll select the varieties. At a basic level, ask yourself if your beer needs aroma or flavor additions. If so, how intense are they? In a 5-gallon (19-liter) batch of beer, I think of ¼ ounce (7 g) as very light, ½ ounce (14 g) as noticeable, 1 ounce (28 g) as strong, and 2 ounces (57 g) as very strong for flavor and aroma. The balance of hop flavor and aroma will depend on what other flavors and aromas are present, obviously, but for most "normal" beers, these quantities are what I use.

If a beer has a strong hop profile, you will often want to use multiple flavor and aroma additions. As in cooking, you are building layers of flavor that add to the complexity of the finished product. Some styles demand this, while others would be overwhelmed by it. Keep the vision of the final beer in mind when choosing the number of additions and the variety of hops.

Select the hop varieties based on flavor/aroma profile and how well they interact with each other and the other components in your beer. Keep in mind that the amount of hop mass can add flavors of its own; if you use a large quantity of hops, you will often get grassy and vegetal flavors in addition to the primary flavor of the hops. You may also get additional tannins and harshness from the vegetal matter, so that's another reason to keep the total hop volume in check.

When you are done selecting malt and hops, you should have the individual ingredients selected in enough specificity that you could place an order. If you want to use grain from a particular maltster, identify the maltster. If it matters which form of hop you use (whole, pellets, other), then specify it. You can always substitute when you see what is available, but you should have a goal in mind. Don't worry about other people being able to get your ingredients; you are picking the ingredients, so select what you want. You should no more say that you want "pale ale malt" than a chef would go to a butcher and say, "give me some beef." Be specific about what you want.

If you are forced to change ingredients because of availability, price, or some other consideration, make note of that in your brewlog but don't change your basic recipe unless you like the new changes better. You should always keep accurate track of what you brew, so keep your as-planned and as-brewed recipes and notes separate.

If my target beer has a particular water flavor profile, then I'll make note of it now—for instance, adding sulfates to get the Burton flavor. If I'm absolutely sure I want the mineral flavors in the final product, I'll use kettle additions. These ingredients are in addition to whatever I decide to do in the mash to bring about proper mash conditions.

Adjust for attenuation. If I'm making an all-malt beer, it might not be possible to get sufficient attenuation, even if I use a mash profile that favors fermentability. In this step, I'm usually asking myself whether I need to add sugars to get higher attenuation, or if I need to add dextrins (CaraPils, oats, etc.) somewhere in the process to get less attenuation. Don't skip this step, because it's what makes a double IPA taste different from an American barley wine, and what gives most Belgian beers their "digestibility." Think about the FG you want, and then see how fermentable a wort you need. Consider the stated attenuation characteristics for yeast, but think more about wort composition as the primary way to control attenuation.

Select a mash method. The mash method may add additional flavors and colors, particularly if you decide to decoct. If you step mash or decoct, you are likely to get higher attenuation as well. The mash rest temperatures will affect wort composition, which impacts fermentability and the body and mouthfeel of the finished beer.

Keep in mind that you may be able to replicate some of these mash effects with other means. You can add sugar or dextrins instead of lowering or raising your mash temperature. You can add aromatic or melanoidin malt instead of decocting. You can adjust the types of crystal malt used if you are trying to get a sweeter finish. Decide if you want to use mash controls, adjust your grain bill, or both.

Sometimes when making dry German and Belgian beers, I'll add dextrin-type malts to get the body I want, and then mash-in at the 144° F (62° C) range. When making German beers using decoction or step mashing, I'll often mash in that low conversion range and then add a rest at 158° F (70° C) to develop dextrins. If I'm using a large quantity of continental Pilsner malt, I'll often add a rest at 131° F (55° C) to improve clarity. I could achieve all of these outcomes with different means, so think about how you want to use the processes to get the desired outcomes. Just remember that some methods or processes have other effects in addition to the main outcome. For instance, decoction will also darken color in addition to developing flavor—which might not be what you want in a *hefeweizen*.

Select a hopping method. Once you are done finalizing the flavor and aroma hop additions, you can calculate their IBU contributions and adjust your bittering addition accordingly to get the final desired IBU level. You don't have to add the bittering hops at 60 minutes, either. You can add them at any time up until about 90 minutes before the end of the boil. Sometimes you can adjust the quantity, so the amounts wind up in easy-to-measure increments, and sometimes you adjust the timing of the bittering hops to reduce potential harshness. Wherever you decide to use the hops, just make sure to recheck the overall IBU level when done. Adjusting the quantity or timing of your bittering additions is the easiest way to change that level.

Some hop methods take a little special handling. First wort hopping adds a huge amount of hop flavor, in my opinion. I calculate the flavor contribution as higher than if I added the same amount at, say, 10 to 15 minutes. You should see what subjective level you get from first wort hop additions, but I tend to cut my additions back between 20 to 35 percent. I tend to calculate the bitterness contribution from first wort hops as if they were a 20-minute addition even though it will measure higher.

Dry hopping and hops added at knockout right before cooling won't add IBUs. My primary concern with choosing a very late hop addition is whether or not I want the fresh, grassy character of raw hops in my beer. Similar to using spices in Indian food, there is a flavor change when the hops get cooked (even if briefly). Decide based on your taste what you'd like; the more I taste beer, the less I like dry hopping. However, I have recently become interested in multiple dry-hop additions for shorter periods of time (say, three days), so I may change my mind on dry hopping.

Adjust water. This is one of the last things I do, and only if necessary. I almost always start with RO water on my system, so I typically do minor water adjustment. My biggest concern is making sure there is some calcium available in the mash. I typically use calcium chloride in malty beers and calcium sulfate in hoppy beers, or possibly a mix of both. I rarely add calcium carbonate.

How you adjust your water is your business, but please at least try making beer with low mineral water. You might be surprised at how good it tastes. If the style you are making is known for having a specific mineral flavor (such as sulfates in Burton-style ales), then by all means use it. But I taste so many beers with overadjusted water nowadays that I'd really like it if brewers backed off on the water adjustments, unless you've tried it without them and had problems.

Final adjustments. I pick a boil method based on any special needs, or just go with a default one. For instance, if I'm brewing a Scotch ale, I might want to caramelize the first runnings. However, I could also get similar flavors by manipulating the grain bill to add more complex and intense malts.

Once you are finished with the recipe, do a "sanity check" on it. Go back through and make sure it meets the style parameters you want and will deliver the outcome you desire. While it is certainly possible to do these calculations and steps on paper, using brewing software will greatly speed up the process, particularly when undertaking revisions. Call me old-fashioned, but when I formulate recipes, I generally do an outline of what I want on paper before turning to the software. I feel this keeps me from having to follow a rigid process and allows my creativity to be unencumbered. Once the concept is honed, I'll use the software to hit the targets and tweak the quantities. But that's just based on how I like to think; you may have a different experience.

I design a recipe for exactly what I want and keep detailed notes of how it turned out. I also update the notes over time, so I know when the beer peaks and if the flavor profile changes. If there is anything I would change, I make note of that. If I subsequently blend or adjust to add something for some reason, I make notes there as well. When I brew the beer again, I try to incorporate these field test notes and lessons learned into the next batch. This is part of homing in on your ideal recipe.

Adjusting Balance

We've covered the basic mechanics of recipe formulation, but we haven't really touched on many of the tradeoffs for adjusting the overall balance of the beer. If you're changing a recipe by scaling it, or making an adjustment to one of your recipes to move it closer to your target, there are some general guidelines to follow.

Scaling Recipes

Suppose you want to create a scaled-up (imperial or double) or scaled-down (session) version of a recipe. How do you go about doing this? The most straightforward way is to do it as if you were scaling batch size. In both cases, you are adjusting the total gravity points you are getting from your mash. Recall that total gravity points are the batch size multiplied by the OG. Increasing either component changes the total; simply use the same percentage of each grain and adjust the total grist quantity for the total points you need.

Adjusting the bitterness is also rather straightforward. You want to retain the same ratio of bitterness units to gravity units (BU:GU) as you scale the gravity units. This will generally give the same balance. Flavor and aroma hops don't need to be scaled the same way, since they will have nearly the same impact in different gravity beers. I will scale the finishing hops maybe 25 percent of the simple linear adjustment (e.g., if I double the gravity of the beer, I might multiply the hops by 1.25 instead of 2). This is a point of personal preference; you should try it sometime and see what ratio you like.

When you scale up recipes, keep in mind that increasing the OG will also increase the FG. A higher FG is not necessarily what you want. This is one mistake I see made time and time again when I see American brewers attempt to brew Belgian-style beers. A Belgian *tripel* is not a blond barley wine; it shouldn't be chewy and sweet. For dry style beers, set the FG first and then determine the OG based on the ABV you want. Many authentic Belgian beers finish lower than 1.010. If you start too high, the beer will seem too sweet just because of the higher final gravity (even if fully fermented). *Duvel* and *Westmalle Tripel* start lower than most people expect, but have high attenuation. The same thing could be said about most of the better American double IPAs.

Contrast Belgian strong golden ale and *tripel* with strong Scotch ale. In the extreme sense, look at some of the historical Scotch ale recipes from Greg Noonan's book, *Scotch Ale*. They start very high and also finish very high. You might have a similar ABV with a *tripel* and a Scotch ale, but they are going to have a completely different balance based on the FG of the beer (as well as the bitterness level). Barley wines and some imperial stouts will also have this character.

If you keep the ABV the same but lower the starting and finishing gravity or increase the attenuation, you are making a beer that's more drinkable. Of course, the hop and alcohol balance will also have to be pleasing, but with all other factors being equal, the beer with the lower finishing gravity and higher attenuation will be more drinkable, while the beer with the higher finishing gravity and lower attenuation will be more of a sipper.

The implication of these observations is that if dryness and drinkability is a feature of the style you are scaling up, you may wish to increase the fermentability of the wort so you can get a higher attenuation, so as to avoid too high a finishing gravity. Adding fermentable sugar (of any type, as long as the flavor profile of the sugar matches the beer style) is the classic way to address this need and is reflected in the recipe formulation of double IPAs and Belgian ales. All-malt beers will become chewier as they scale up (think traditional bock versus *doppelbock*, or American IPA versus American barley wine). If this is the character you want, then by all means go all malt. If you want to preserve the dryness and drinkability, mash lower and add sugar.

I tend to mash very large beers fairly low (144-150° F, 62-66° C), since I will be getting a higher final gravity due to the higher starting gravity. I treat excessive sweetness in a big beer as a fault, so it's one I try to avoid.

Adjusting Final Gravity and Attenuation

Final gravity is a measure of sugars and dextrins remaining in beer. Sugars have a sweet flavor, but dextrins do not. Both add body and viscosity to beer. Sweetness balances bitterness, but dextrins simply give a fuller mouthfeel and chewiness to beer. Both make a beer less refreshing and somewhat harder to drink if used to excess (think about drinking whole milk versus drinking water), but their absence can make a beer seem watery and insipid.

If you want to increase final gravity, you can either add dextrins (through mash temperature control, by mashing starchy adjuncts, or by using CaraPils or dextrine malt), add crystal malts (which will also add sweetness), or raise the original gravity. The method you choose depends on whether you want to change the sweetness or just the body, and whether you think the attenuation level is appropriate.

If you want to lower the final gravity, you can increase the fermentability of the wort (mash lower to increase the proportion of maltose), add sugar, or lower the original gravity. The fermentability of the wort is what primarily drives attenuation; using an attenuative yeast can help somewhat, but your first focus should be on the wort composition. Proper fermentation management should attenuate your beer to near the limit of fermentability.

Balancing Bitterness, Alcohol, and Tannins

Bitterness can balance maltiness and sweetness in beer, and is measured in International Bitterness Units (IBUs). However, there is a big difference between measured IBUs and perceived bitterness. A rich, full-bodied, sweet beer can handle many more IBUs and seem more drinkable and balanced than a crisp, dry, well-attenuated beer can.

There are two measures that you can use to capture the perceived bitterness in the overall balance of the beer. The first one has been around for a while, and is the ratio of IBUs to starting gravity (usually written as BU:GU). The second one is relatively new (to me, at least), and is the ratio of IBUs to finishing gravity (or BU:FG). Each has its place and can allow for some more interesting comparisons between beer styles and recipes.

The BU:GU ratio is more useful for comparing the relative balance of two different beers or styles that have some similarity (gravity or bitterness), or for telling whether a beer is predominantly malty or bitter in the balance. I like the BU:FG measure for preserving the perceived bitterness of a beer as the gravity scales, or for comparing the perceived bitterness level of different beers or styles.

Both measures provide useful information and should be calculated for each of your recipes. If you are trying to match a certain profile, look at these ratios and see if they can provide some insight. Another more qualitative measure is to consider the relative maltiness of the grist; a richer, more malty beer can mask IBUs almost as well as sweetness. Düsseldorf *altbiers* (especially *Zum Uerige*) can have a much higher measured IBU level than they seem to, not because they're sweet (they're often bone dry) but because they are simply so malty. I don't know a good way to measure this, but keep it in mind as you adjust your recipes. You may have to increase the bitterness level of very malty beers to have the same level of perceived bitterness when compared to a beer made with neutral-tasting malt.

Balancing alcohol is tricky, because the character of the alcohol depends on age and condition. Higher-alcohol beers that haven't been adequately aged can have a hot character, a flavor of alcohol, and increased bitterness from the alcohol. The same beer when aged properly becomes much smoother, and the bitterness and flavor from the alcohol fades.

Aging tannins can also play a role in the smoothness, as they do in red Bordeaux wines. Astringency from tannins has a harshness and a mouth-puckering mouthfeel but also some bitterness. Smooth tannins and alcohol add to the complexity of a beer as they do to wine. When young, these components can seem unbalanced.

The impact of alcohol and tannins on the balance is therefore first a function of age and condition. Yes, the absolute alcohol and tannin levels are the primary reason, but the quality of those flavors and mouthfeels changes significantly with proper conditioning. Big beers of mine will often seem unbalanced for the first six months to two years but then come into balance as they age. If I'm targeting them to be served at a younger age, I'll try to adjust the recipe to reduce alcohol (lower gravity) and tannins (reduce quantity of hops and darker malts, or handle them in a way that reduces the harshness).

Sweetness and malt flavor balance alcohol content and tannins just as they balance bitterness. This is one reason why young barley wines sometimes seem balanced, then unbalanced, then balanced as they age. If the beer is young, it could have more residual sugars that balance the more bitter components. As the beer continues to attenuate as it conditions, the balance changes to make the bitterness more apparent. As the beer continues to age, the alcohol and tannins smooth out and the bitterness drops. Keeping these changes in mind as you target your recipe is vital. I tend to brew my big beers to age a long time, since I really enjoy the complex flavors that develop. So I trade off short-term drinkability for long-term storage. I compensate for that by "laddering" my big beer brewing, so I'm always replenishing my stock well before the old batches are gone.

Interactions

When adjusting a recipe, you can change multiple variables, but you need to be aware of their interactions. For example, if you think your beer needs more bitterness, you can increase the hop bitterness, you can increase the attenuation to dry it out, or you can lower the gravity to make it finish lower. Each of these will change the balance of bitter versus sweet. If you increase the bitterness and also increase the attenuation, you could be fixing the problem twice and overshooting your target balance.

When making changes, don't automatically assume that you need to directly control the most obvious variable. For our previous example, don't assume that the best way to make a beer seem more bitter is to increase the IBUs. Remember that you are primarily concerned about the perceived bitterness in the overall balance of the beer, and that you can often achieve that goal in multiple ways.

Understanding interactions between the variables you can tweak and how they finally balance is your goal. Keep in mind that most changes have interactions and ripple effects. Go easy on changes unless you understand them well, and if possible, only make changes that don't interact with each other. If some changes have side effects, try to select the adjustments that most closely match your desired end state. Think about what components in beer provide what you perceive, and seek to keep them in balance per your recipe target.

Avoiding Clashing Flavors

Once a beer is balanced properly, you still have to worry about overall drinkability—clearly, a subjective topic. However, there is one certain way to improve drinkability: avoiding clashing flavors. If you understand common flavor clashes and how flavors balance and complement each other, you can avoid most of these problems. While there are probably many examples I could cite, here are ones that tend to show up most frequently in commercial beers that I try or in beers that I judge in competition.

- **Phenolics and harshness.** Avoid using harsh hops or grains with phenolic yeast, or in using multiple sources of phenolics or harshness in a beer. Highly sulfate water can make hops harsh, and water with a high pH can extract harshness from grains. Certain hop varieties can be harsh, as can using lots of hops in long boils. Combine this harshness with a Trappist or *weizen* yeast, and the result will be amplified.

- **Dark malts and citrusy/piney hops.** Sometimes found in stronger stouts, I'm not a fan of this flavor combination. The acidity clashes, and the citrus flavors make the dark malts seem like stale, bad coffee. Wonder why black IPAs go easy on the dark malts? It's because they're avoiding this combination.

- **Yeast, spice, or fruit and bitterness/late hops.** Have you ever noticed how most beers with a lot of yeast character tend to have low bitterness? Think of *weizens*, *witbiers*, and *lambics*, as well as fruit and spice beers. If you add too much bitterness or too many late hops, the hops can step on the yeast, spice, or fruit. Worse, you might still get both, but they could clash. Unless you have found a combination you know works, it's best to avoid trying to overhop these type of beers.

- **Fruit and spice.** Using fruit and spice is a classic pairing. However, keep in mind the combinations need to work just like they do in food. For example, plums might work with cinnamon, but not with rosemary.

- **Sour and bitter.** Sour beers usually aren't bitter. Those two flavors are not naturally appealing to the palate (our lizard brain tells us they are markers for poison), so combining them makes for a difficult flavor combination. Acidity and sourness can come from unlikely sources, so be sure to account for the use of any fruit, large amounts of dark grains, and citrusy hops. Taste your raw ingredients, and see if you can characterize their contributions.

- **Harsh and harsher: spices and coffee.** I like spiced and specialty beers, but I've seen brewers mishandle spices and coffee too many times to count. You can pick up significant tannins from spices, since they are typically the bark or seeds of plants. Likewise, coffee can take on tannic and acidic notes when boiled. If you use these products in your beer, be sure you are handling them properly. I tend to cold-press coffee and add it at knockout, and I tend to make teas from spices and blend in to taste. In my experience, spices need some heat—but only for a short time—to reach their peak flavor (similar to making Indian food). Extended cold steeping of spices (as in the secondary) seems to draw out tannins. Adding coffee too early makes it seem like that coffee at work that someone left on for hours and no one wants to drink. There can be some harshness already in beer from hops, so be careful about piling on the harsh flavors when using spices and coffee.

- **Bitterness and alcohol.** If you do palate training and spike beer with vodka, one of the things you'll notice is that the bitterness level rises sharply. If you serve a high-alcohol beer before it is properly conditioned, the alcohol may seem hot. If you get the flavor of alcohol in a beer, it can add to the perceived bitterness level. You'll need to balance the bitterness of the hops (and sometimes malt) with the added bitterness from alcohol, or your beer will seem out of balance.

- **Spicy/hot and bitterness/alcohol.** If you make beers that contain hot spices (cinnamon, ginger) or use chile peppers, be aware that these flavors can amplify the inherent bitterness and alcohol impression in your beer. Spiciness can be confused with fusel alcohols, so if your beer has an alcohol edge, you may be tricking tasters into thinking it is flawed. You may need to raise the residual sweetness in beers that have a spicy/hot component to provide some balance.

At the 2004 NHC in Las Vegas, Vinnie Cilurzo of Russian River Brewing Company handed out a sheet of tips for making better hoppy beers. In this guide, he said that crystal malt and American hops (such as those found in American IPAs) do not mix. He recommended keeping crystal malts below 5 percent of the grist, preferably in the 3.5 to 4 percent range, and to use crystal malts in the 40 to 45 Lovibond range when making American IPAs or double IPAs. *Pliny the Elder* is one of the best beers I've ever tasted, so far be it from me to argue. Personally, I find that too much crystal malt tends to make these beers too sweet, when the style profile screams for high attenuation. I find that flaw much more objectionable than a flavor clash, but maybe I don't normally use hops in the same concentration that Vinnie does. I could see how darker crystal malts bring more acidity and darker malt flavors, which trigger some of the clash warnings from my list. Perhaps that is what he means, as well.

Recipe Formulation Examples

I've discussed the general background and approach that I take with recipe formulation, but I think it would be more helpful to walk through several real-world examples. I picked out a few recipes of mine that I will use as examples while discussing some of my experiences in formulating the recipes.

Example: Cloning a World-Class Beer

Last year, I wanted to brew a Belgian pale ale similar to the *De Koninck* I enjoyed so much in Belgium. It's moderately bitter and dry but smooth, with a light earthy hop note and great malt flavors. It's so nicely balanced and drinkable that I could easily drink it all afternoon. We can only occasionally get it in the United States, and when we do, it's expensive and almost always poorly handled. So how did I start in my quest to recreate this beer? What resources did I use?

First, I tried to get the general style parameters identified. I took a look in Michael Jackson's *Great Beers of Belgium* and found several great clues: it's a 1.047 beer with 25 IBUs; it doesn't use adjuncts; it contains Pilsner and Vienna malts; and it has three additions of Saaz hops. A visit to the brewery website confirmed that it is 5% ABV. I also happened to know that White Labs WLP515 Antwerp ale yeast is the *De Koninck* strain. The brewery says that the beer ferments at 25 to 27° C (77-81° F), which seems pretty aggressive to me. I figured I would start in a more comfortable range and try that first before trying something that bold. I hadn't used the *De Koninck* yeast before, so I was afraid to go that warm. If I would ferment like that, I'd probably use the Wyeast 3522 Ardennes yeast instead (the Achouffe strain), since it can take warmer temperatures. Still, I'd be afraid of doing that unless using a very shallow open fermenter, or unless someone else had told me they had used the strain that warm without throwing off fusels, phenols, or other funk.

The brewery website also has a picture of the beer, which gave information about the color. I also had my tasting notes and photographs from Belgium, which I relied upon heavily. When I tasted the beer, I got a couple of very distinctive malt flavors: the unmistakable flavor of biscuit malt—a crackery, dry flavor—and the color and flavor of CaraMunich malt, which adds some coppery color and some plum flavors. I wanted to make sure both of those malts were noticeable. I used proportions similar to English beers as a starting point. The beer also has a light taste of malty sweetness to offset the hop bitterness and flavor, as well as some fruitiness, which could come from the malt and/or the yeast.

I took the information about the Saaz hops at face value; they are commonly used in Belgian brewing, so it wasn't a surprise. Three additions are stated, so I used them as bittering, flavor, and aroma. I targeted the 25 IBU value and kept the flavor and aroma additions moderate. From past experience, a half ounce of finishing hops tends to give a noticeable but not overwhelming flavor or aroma. So I started there and used them at 10 to 15 minutes for flavor and 2 to 5 minutes for aroma.

Vienna malt should add some toasty maltiness, but I also added some aromatic malt to make sure it came across as malty. I could have used Belgian Pilsner malt but I often find that I have to step mash Pilsner malts to get them to have a good clarity. In darker beers, I'll often just use Belgian pale ale malt instead. That's what I do in a *dubbel*, so I tried that here. Most breweries I toured in Belgium seemed to use Dingeman malt, so that will be my first choice where possible. I adjusted the malts to hit a roughly 1.048 gravity, which is fairly normal for a pale ale. I'm glad that I read that it's an all-malt beer, or I might have been tempted to use some sugar, as in a *dubbel*.

One final adjustment I made was to use a little bit of debittered black malt to add some reddish tones. I use this trick in my *dubbel* recipe, and it also made sense here. You shouldn't taste the malt, but if you want a coppery-red color, you need to use a little bit of something dark. I made sure to use a huskless malt, since I didn't want any roast at all, and only put it in the vorlauf until the color is correct.

As far as mash profile, Belgian beers are typically fairly dry, so I tried mashing at 151° F (66° C). I chose a balanced water profile with a light mineral addition of sulfates and chlorides; I don't get a minerally flavor with *De Koninck*, so I didn't give it as much sulfates as I'd use in an English pale ale. As usual, I started with RO water for my strike water and adjusted my sparge water with phosphoric acid to pH 5.5.

So that's how I approached creating this recipe based on the information I could find and my experiences in brewing related beers. While I could find out quite a bit of information on the ingredients and specifications, I still had to estimate the percentages of malts based on experience. I mostly used my notes on brewing Belgian *dubbels*, English bitters, and American amber ales to come up with a general idea, always comparing source ingredients with target profile and adjusting accordingly.

The King—Belgian Pale Ale

Recipe for 5.25 gallons (19.9 liters)

7 lbs. (3.2 kg) Belgian pale ale malt

3 lbs. (1.4 kg) Vienna malt

6 oz. (170 g) biscuit malt

10 oz. (283 g) CaraMunich malt

8 oz. (340 g) aromatic malt

0.4 oz. (11 g) debittered black malt

1 oz. Saaz whole hops, 4% alpha acid, at 60 min.

½ oz. (14 g) Saaz whole hops, 5.8% alpha acid, at 15 min.

½ oz. (14 g) Saaz whole hops, 5.8% alpha acid, at 5 min.

WLP515 Antwerp ale yeast

OG: 1.048

FG: 1.010

25 IBU

5% ABV

RO water with ½ tsp. $CaSO_4$ and ½ tsp. $CaCl_2$. Mash at 151° F (66° C). Collect 7.5 gallons (28.4 liters). Add ¼ tsp. $CaSO_4$ and ¼ tsp. $CaCl_2$ to the boil. Boil 90 minutes; final volume 5.5 gallons (20.8 liters). Pitch at 60° F (16° C) and ferment at 64° F (18° C).

I thought this turned out quite close to my goal and very similar to my memory of the beer. I haven't tried them side by side, but I would try to repeat this recipe as is rather than tweaking it. It's pretty rare that I make a beer and don't have some adjustments I want to make in the next batch, so I'll call this one a success. The beer was very good when fresh and young, so I also think this would be a good recipe to have as a house beer that doesn't require much aging. The yeast is currently a seasonal strain, so plan on making it in the fall. If you want to experiment on your own, try making a Winter Koninck, a darker, 6.5 percent version of the same beer. I might give this a go next time I make it, boosting the CaraMunich and aromatic, and possibly using a touch of orange peel to give it a Belgian Christmas beer character.

Example: Modifying or Improving Someone Else's Beer

Another way of formulating a recipe is to taste a beer made by someone else (a friend or a commercial brewery) and think of how you could improve it. If you can get the recipe (in many cases, you can just ask for it), you can then start to tweak it to your own taste. This is exactly what happened with my standard oatmeal stout recipe.

This story and recipe date from my earlier days of brewing, 1999 to be exact. I was traveling on business and visited the sadly now defunct North Channel brewery in Michigan. My longtime friend and early brewing influence Doug Beedy was the brewmaster, and I wanted to check out his lineup and talk to him about his beer.

I remember enjoying his oatmeal stout immensely, but I thought it was just a touch too bitter and would be improved with a little more oatmeal flavor. Doug wasn't entirely convinced, and also said the owner liked the beer and wouldn't let him change it, anyway. So I asked him for the recipe, which he readily provided. It was scaled for a professional system, so I just made note of his grist percentages, hop schedule, and overall specifications.

I kept the gravity the same but lowered the IBUs from his original 30 to 32 down to 25. I also increased the oats by 50 percent. I used the same malt and hop varieties that he did and tried to keep the other grains in the same proportion but scaled to my system. I even took home some of his yeast to use. Since I was making the beer for critical review, I used the no-sparge technique and didn't mash the dark grains, so as to get the best malt flavor possible.

After the beer was finished and had conditioned, I took a sample up to him in a growler. We tasted it together and compared my beer with his. It had the same house character, but you could tell the balance was different. I was very happy to hear that he liked the changes and thought they were an improvement. I'm not sure if the owner let him change the recipe, but at least my palate was vindicated, and I had a great stout recipe from it.

Lakeside Stout—Oatmeal Stout

Recipe for 6 gallons (22.7 liters)

12 lbs. (5.4 kg) Maris Otter malt
1.5 lbs. (680 g) flaked oats
1 lb. (454 g) crystal 80° L
¼ lb. (113 g) crystal 40° L
¾ lb. (340 g) chocolate malt
½ lb. (227 g) roasted barley
.8 oz. (23 g) East Kent Goldings whole hops, 6.2% alpha acid, at 60 min.
.6 oz. (17 g) East Kent Goldings whole hops, 6.2% alpha acid, at 30 min.
Wyeast 1.318

OG: 1.062

FG: 1.018

25 IBU

5.8% ABV

No-sparge technique. Add dark grains during vorlauf. Mash at 153° F (67° C). Collect 8 gallons (30.3 liters). Boil for 90 minutes. Final volume 6 gallons (22.7 liters). Ferment at 68° F (20° C).

Example: Brewing a Style Not in the Guidelines

OK, this example doesn't really create a new style (actually, it's quite old), but it is based on one that isn't described in the BJCP Style Guidelines. Regardless of the source, this method of recipe formulation is what you do when you don't have detailed style guidelines to explain the profile of the beer. You still need to have a vision for your beer, but how do you proceed? I'll get to that in a moment, but first let me tell you a bit about how the beer was made.

This is a great homebrewing story, since I couldn't have made this beer without the help of the AHA. At the National Homebrew Competition finals in Oakland, California, in 2009, one of the big surprises at the awards ceremony was the announcement that any brewer winning a gold medal would get a Golden Ticket to Sierra Nevada Beer Camp. Ken Grossman, the founder and owner of Sierra Nevada Brewing Company, was the keynote speaker and graciously donated the prizes.

Sierra Nevada Beer Camp is a chance for a group of people to formulate and brew their own batch of beer on Sierra Nevada's 10-barrel pilot system. Before a bunch of homebrewers descended on them, Beer Camp had been reserved for industry insiders. I'm sure it was a different experience for them to have a dozen experienced brewers with our own ideas get together to hash out a recipe.

We hadn't agreed on a style, theme, or concept before we showed up. Our first constraint was that we had to use Sierra Nevada's house yeast (what we all know and love as Wyeast 1056 or WLP001) for the beer. So we were making an ale. We then asked for a list of the malts and hops they had in-house, so we could see which raw ingredients we could use. The list was shorter than what you'd find in a well-stocked homebrew store, and it didn't have many truly unusual varieties. We asked about the newer Citra hops that were being used in the *Torpedo IPA*; nope, there weren't any we could use. We also were limited in the amount of continental Vienna malt, since the next beer camp had reserved most of it. The Munich malt was domestic, not continental, so we didn't want to feature that, either.

There was a lot of arguing about the basic concept of the beer. Some wanted to do a Belgian-style beer or a Belgian/American IPA, which would be difficult with the yeast we had on hand. Others wanted to include as many unusual ingredients as possible, including cherrywood-smoked malt and rye. The less confrontational among us even suggested incorporating one idea from everyone (I called that beer "Chico Trainwreck"). In the end, the concept of a fuller-bodied malty beer with a firm hop bitterness and some interesting malt flavor won out. We understood we would be drinking the beer in the late fall or early winter, so we wanted something appropriate for the season.

There were different possible styles we could make, including old ale, Scotch ale, barley wine, imperial stout, and so on. We didn't want to make the same style that any of the beer camp brewers made in the NHC, so that ruled out several styles. We also wanted to do something different from other beer camps, which took out most of the rest. We finally settled on what I called an American stock ale, or sort of an Americanized old ale—something of a throwback beer, perhaps a little like an *Arrogant Bastard* but with a balanced rather than aggressive bitterness.

We next set a target ABV, something in the 7 to 7.5 percent range. We set about picking the malts, specifying percentages. For the base malt, we decided to use a blend of Weyermann Pilsner and Crisp Maris Otter. We would have preferred to use Vienna or Munich instead of Pilsner, but those weren't available in the quantity or from the source we wanted, so we used smaller percentages of each instead to add to the maltiness. The Pilsner malt would cut some of the strong, bready flavors of the Maris Otter and help allow the specialty malts to show through. The flavor malts would be CaraMunich, Special "B," and chocolate. We wanted the CaraMunich to be more dominant, with the Special "B" and chocolate adding background complexity and color. While seven malts seem like a lot, we were trying to build complexity without having clashing flavors.

Since the beer was going to have a fairly strong malt flavor, we wanted a clean bittering hop that wouldn't clash; German Magnum was the obvious choice. For flavor hops, we chose German Perle and Sterling, which would give spicy and floral flavors. For aroma hops, we wanted to pick something we hadn't used before. A trip to the hop room led us to choose two New Zealand hops, Pacific Hallertauer and Southern Cross. Half of the aroma hops would be used in the kettle at knockout, and the other half would be used in the hopback. We were Beer Camp #13, so Sierra Nevada pilot brewmaster Scott Jennings adjusted the quantities so that we'd use 13 pounds (5.9 kilograms) of hops in one 10-barrel (1.2 hectoliter) batch.

We mashed on the high side (154° F, 68° C) to try to hit a finishing gravity of approximately 1.016. We wound up quite a bit higher than that (1.022), since the malts we used responded a bit differently to mashing than those Sierra Nevada typically uses. If this had happened to me at home, I probably would have added some sugar in the fermenter to be able to drive attenuation lower. However, the beer wound up very nice, if a bit chewier than expected.

Sierra Nevada served this beer in their taproom in addition to sending it to the brewers. They created a sell sheet for their bar that described the beer as "an interesting example of the nearly forgotten Stock Ale style of beer. It is full-bodied with sweet malt aromas reminiscent of raisins and toffee. The flavor is rich with complex malts with notes of caramelized sugar and toasted walnuts. This English-style beer is clean and balanced with a restrained hop finish."

Old Cantankerous—American Stock Ale

Recipe for 5 gallons (19 liters)

6 lbs. (2.7 kg) Pilsner malt (Weyermann)

5 lbs. (2.3 kg) Maris Otter (Crisp) malt

1.25 lbs. (567 g) CaraMunich malt (Weyermann)

1.5 lbs. (680 g) Munich malt (Briess)

1 lb. (454 g) Vienna malt (Weyermann)

2.25 oz. (64 g) Special "B" malt (Castle)

2.25 oz. (64 g) chocolate malt (Crisp)

0.6 oz. (17 g) German Magnum whole hops, 13% alpha acid, at 60 min.

1 oz. (28 g) Perle whole hops, 6.6% alpha acid, at 20 min.

1 oz. (28 g) Sterling whole hops, 5.5% alpha acid, at 10 min.

½ oz. (14 g) Pacific Hallertauer whole hops, 6.4% alpha acid (see note)

1¼ oz. (35 g) Southern Cross whole hops, 11% alpha acid, (see note)

Wyeast 1056 or White Labs WLP001

Note: If you can't get the New Zealand hops, substitute any noble hop. Sierra Nevada uses whole cone hops. Use half the finish hops at knockout, and half in a hopback, or add all at knockout.

Use water treated to pH 5.5 at 154° F (68° C). Using RO water, add 1 tsp. $CaSO_4$ and ¼ tsp. $CaCl_2$

Mash-in at 140° F (60° C), slowly raise to 154° F (68° C). Mash-out at 170° F (76° C). Sparge, collecting 7 gallons (26.5L). Boil for 90 minutes.

Chill and pitch at 62° F (17° C), ferment at 68° F (20° C).

OG: 1.075

FG: 1.020

41 IBU

7.2% ABV

This beer was made in early September and released in early December. I bought three half-barrels and saved one to bring to the AHA National Homebrew Conference the following June. It aged beautifully and was even better than when it was fresh. My good friend Thomas Eibner, a co-brewer of the batch, pretty much poured the beer continuously from the time we tapped it in the hospitality suite until it was gone less than two hours later. I was happy to be able to share it with my fellow homebrewers, and with so many of the co-brewers of the beer in attendance.

Example: Creating a Beer Based on a Food Idea

This is a specialty-type beer that was inspired by a chai tea latte I had once at Panera. That drink had such a great burst of spices and blended so well with the underlying tea that I immediately thought it could be turned into a beer. I've made it several times, and it's always a big hit at parties or festivals where the unusual beers stand out. When I was later technical editor on *Radical Brewing*, I thought this recipe fit in very well with Randy Mosher's concepts, so I was very happy to have him publish it there first. Since then, I've had several people tell me they've enjoyed making it. This recipe is an updated version of the one that originally appeared in *Radical Brewing*.

The general concept is to make a sweetish, slightly creamy, Northern English-style brown ale and then blend in a spiced tea to taste. Many spiced beers are quite heavy (Christmas-type). This one is different, since it's a lighter beer that's enjoyable in the summer (basically as an alcoholic substitute for a chai iced tea).

Given this vision, I went about modifying a Northern English brown ale recipe of mine. As a general rule of thumb, I find one-quarter pound of chocolate malt is about right in a brown ale to give nuttiness without much chocolate flavor. So I left that alone. Rather than using Maris Otter exclusively as the base malt, I substituted half Durst Vienna malt to boost the toasty, malty flavors. I added some honey malt and increased the crystal-type malts considerably to give a richer and sweeter flavor. Finally, I added some flaked oats for more body and mouthfeel and a little lactose for body, sweetness, and milky flavor. Using a trick from *Radical Brewing*, I now toast the oats for additional flavor. I keep the hops restrained and probably at a lower level than if the beer weren't spiced. I didn't want the hops to compete with the spices, so I removed any late hop additions. I also used Saaz instead of an English hop, since I thought any spiciness that was present would be more appropriate than English hop flavors.

The chai spices were a blend that I put together based on some Internet research on making your own chai tea at home. I found several recipes and looked for common elements, then selected the spices that I personally like. Vanilla, cinnamon, nutmeg, and clove are spices I use frequently, particularly when I'm making my Apple Pie Spiced Cyser. I love the flavor of cardamom and star anise, so I definitely wanted those to be featured. Black pepper, ginger, and fennel added additional kick and complexity. Warmer spices are needed when competing with the sweetness of the underlying beer.

Given there are so many different spices, getting the right balance was a bit tricky. I make it easier on myself by making a tea from the spices first. I pour boiling water over the spices as if I were steeping tea. I let them sit for between 5 and 15 minutes, covered, to develop flavors but not to extract much tannin. I strain out the spices, reserving the liquid, and then cool it down, covered. The resulting tea is packed with flavor and can then be blended with the finished beer or adjusted with additional spice additions. I liked this combination, so I just used it as is. I blended it with the beer to taste, with the spices being noticeable but not dominating the beer. You want it to be recognizable as chai, but you also need to know you're drinking a beer.

Chai Tea Brown Ale—Spiced Beer

All-grain recipe for 6 gallons

4 lbs. (1.8 kg) Maris Otter malt
4 lbs. (1.8 kg) Vienna malt
1 lb. (454 g) honey malt
1 lb. (454 g) CaraVienne malt
1 lb. (454 g) U.K. crystal 80° L malt
¼ lb. (113 g) U.K. chocolate malt
¾ lb. (340 g) Quaker Oats, toasted 20 minutes at 250° F (121° C), cooled
½ lb. (227 g) lactose at 15 min.
1¼ oz. (35 g) Saaz whole hops, 4% alpha acid, at 60 min.
White Labs WLP002

Mash at 150° F (66° C) for 1 hour. Mash-out at 170° F (77° C).

Boil for 90 minutes. Ferment at 67° F (19° C).

Post-fermentation, blend in tea to taste.

Keg and force carbonate.

OG: 1.048

FG: 1.016

18 IBUs

4.2% ABV

Chai Spiced Tea:
1 vanilla bean, split and scraped
2 cinnamon sticks
2-inch piece of ginger, peeled, sliced
5 whole cloves
2 star anise
24 green cardamom pods, split
1 black cardamom pod, split
2 tsp. black peppercorns
½ whole nutmeg, roughly chopped
¼ tsp. fennel seeds

Bring about 1 quart filtered water to a boil, then pour over spices and cover in a separate container. Let steep for 15 minutes, then strain to remove spices. Cover tea and keep chilled until used. I blended in about 2 cups (473 milliliters) of this liquid in the 5-gallon (19-liter) batch. But you want to do it slowly, mix it well, and taste it. Different people have different tastes, so you're looking for a nice balance without being overpowering with the spices. Don't use tea—it has too much tannin.

In competition, I enter this as a Spice/Herb/Vegetable beer and describe it as a "brown ale with chai tea spices." I don't list the individual spices, since I don't want judges trying to individually identify them. I don't say what kind of brown ale it is because I don't want judges to say "good spice beer, but not a great Northern English Brown Ale." I don't call it a "chai tea brown ale" because I don't want judges to think that there is actual tea in it (and then ding me because they don't get any tannins or tea flavor).

This brown ale is midway between a Northern English brown ale and a Southern English brown ale. It has more sweetness and less bitterness than a Northern English brown ale but has the same nutty flavor profile. The addition of oats gives it more body, which is reminiscent of the latte.

Example: Building a Recipe From Historical Research
This beer won a gold medal in the second round of the 2008 NHC; I was proud to have Randy Mosher as one of the judges on the panel that selected it. After the judging was over, Randy and Drew Beechum came up to me and gave me a sample. The conversation went something like this. Randy: "You've got to try this! It's a colonial stock ale with spruce tips." Me: <sip> "Mmm, I'm familiar with that." Drew: "Dammit! Is it too late to change our decision?" Priceless.

This beer also has a great story behind it. I first made it on Big Brew Day in May 2006. I had read an article describing Tony Simmons' research and development of the Poor Richard's Ale recipe. I thought it sounded great, since it was described as a cross between an old ale and a strong Scotch ale, two of my favorite malty beer styles. I also liked the unusual ingredients (molasses and corn) that were included. But, reading his research, I thought the recipe he offered was simplified to make it easier to brew; I wanted to make the real McCoy.

It sounded like he wanted to use more blackstrap molasses and malt but was afraid people wouldn't like it. I also knew that colonial beers were often spiced with spruce tips as a locally available ingredient. Lucky for me, I have three nice Colorado Blue Spruce trees in my backyard, and they had new growth around the time I was making the beer. Finally, I wanted to add a touch of smoked malt, since I thought malts of that era would likely be kilned over wood fires and might have that quality.

I had used molasses and smoked malt before, so I had no problem adding them to the recipe. I know blackstrap molasses is intense, so I went light on it. However, I didn't have a clue as to how to use the spruce tips. This is when I remembered my good friend Pete Devaris' talk from the 2004 Las Vegas National Homebrewers Conference on using spruce tips. I was judging, so I didn't get to hear the talk, but I emailed Pete and asked him to summarize his tips (pun not intended) for me. His information was so useful, I'll just repeat his entire message:

Glad you caught me. With spruce, it is all about timing.

Pick your tips at the peak of "brilliance." This is after it (the tree) has shed the reddish-brown woody hood, exposing the brilliant light green new growth. You will want to pick within a few days of the tips "blowing" their hoods. The tips should be soft and supple, like a paintbrush. If they are stiffer and unpleasant when brushed over your cheek, sap has started to flow into the new growth and they will be unsuitable for brewing (i.e., have a medicinal flavor). FYI, the reddish woody hood is very bitter. If it is a dry day, shaking the limbs will allow the hoods to float away in the wind. If picking in the rain, loose hoods tend to stick to the tips. They can be removed by throwing your tips in a bucket of water. The hoods will float and can then be skimmed.

The tips can be used fresh or frozen (preferably vacuum-sealed) and will last two years.

Use spruce tips in the boil only. It takes some real energy to extract the sugars (a mix of short and long chain, the long chain being very complex). I add to the last 60 minutes of the boil, no more, no less. From experience, I found this to be ideal for maximizing sugar extraction while minimizing vegetable and chlorophyll extraction.

How much? First, measure by volume, not by weight. The weight of tips will vary up to 30 percent depending on if you pick in the rain or not, dry or wet season, etc. However, although water content fluctuates, sugars are relatively constant. For subtle background flavors, I use 1 quart by volume (quart canning jar—full but not packed down) per 5-gallon batch. I have used twice that for barley wines.

Remember, spruce has a wonderful, floral, citrus flavor, not piney like the extract imposters sold in homebrew shops. The bulk of the sugars are very complex long chain, and so you should expect a lot of residual sweetness and a bump in both OG and terminal gravities. One quart of spruce is about like adding a pound of two-row to the grain bill.

Let me know how the beer turns out. Bring samples. I have had great blue spruce beers from trees in Michigan. Tip flavor is more sensitive to soil quality and acidity than other species. Good luck!

With this information, the last piece had fallen into place. If I hadn't spoken to Pete, I probably would have used the spruce tips as if they were late hops, which is apparently the wrong thing to do. I decided to use 1 quart of freshly picked spruce tips, and switched the hops from Kent Goldings to Simcoe and Amarillo to better match the spruce character. The pairing of spruce with Amarillo was advice from Pete; the Simcoe addition was my idea. Finally, I fermented this beer warmer than the 68° F (20° C) originally recommended, because I wanted to enhance the fruity character.

Ben Franklin's Ale—Specialty Beer

Description for judges: "Colonial Stock Ale with molasses and spruce tips (citrusy taste). 7.8% ABV, 2 yrs. old."

Recipe for 6 gallons (22.7 liters)

10 lbs. (4.5 kg) Maris Otter malt

3 lbs. (1.4 kg) flaked maize

1 lb. (454 g) Durst Vienna malt

1 lb. (454 g) Dingeman CaraVienne malt

1 lb. (454 g) Weyermann Rauchmalz

1½ lbs. (680 g) U.K. biscuit malt

2 oz. (57 g) Crisp chocolate malt

2 oz. (57 g) Special "B" malt

1 qt. (946 ml) fresh Colorado Blue Spruce tips at 60 min.

4 oz. (118 ml) light (normal) molasses at 15 min.

1 Tbsp. blackstrap molasses at 15 min.

½ oz. (14 g) Simcoe whole hops, 12% alpha acid, at 60 min.

½ oz. (14 g) Amarillo pellet hops, 7% alpha acid, at 10 min.

½ oz. (14 g) Simcoe whole hops, 12% alpha acid, at 5 min.

½ oz. (14 g) Amarillo pellet hops, 7% alpha acid, at 0 min.

White Labs WLP002

Mash-in all grains at 154° F (68° C) until converted. Collect 9 gallons (34.1 liters). Boil hard for 90 minutes. Final kettle volume 6.5 gallons (24.6 liters). Ferment at 72° F (22° C).

OG: 1.070

FG: 1.010

7.99% ABV

This beer takes some aging to hit its peak. I didn't like it much when it was less than six months old, but then it started to smooth out and develop a great complexity. It was at its best when it was a year and a half to two years old. The smoke is very subtle and blends in with the molasses; you can't detect smoke on its own, which is a good thing since the beer has enough complexity. It's the molasses flavor that takes a little time to age out; the spruce character is best when young.

I found that there is about a one- to two-week window for picking new growth on spruce trees. Get the tips while they are young and very pale green. Once they start to darken and get stiffer, the flavor is already suffering. I hand-picked them into a 5-gallon plastic bucket. You snap or pinch off the tips with two fingers, like when picking herbs. Wash and store in plastic bags in the refrigerator until use, then freeze the remainder for another batch.

To complete my original story, after I had made the beer in 2006, I cellared it for a while, then drove the keg of it 1,200 miles to Denver for the 2007 NHC. I knew Tony Simmons was giving a talk on the beer, so I wanted him to try it and give me his impressions. I was thrilled when he told me he thought my version was the best homebrewed version he had tried, and that he thought my additions were well thought-out. I went on to serve that keg at Club Night, then drove it back to Ohio. I also took that keg to the Beer & Sweat competition in Cincinnati that year. Beer & Sweat is the world's largest keg-only competition, so that was another chance for people to kill my keg. Luck must have been on my side, because I still had some left to enter in the 2008 NHC, where it took gold. I'm amazed it held up so well given how it was handled; maybe that's part of the secret?

Example: Make a Reference Beer, Then Adjust

If you can't find any good source material on a target clone beer, one approach is to make a beer of a similar style and then do a critical side-by-side comparison of the clone beer and the target beer. Take good notes and use them to adjust your next batch. Here is an actual example from a batch that I made in 2001 that illustrates this point nicely.

A friend of mine requested that I brew a batch of his favorite beer, *J.W. Lee's Harvest Ale*, for his fiftieth birthday party. I love that beer, too, so I was happy to give it a go. Here was my first attempt at the recipe. As you can see, I didn't do much research on the actual beer, and I was using ingredients I had on hand.

Randy's Old Ale—English Old Ale

Recipe for 5 gallons (19 liters)

6 lbs. (2.7 kg) Maris Otter malt
9 lbs. (4.1 kg) Vienna malt
¼ lb. (113 g) crystal 120° L malt
½ lb. (227 g) crystal 80° L malt
1 lb. (454 g) CaraVienne malt
½ lb. (227 g) CaraPils malt
¼ lb. (113 g) Kiln Coffee malt
¾ lb. (340 g) biscuit malt
1 lb. (454 g) malted wheat
1 can (454 g) Lyle's Golden Syrup
2 lbs. (907 g) raw brown sugar
1 oz. (28 g) Tomahawk whole hops, 16.3% alpha acid, at 60 min.
½ oz. (14 g) Tomahawk whole hops, 16.3% alpha acid, at 30 min.
1 oz. (28 g) Saaz whole hops, 4% alpha acid, at 10 min.
1 oz. (28 g) Saaz whole hops, 4% alpha acid, at knockout

Repitched yeast from previous batches, contained White Labs WLP002, Wyeast 1968, and Wyeast 1187 (WLP002 and Wyeast 1968 are essentially the same yeast).

Mash-in at 149° F (65° C) for 90 min., raise to 158° F (70° C) for 15 min., mash-out at 170° F (77° C). Collect 8.5 gallons (32.2 liters). Boil hard for 90 minutes.

Final kettle volume 5.5 gallons (20.8 liters). Ferment at 68° F (20° C).

OG: 1.094

FG: 1.020

50 IBU

9.7% ABV

This beer is a decent old ale, although I probably would boost the darker crystals to have it score better if I were brewing it today for competition. That's not the point, but feel free to try the recipe yourself. What is interesting are the actual notes I found in my brewlog when I tasted the beer alongside a *J. W. Lee's*. This gives some insight into the kinds of observations you might make when comparing beers, and how to turn them into something actionable. As you can see, you don't need to be totally precise, but you do want to record all your observations and identify the components that need to be nudged in the right direction:

- less bittering hops (50 IBU → 35 IBU)

- less sugar (2 lbs. → 1 lb.)

- more malt (1.094 → 1.110+)

- darker (maybe try a touch of Carafa)

- age longer

- more body

- sweeter finish.

Ironically, if I wasn't trying to clone a specific beer, this recipe would have been perfectly acceptable. People really enjoyed it, and the beer was finished quickly at the party. But I had a slightly different vision in mind, so I kept adjusting the recipe based on these notes. After another two batches, I wound up with the barley wine recipe in the introduction to this book. If you compare the two recipes, you'll see how much it changed. This demonstrates that the cloning process can be much more iterative if you don't do the initial research to establish the basic parameters of the style.

This recipe makes a good, drinkable example of the darker English barley wine style, and one that can age well. You can also make paler and more bitter examples of the style in the vein of *Thomas Hardy's Ale* (my recipe for that beer is listed in the Mastering Techniques chapter). I've also had fun blending the two types of English barley wines to get an even more complex beer, as well as blending different vintages of the same beer for additional character.

Conceptualizing New Styles

If you brew for homebrew competitions, you have no doubt heard of "brewing to style." That is, you brew your beer to be a good match for a defined style in the BJCP Style Guidelines. Brewers who brew to style tend to do better in competitions than those who don't, even if they all produce solid beers. However, brewing to style only gets you so far. What do you do for the Specialty Beer category, where the only limitation is your creativity?

Some beers that fall into the Specialty Beer category (BJCP Category 23) are fairly straightforward, like making "imperial" versions of existing styles, cloning commercial beers, adding unusual adjuncts, or making traditional or historical styles that don't yet have a description. I've already discussed most of those, but what about combinations of existing styles, or what I call "Fusion Beers"?

This is an advanced topic for recipe formulation, since it involves creativity, imagination, and brewing skill. There are several ways to create a fusion beer, but this focus is on a combination of two or more existing BJCP style categories, or a variation of an existing BJCP category by using ingredients, processes, or techniques from other styles.

Getting Ideas

I discussed the concept of "style space" in the last chapter. This is an important consideration when creating a recipe for a new style. You want to avoid creating something that hits or narrowly misses the style space occupied by another beer. For example, if your concept is a "darker American pale ale," then you are probably describing an American amber ale or an American brown ale. A description alone won't make it a special beer; you have to come up with something different. If you enter a beer like that in competition, judges will likely tell you that you miscategorized the beer, or they will think that you tried to make one style but missed and are now trying to cover it up by calling it something else. Either way, you lose. Your best bet is to think about the style space when you are conceptualizing your beer, and look for a place with no clear fit. It helps to get other opinions about your concept, particularly from beer judges. They should be able to tell you if the idea sounds unique or not.

It's a lot easier to clone an existing beer or brew a beer within a well-established style than it is to come up with a new idea. Fortunately, you don't have to be completely original—you can "borrow" ideas from other sources if you aren't getting a flash of inspiration. One thing you can try is to sample commercial examples that don't fit established styles and see if you get any ideas. You don't have to try to replicate a commercial beer; you can try one and then decide to take it in another direction. For example, I brew a brown IPA but it's not like *Dogfish Head Indian Brown Ale*; mine is hoppier. All you need is inspiration from one of the commercial examples; you can decide on your own recipe later.

If you are a BJCP judge, you can ask to judge specialty beers (or fruit/spice beers) at competitions that get a lot of entries. The organizers will love you, since few people ask to judge these styles, and you may get some great ideas. The NHC second round is a wonderful place to judge these styles; all the really bad ideas have been weeded out in the first round.

You could also think about food and wine concepts. Think of food pairings you like, or food and wine matches that work well. See if you can take the dominant flavorings from some of these examples and apply them to beer. Tasting is tasting, and if a flavor combination works in one realm, it will work in another. If you like spicy and malty flavors together, see if you can work that into a recipe.

If you do have an idea about mixing two commercial styles, here's an easy way to see if you like it. Get two commercial (or homebrewed) beers of the styles you'll be fusing, and blend them. Taste the blend, and see if you like the results. You may have to vary the amounts you blend of each beer to get an idea of how well it works. But if you want to know what an IPA with Vienna malt tastes like, try blending an IPA and an Oktoberfest. It won't be an exact match with your recipe, but it will allow you to quickly test if the concept is sound or not.

Keep in mind some pairings that are known to work well. Hoppy, pale beers work well, as do malty beers with low bitterness. Watch out for known clashes. I dislike burnt, deeply roasted grains with citrusy hops. Beers that are spiced or are sour rarely have high levels of bitterness or hoppiness. That's for a reason.

Sour and bitter clash; sweetness balances both. It's as true in food as it is in beer. When you use harsh grains and harsh hops, you get an extra-harsh beer. Garrett Oliver's *The Brewmaster's Table* is a good reference for understanding the interaction between food and beer, as well as flavor components in beer.

If you're still short on ideas, here are a few commercial examples of beers fitting the experimental fusion beer theme. Look at the descriptions and try to categorize them into the BJCP Style Guidelines; they simply don't fit. Then try to describe them in a single sentence using existing styles as a shorthand— that's much easier.

- *Dogfish Head Indian Brown Ale* is a 7.2% ABV, 50 IBU cross between Scotch ale, IPA, and American brown ale made with brown sugar.

- *Surly Bender* is a 5.1% ABV, 45 IBU oatmeal brown ale made with Belgian and U.K. malts.

- *Chouffe Houblon Dobbelen IPA Tripel* is just that; a 9% Belgian *tripel* hopped like an American IPA, using Tomahawk, Saaz, and Amarillo hops.

On my last trip to Belgium, I visited a very small artisanal brewery, Millervertus. It was very creative in creating beers that blended styles. I tasted a bitter *witbier* with plum, a beer that tasted like a strong Düsseldorf *altbier*, a bready *tripel* (sort of like a cross between a *tripel* and a Belgian pale ale), and a smoked beer. The brewer used the Orval yeast, so his Germanlike beers all had a Belgian character.

As you can see, American craft brewers and Belgian artisanal brewers don't care much about hitting styles. They're just trying to be creative and come up with interesting, tasty beers for their customers to enjoy. That's good advice for any homebrewer.

Creating a Fusion Recipe

Once you have a concept in mind, it's time to start formulating a recipe. There are two basic models you can follow: You can either make a variation of an existing base style by adding elements from another style, or you can attempt to combine attributes of two or more separate styles to create something completely different. I'll address the variation option first, since it's easier.

This might be an obvious step, but it bears repeating. Make sure you have a good recipe for your (unmodified) base beer style. Adding more ingredients isn't going to make it better, so please be sure you're happy with your original beer. You can even use it as a control batch against which to judge your experimental fusion beer.

Examine the attributes of the variation style (that which you are fusing with the base style). It helps to understand what makes a recipe fit a certain style. Compare recipes of similar styles to help identify the key differences (for instance, what makes a porter different from a brown ale?). Jamil Zainasheff and John Palmer's *Brewing Classic Styles* is a great resource for this exercise. In many cases, it's just a difference in specialty grains. Look at the base grains, the specialty grains, the yeast type, the hop varieties, the bitterness level, and the overall strength of the beer.

Identify what ingredients you want to vary. Pick the attributes that make the style unique, then think about how you want to fuse them with the base style. In my example of a brown IPA, I took the specialty grains that can make a brown porter (various crystal malts and chocolate malt) and fused them with my base IPA recipe.

Many brewers in the United Kingdom are creating new pale ales by using American hops. They leave everything else the same but change the hop varieties. It's still not an American pale ale, since the grain and yeast are British, but it has a different character. You can create interesting beers by following a similar pattern of changing the country of origin of some of the ingredients. Try making an Oktoberfest or *dunkelweizen* but use a Belgian Trappist yeast, for instance. That would be sort of like merging the German beers with a *dubbel*.

In addition to the country of origin (United States, United Kingdom, Germany, Belgium) of the ingredients, you can also vary the strength of the beer and the use of adjuncts. If you fuse styles of different strengths, you can decide how strong to make the result. You can add distinctive grains (e.g., rye, spelt, buckwheat, oats) or fermentables (e.g., honey, molasses, brown sugar, sorghum, maple syrup). Don't make too many changes at once; remember you still need an easy-to-describe concept.

When merging two styles, look for the common elements between them. It's helpful to use two recipes representing the styles, then analyze the similarities and differences. Do they use the same base malt or the same yeast? Are they the same gravity or bitterness level? Pick out all the things are the same between them and put that in your fusion recipe. Then start taking a look at the differences. You'll want to borrow enough from each recipe so that your fusion beer reminds the taster of both styles, but not so much that all the flavors become muddled. It might help to consider base malts, specialty grains, adjuncts, bitterness level, strength, late hops, yeast, and fermentation technique separately. Fill each of those attributes with one element from either of your parent styles, and see if the combination is appealing to you. It will take some trial and error, as well as some imagination.

Avoiding Stupid Ideas

So now you have a basic recipe. Time to brew it, right? Not so fast. You need to take a moment and think about what you're going to brew. Does it make sense? Does it sound good? Remember that just because you can combine two styles doesn't mean you *should*. Some concepts are simply bad ideas that could taste horrible. It reminds me of the old "Friends" episode where Rachel is cooking an English Christmas dinner. But two pages of her recipe book stuck together and she wound up making a dish that was half English Trifle and half Shepherd's Pie. Ross said that it "tastes like feet." Don't let your beer wind up that way! Run through a mental "sanity check" before brewing your beer.

A good fusion beer needs to succeed in both concept and execution. I've discussed the conceptual side, but not as much the execution. Here are some common pitfalls in making these type of beers and how best to avoid them.

The keys to a great Specialty Beer are balance, flavor, and drinkability. Whatever you do, your beer needs to be enjoyable to drink. The flavor profile should be clean, and any special ingredients should be well balanced. When in doubt, err on the side of restraint. Many good concepts are ruined because brewers overemphasize the special nature of the ingredients at the expense of overall drinkability.

Take another look at the section in this chapter on Avoiding Clashing Flavors, and make sure you aren't falling into those traps. If you start experimenting with ideas that are known to work, such as blending fruits and spices, making darker variations of normally pale beers, making Belgian versions of American, English, or German beers, using German base malts in American beers, brewing ales as lagers and vice versa, making pale beers hoppy and bitter, or making dark beers malty and with lower bitterness, then you will have a better chance of success. Remember to apply your recipe tweaks sparingly, and to keep good notes. Don't change too many variables at once, and keep experimenting. Finally, if you brew a combination you don't like, let it age for a while. Some flavors take a while to meld, and many beers improve with time.

If you subsequently enter your fusion beer in a competition, it's very important to be able to succinctly describe your concept to the judges. For example, "brown IPA" or "a cross between a brown ale and an IPA" would be understood by judges to mean an IPA with a darker color and some chocolate and caramel flavor. The judges would quickly grasp your intent and then be able to judge the beer without having to think about it too much. Think about descriptions of recipes on menus in restaurants. The best ones will have simple descriptions. The more difficult ones will go into long details about the ingredients, the preparation, and the chef's ego. Yup, it will come off the same way with beer judges. Talk about your beer too much, and you'll likely irritate the judges by making them think you're pompous or that you are trying to hide something. You're giving them a description of your beer, not the recipe; remember that.

If you spend too much time explaining your beer, you're also giving the judges more reasons to deduct points. If you mention ingredients, judges will expect to find them. If you give them a general concept, they will automatically give you more leeway. My best advice is to be specific enough so that they understand you, but general enough so that they give you the benefit of the doubt. Look at the description I used for my *Ben Franklin's Ale*, earlier in this chapter. I gave a one-sentence description with specific information and a general impression. I didn't talk about how I handled the spruce tips, or that it had several other unusual ingredients. I mentioned the ones you could taste and gave some general guidelines to set their mind properly before they tasted it.

I've included two recipes to give you an idea of how to put these concepts into practice, a brown IPA and a black *witbier*. The brown IPA is a fusion between an American IPA and a Northern English brown ale. The black *witbier* is a fusion between a Belgian *witbier* and a *schwarzbier*. Both have additional ingredient substitutions to account for flavor differences and to provide a more pleasant end product. You could easily create a black IPA recipe by taking the darker grains and associated methods from the *witbier* recipe and swapping them for the darker malts in the IPA, cutting back on the sugar and lowering the crystal malts. Alternatively, using some light molasses might be interesting, but keep in mind that molasses can be a strong flavor, so go easy.

My first fusion beer recipe is for a brown IPA, which is my normal IPA recipe with the addition of some darker malts and using brown sugar instead of honey. It uses late hopping for bitterness and adds the darker malts during the sparge, both of which should cut down on the clash of malt/hops that can happen in hoppy darker beers.

Julius Erving—Brown IPA or India Brown Ale

Recipe for 6.5 U.S. gallons (24.6 liters), 75% efficiency

11 lbs. (5 kg) Maris Otter malt
0.5 lb. (227 g) Munich malt
0.5 lb. (227 g) wheat malt
1 lb. (454 g) CaraVienne malt
1 lb. (454 g) crystal 40° L malt
0.5 lb. (454 g) chocolate malt
0.25 lb. (113 g) Special "B" malt
1 lb. (454 g) turbinado sugar
1 oz. (28 g) Centennial whole hops, 10.5% alpha acid, FWH
2 oz. (57 g) Tomahawk whole hops, 16% alpha acid, at 20 min.
2 oz. (57 g) Cascade whole hops, 5.8% alpha acid, at knockout
2 oz. (57 g) Centennial whole hops, 10.5% alpha acid, dry hop
Wyeast 1272 American Ale II yeast

Mash-in base grains at 152° F (67° C). Add crystal malts and dark grains during recirculation and sparging. Run off 8 gallons (30.3 liters). Add sugar to the boil. Use a 90-minute boil, hopping according to schedule. You'll probably lose some volume to hops soaking them up. Ferment at 68° F (20° C).

OG: 1.070

FG: 1.014

7.4% ABV

66 IBU

My second fusion beer recipe is for a black *witbier*, which is my normal witbier recipe with darker malts and a slight tweak in spicing. Darker malts were used, but again, only during the sparge. I changed the usual coriander and orange peel to star anise and tangerine, since I thought those spices would match better with a darker grain bill. I was actually thinking about a Chinese red braised beef dish for the flavorings, and wondered how they would fit.

RIP MJ—Black Witbier

Recipe for 5 U.S. gallons (19 liters), 75% efficiency

4.5 lbs. (2 kg) Belgian Pilsner malt
4 lbs. (1.8 kg) flaked wheat
0.5 lb. (227 g) flaked oats
0.25 lb. (113 g) Carafa Special II malt
0.25 lb. (113 g) pale chocolate malt
0.25 lb. (113 g) CaraVienne malt
0.75 oz. (380 g) Hallertauer whole hops, 4% alpha acid, at 90 min.
¼ tsp. dried chamomile flowers
Zest of 2 tangerines
1 whole star anise, crushed
Wyeast 3944 Belgian white beer yeast

Step mash Pils malt, wheat, and oats: 122° F (50° C) for 10 minutes, 148° F (64° C) for 60 minutes. Add dark grains during recirculation and sparge. Collect 6.5 gallons (24.6 liters). Use a 90-minute boil. Add spices at knockout, and steep for 5 minutes. Ferment at 68° F (20° C).

OG: 1.052

FG: 1.012

5.3% ABV

15 IBU

Ingredient notes: Get chamomile flowers at a spice store, health food shop, tea shop, or craft store. Google "buy dried chamomile flowers" to find online sources. Chamomile tea is usually made of pure chamomile flowers (check the ingredient list).

Use only the orange zest of the tangerines. Do not use the white pith.

Using broken pieces of star anise is cheaper; use the equivalent of 1 whole star.

CHAPTER 7
troubleshooting

Life. Don't talk to me about life.
—Marvin, the paranoid android,
The Hitchhiker's Guide to the Galaxy, by Douglas Adams

Unfortunately, life isn't perfect. Once you've brewed, you aren't really done. You have to check your beer to make sure it doesn't have any problems. If it does, you should try to fix them, or at least learn from your mistakes so you can avoid them next time. This is the essence of troubleshooting, or trying to determine what went wrong when your beer didn't turn out perfectly. It's a problem-solving discipline that requires an in-depth knowledge of the system and processes.

Most faults for advanced brewers don't present themselves like they do in a spiked beer on a BJCP exam. Faults don't always pop up and ask to be noticed. Subtle things can be wrong; they are often hard to notice and may be more stylistic than technical but still have a technical (brewing process) issue as the source of the problem.

Beer judges don't have recipe or process information, so they often guess at problems in beer. If you're the brewer, you should be able to troubleshoot your own beer with perfect information. The only things you need to know are how to identify the faults and what you can do to address them. Can you fix the flaws on the fly during your brew day? What can you do after fermentation is complete? How do you know your beer is unsalvageable and should be dumped?

Your goal should be to be able to detect faults at various places in the brewing process. If you are able to fix (or at least partially mitigate) these faults, then your beer may still be drinkable or even quite good. If you aren't able to fix the faults, you should consider them part of a learning experience, so that you can either adjust your recipe the next time you brew it, or investigate your equipment, ingredients, or processes to remediate the root cause of the problem.

I've categorized faults into two major groups: technical brewing faults and style-related faults. A list of common faults is provided, along with how they are perceived and what solutions might be applied. A proper diagnosis of the problem is critical to selecting the right approach for addressing the problem. Randomly applying "fixes" without knowing the source of the problem can often create more severe problems and rarely solves the original issue.

It bears repeating that most brewing faults can be avoided by using fresh, clean ingredients, following good wort production practices (proper level of free amino nitrogen and yeast nutrients, proper level of maltose), providing a sufficient quantity of fresh, high-quality yeast with proper aeration, controlling fermentation conditions, keeping oxygen out of the cold side of the brewing process, and following good sanitary practices. Those are the key control points in brewing; if you follow those practices, you are likely able to avoid most technical faults.

Detecting Beer Faults

Before we delve into specific faults, know that some faults are temporary and others are permanent. Temporary faults will sometimes go away on their own or can be coerced into going away, while permanent faults often lead to dumping your beer. Be careful about writing off a batch of beer unless you know it contains an unrecoverable fault. If a beer is too bitter, too roasty, too estery, or too alcoholic, those features tend to fade with time, so simple aging under proper storage conditions will likely mellow those faults. Sour, medicinal, or oxidized flavors are usually there to stay; toss those.

Dealing with faults in a beer is similar to how a doctor treats an illness. You start with the symptoms (i.e., the faults in the beer), you diagnose the problem, and you prescribe treatment for the underlying problem. Anybody can "tell you where it hurts," but a doctor goes to medical school to understand how to identify the important symptoms, understand what condition this represents, and decide what to do about it.

Fortunately, fixing a beer is much less complicated than healing a person, but knowledge and experience still are required. As the brewer, you have some inside information that will help; you know the ingredients and process used. If you can combine that with your beer style knowledge, sensory skills, and knowledge of common faults, you are well on the way to solving your brewing problems.

Common beer faults are identified using their perceptual characteristics; simply use structured evaluation (described in Chapter 5) to isolate the faults, then reference the fault list later in this chapter to help determine cause and effect. A complicating factor is that some faults can come from several different sources. Consider the most likely causes of faults rather than those that are rare, and look for multiple clues toward underlying problems. Again, think of those faults you perceive as symptoms of an underlying problem, and try to determine what went wrong. It can be somewhat of a detective game.

One problem with identifying faults and problems with beer is that some faults are confused with seemingly positive features. For example, if you detect caramel and fruitiness, you could be drinking an English beer, or you could be sensing early forms of oxidation. Heavy caramel (especially kettle caramelization) is sometimes confused with diacetyl. Be careful about jumping to conclusions prematurely, and look for confirming evidence of your diagnosis.

Some balance-related faults are temperature-dependent. If you serve a bitter beer too cold, it will seem even more bitter, since the balancing malt is suppressed. Warming it up might bring it into balance. Warm temperatures can exaggerate the impression of esters, alcohols, and other volatile aromatics. Try to assess the beer at proper serving temperature for the beer style in question.

You can simplify the diagnosis by leveraging your knowledge as the brewer. For example, if you know the fermentation was sluggish or that the target gravity wasn't met, use that to prune the possible choices for the faults you detected. If you think the problem is ingredient-related, do you have any other beers made with the same ingredients? Do they have problems, too? Likewise for process. What are the common elements between different batches? Think of this as the "medical history" part of the investigation. If you made recent changes or have a recurring problem, see if that information can lead you to the source.

For subjective faults, broader input is often useful. Get feedback from other knowledgeable brewers, tasters, beer judges, etc. Are their observations consistent, or are they giving you widely varying opinions? Some beers can invoke love-it-or-hate-it responses from tasters.

Technical Brewing Faults

Technical faults are what most people think of as flaws in beer; they are either single faults or a combination of faults that are derived from the brewing process, often from fermentation. These are more obvious faults that many people can find; basic tasting skills and quality control can often catch them. Sensory thresholds for the different chemical substances associated with the brewing faults can vary by individual, based on genetic or physical limitations, individual perceptual differences, and insensitivity to certain substances. It helps for you to know your own limitations.

Newer brewers often have beers that show multiple faults. The flavors I often detect in their beers are derived from weak fermentations; there are off-flavors of varying levels, poor attenuation, general unclean or muddy flavors, and vegetal notes. A slow start can allow spoilage bacteria to grow. Weak fermentations can cause the yeast to throw off many off-flavor by-products and not be able to clean them up. Stale extract has a tangy flavor. Oxidation of ingredients and the beer at various stages is frequently evident. Stale, dull flavors are common. Infections can exist in different forms. Some are from wild yeast and tend to be phenolic, others are tart, others are vegetal. General spoilage bacteria can take root after the wort is cooled and before the yeast starts active fermentation. Poor ingredients, inattention to oxidation, long lag times, weak fermentations, and poor handling of the finished beer all contribute to lame flavors and a poor drinking experience.

This discussion of faults is an elaboration on material I helped develop for the Beer Judge Certification Program's instructional information for beer judges, and covers the most common technical flaws found in homebrewed beer.

Acetaldehyde. A fermentation-derived character perceived as an aroma and flavor of fresh-cut green apples, or as a grassy, rough, green, immature beer flavor. It is an intermediate fermentation compound and a precursor to alcohol. It is a common green beer flavor and a marker of beer maturity (it increases during fermentation, then decreases as the beer conditions).

It can be controlled by proper fermentation (pitching rate, oxygen, nutrients) and conditioning practices to allow the fermentation to finish and to let the yeast naturally reduce the acetaldehyde levels. Yeast must remain in contact during these phases to do their job. Ensure yeast remains healthy and in sufficient quantity to start fermentation quickly, then subsequently finish fermentation and achieve full attenuation. Allow sufficient conditioning time in contact with the yeast. Some yeast strains are known for producing higher levels of acetaldehyde, in which case selecting another strain is the solution.

Reducing head pressure during fermentation and conditioning can allow the aldehydes to blow off, as they are easily volatilized. Avoid oxygen during packaging; alcohol oxidizes back to aldehydes, which can then cause stale beer flavors. Light and heat can also catalyze this process.

Levels can be increased in primary fermentation by having an intense fermentation, increasing fermentation temperature, increasing pitching rate, increasing fermentation pressure, reducing aeration, and by stirring up the yeast. Levels can be reduced after fermentation by having an active secondary fermentation and conditioning, warm conditioning, increasing yeast concentration during conditioning, and reducing aeration.

Alcoholic/hot. A fermentation-derived character that can be perceived as an aroma, flavor, and mouthfeel. Although ethanol is relatively tasteless, it can be tasted (think of the flavor of vodka). It is often found with other higher alcohols and can have a spicy, vinous aroma and flavor and a warming sensation in the mouth and throat. At higher levels, the warming can seem hot or burning. Alcohol also adds bitterness to beer. Since ethanol is the primary objective of fermentation, it by itself is not a flaw unless it is unbalanced or insufficiently aged. However, it is often accompanied by other flavors from higher alcohols (see Solvent/fusel for more detail).

Conditions that favor development of ethyl alcohol also can lead to fusel alcohols being formed. Reducing the alcohol level can control this character, which can be accomplished by reducing the starting gravity of the recipe, reducing the fermentability of the wort (raising the mash temperature, using less sugary adjuncts), or using a less attenuative yeast strain.

Conducting a healthier fermentation can produce cleaner alcohols. Lower fermentation temperature, ensure proper fermentation conditions are met, check yeast health, and select a yeast strain that produces less alcohol character. Follow good sanitation practices to avoid infection, which can increase attenuation and alcohol production.

Finally, let the beer condition and age longer before consuming. Beers with a higher alcohol content often need considerable cellaring before they become smooth and drinkable.

Astringent. A mouth-puckering mouthfeel with a lingering, bitter harshness and a husklike, grainy flavor. Astringency is primarily a mouthfeel but is accompanied by telltale flavors. It is typically derived from a combination of the ingredients and brewing process. Astringency in beer is caused by tannins; controlling tannin extraction controls astringency.

Tannins can come from grain husks and can be extracted during the mash, sparge, and boil. Don't oversparge; attempting to get every last bit of extract from the grain can cause a husky flavor. Don't overcrush the grain; husk particles can carry over to the boil and have more surface area for tannin extraction. Don't boil grain. Don't sparge with water above 170° F (77° C) and with a high pH (above 6). Use a lower amount of dark grains (especially black malt).

The vegetal matter in hops is also a source of tannins. Use a lower quantity of whole hops (especially high-alpha hops). Use water with lower sulfate content, since sulfates can accentuate bitterness and harshness associated with tannins. Avoid the use of raw spices, fruit pith, and fruit skins, which are also sources of tannins.

Diacetyl. A fermentation-derived character that can be perceived as a flavor and an aroma. It has a flavor like butter, butterscotch, or movie theater popcorn (artificial butter uses diacetyl as a flavoring). It sometimes has a slick mouthfeel as well. It is an intermediate yeast by-product, typically reduced by yeast during fermentation. Warm fermentation temperatures and high levels of aeration can increase diacetyl but also can lead to later reduction, if enough healthy yeast is present.

Control diacetyl by following good fermentation practices (adequate pitching rate of healthy yeast, aeration, nutrients) and avoiding low nitrogen adjuncts (which can reduce available yeast nutrients). Removing the yeast prematurely can leave high diacetyl levels. Don't crash-cool the yeast, or rack, filter, or fine too early. Allow the beer to rest on the yeast until fully attenuated. Avoid adding oxygen during fermentation. Reduce primary fermentation temperature to control the production.

Diacetyl can be removed by stimulating yeast activity in the absence of oxygen (i.e., a diacetyl rest, more commonly conducted for lagers), or by raising the temperature or extending secondary fermentation (warm conditioning). Bacteria, wild yeast, and mutated yeast can also produce diacetyl, so good sanitation and yeast-handling techniques are important for control. Some yeast strains are known diacetyl producers; avoid those if you wish to control this character. Bottle-conditioning beer at cellar temperatures also gives the yeast additional time to reduce the diacetyl.

DMS (dimethyl sulfide). Perceived as the flavor and aroma of creamed corn, cooked corn, cooked vegetables (often sulfury vegetables like cabbage). Derived from malt (S-methyl methionine, SMM) during germination. Highly kilned malts produce less SMM, so paler beers will have more DMS. Above 65 to 70° C (149-158° F), SMM is converted to DMS, but DMS is volatile and can blow off with rising heat (as in a proper boil).

Control at the source by reducing the amount of SMM (reduce Pilsner malt and other very pale malts). Drive off any DMS created from SMM by using a long, vigorous, rolling, open boil. When DMS has not been fully volatilized during the boil (nonvigorous boil, insufficient boiling time, covered boil), it will remain in the beer. DMS can also be created after the boil, unless the wort is cooled rapidly. Long whirlpool times or extended time before chilling can create DMS.

DMS can also come from infections. Make sure you use a healthy, vigorous yeast starter and follow good sanitation practices. Cool quickly, and pitch yeast shortly afterward.

Estery. Perceived as a fruity (strawberry, pear, banana, apple, grape, citrus) aroma and flavor, it is generally fermentation-derived (not counting esters that come directly from malt or hops). Esters are commonly associated with

English and Belgian ales but are unwanted in most lagers. At excessive levels, esters can take on an unpleasant, solventy character.

Ester formation is quite complicated and depends on many factors. Esters are derived from an alcohol and a fatty acid. Not all esters are produced in the same way. Ester production is influenced by yeast strain, wort composition, and fermentation conditions. Contradictory evidence exists as to the effect of pitching rate on esterification. The optimal pitching rate to maximize esters may differ by strain.

When factors favoring growth (oxygen, lipids, stirring) are present, yeast tend to grow more and produce fewer esters. Fermenting at a high temperature and adding new wort to an active fermentation stimulate ester production. Conditions that stimulate fusel production (temperature, zinc) also contribute to esterification. Many esters are formed from fusel alcohols as well as esters.

Lager yeast produce fewer esters, but low fermentation temperatures may be the primary cause. Warm-fermented lagers will be quite estery. Many ale yeasts produce a significant amount of esters, particularly strains associated with English and Belgian beers.

Carbon dioxide pressure during fermentation is a common way of influencing ester production. High levels of carbon dioxide inhibit ester production. Tall, cylindrical tanks increase pressure on the yeast but also produce natural convection currents that limit esterification. Shallow fermenters tend to maximize ester production (e.g., in German *weizenbiers* and Belgian ales).

Ester production can be increased by selecting a yeast strain known for esters, using flocculent yeast, adjusting the pitching rate (high or low, depending on the strain), and from yeast mutations from generation to generation. Esters can also be increased by reducing oxygen in the wort, raising the gravity of the wort, reducing fatty acids present, and increasing zinc levels. Higher fermentation temperatures, decreased pressures, and decreased stirring can increase esters. In general, stressing the yeast during fermentation can increase esters.

Bottle conditioning and aging the beer longer at cellar temperatures on the yeast can reduce esters. Slow oxidation during storage can increase esters.

Grassy. Perceived as the flavor and aroma of fresh-cut grass or green leaves. Generally a hop-derived character produced by the prolonged contact of beer with the vegetal material in hops, or through contact with raw hops (as in dry hopping).

Control by reducing or eliminating dry hopping, possibly substituting another late-hop technique instead. Also can be controlled by reducing the quantity of whole hops used throughout the beer. Avoid post-fermentation oxygen pickup, which can give a harsher, grassy character to hops. Check hops and malt for freshness; stale, oxidized flavors can sometimes have a grassy component.

Light-struck. Perceived as a skunky or catty aroma and flavor. Certain wavelengths of visible light striking hop chemicals cause a physical change that produces mercaptans, the same chemical skunks produce to defend themselves. Humans are extremely sensitive to these sulfur compounds and can detect them in concentrations as little as parts per billion.

Since light-struck beer is caused by exposure to sunlight, avoid allowing direct sunlight to strike the beer after hops have been added. Store beer in brown bottles, since clear and green bottles are up to eight times less effective in blocking the critical wavelengths. Avoid extended exposure of packaged beer to sunlight or fluorescent light. Brown bottles can reduce the transmitted light but are not opaque; given enough time, beer in brown bottles can skunk, too.

Some hop varieties (such as Cluster) can have a catty aroma; avoid their use in late additions. This isn't exactly the same as light-struck but can have a similar character.

Medicinal. Perceived as the flavor and aroma of Chloroseptic lozenges, disinfectant, or other harsh medicines or cleaners. Caused by chlorophenolic substances, derived from a combination of chlorine and phenols. One of the most offensive flavors in beer.

Control by removing chlorine from the water supply. Avoid water with chlorine or chloramines (use RO water, if necessary). Filter supply water with activated charcoal filters. Use Campden tablets to neutralize chloramines. Avoid chlorine bleach sanitizers.

Control by reducing sources of phenols. Reduce astringency/grain husk sources. Avoid excessive whole hop use. Practice good sanitation to reduce infections, particularly from wild yeast strains. Avoid yeasts that produce phenols, such as *weizen* strains and some Belgian yeast.

Metallic. Perceived primarily as the flavor of iron, copper, coins, or blood. Can be detected in the aroma in high enough concentrations. Typically caused by impurities in the water source or defects in equipment. Can also come through intentional or unintentional chemical additions.

To control, check your water supply for metallic ions, particularly iron. Get your water tested. Reduce salt additions to brewing liquor. Check the condition of your brewing equipment, looking in particular for rust. Make sure stainless steel equipment is properly passivated. Fully rinse any sanitizers. Try using RO water if your water supply is suspect, and only add the brewing salts necessary.

Musty. Perceived as the flavor and aroma reminiscent of a stale, moldy cellar. Carries the impression of age, filth, dirt, and general lack of cleanliness. Can be due to mold in the ingredients, stale ingredients, oxidation, or infection.

Avoid oxidation (see Oxidized). Follow proper sanitary practices. Avoid peat-smoked malt. Check water for freshness and taste; use an activated charcoal filter or use RO water. Use fresh ingredients (especially malt and hops); sometimes the staleness carries through from the source. Avoid the use of corks when bottling; the cork itself can cause off-flavors (a flavor known as "corked" in wine tasting). Check equipment or supplies (like bottle caps) for contamination and cleanliness.

Oxidized. A common problem, can be perceived as a stale, papery, or wet cardboard aroma and flavor; this form of oxidation is always bad and is not recoverable. Slow oxidation of alcohols are sometimes desirable, and can provide a pleasant sherrylike character in some styles, such as barley wines and old ales. Controlled oxidation of tannins can soften astringency in red wine and hoppy beers. Esterification of harsh fusel alcohols during aging can also lead to improved flavor and aroma.

Oxidation from slow aging can cause beer to take on sweeter or more caramelly flavors and can cause esters to increase. Not all oxidation will be like paper, cardboard, or sherry. Some might cause increases in these other flavors that take a beer out of balance before ultimately becoming dull, stale, and old-tasting.

To control, avoid introducing oxygen into the beer during the second half of fermentation or later. Don't let airlocks run dry. Don't splash the beer when racking or bottling; blanket the beer with carbon dioxide after racking. Check bottle caps and keg seals for good fit. Use oxygen-scavenging caps. Purge bottles and kegs with CO_2 prior to filling. Bottle-condition beer; yeast will take up oxygen. Store beer cold to slow the rate of oxidation (and other chemical reactions). Drink beer when fresh.

Plastic (phenolic). Perceived as the flavor and aroma of adhesive bandages, electrical tape, or styrene plastic. Typically caused by a wild yeast infection but also can be produced by some yeast strains when fermented at very high temperatures.

Follow proper sanitary practices, avoiding infection by wild yeast. Use a different yeast strain or form. I've had off-flavors from some older dry yeast products. Make sure your yeast is healthy and active, and follow good fermentation practices. Avoid a long lag time at the start of fermentation. Reduce fermentation temperatures.

Solvent/fusel. Perceived as a hot burning sensation on the palate, and an alcoholic, spicy, hot, vinous, and solventlike aroma and flavor. Can cause headaches, especially in the temples. Fusel alcohols are fermentation-derived.

Ethanol is relatively tasteless. Fusel alcohols (or higher alcohols) are more aromatic than ethanol. In general, conditions that promote rapid yeast growth can foster fusel alcohol production. Fusels are produced when yeast growth stimulators create demands for amino acids beyond the quantity of amino acids in the wort.

Factors that favor increased fusel alcohol production include increased dissolved oxygen, stirring/convection currents (using tall fermenters), high fermentation temperature, high-gravity wort (greater than 13 °P, 1.052), low pitching rate, low-pressure fermentation, and yeast strain (certain strains, especially ale strains, produce more fusel alcohols).

If performing a higher-gravity or warmer fermentation, increasing pressure in the fermenter can inhibit fusel alcohol production (as well as esters). To control, take steps to reduce the rate of yeast growth. Lower fermentation temperature or use a different yeast strains. Using glucose adjuncts (no nitrogen) increases fusel production (hello, malt liquor). Follow proper sanitation practices, since infections can also cause fusels to be produced.

Sour/acidic. One of the five basic tastes, it can also be perceived as an aroma and a mouthfeel. Different acids have different aromas and flavors and a different overall balance. Lactic acid can have a clean sourness, citric acid a sharp sourness, and acetic acid a harsh, vinegary sourness (see Vinegary for a description).

Follow proper sanitation practices to reduce the chance for infection. Check your equipment for nicks or scratches that can harbor bacteria. If you make *lambics* or otherwise intentionally use acid-producing bacteria, segregate your equipment. Select a different yeast strain. Don't mash for long periods of time at low temperatures (this is called a *sour mash*).

Smoky (phenolic). Perceived as a smokelike, charcoal, or burnt flavor and aroma. Can be caused by infections or by ingredients or processes that involved burning.

Follow proper sanitation practices to avoid infection. Select a yeast strain that produces fewer phenols. Adjust the fermentation temperature of your yeast (either up or down, depending on the strain). Check for a scorched mash or boil; clean equipment of residue from previous batches, stir decoctions constantly, control heat applied to kettles and tuns. Reduce the use of dark malts or *rauchmalz*.

Spicy (phenolic). Perceived as the flavor and aroma of spices, such as clove, pepper, vanilla, etc. These are often positive phenols, and are produced by yeast or are derived from ingredients or processes.

Certain yeast strains and hop varieties can produce spicy characteristics, such as clove and pepper. Adjust fermentation temperature (sometimes higher, sometimes lower, depending on yeast strain and beer style). Oak aging can increase the vanilla character in beer.

Sulfury. Perceived as the flavor and aroma of rotten eggs or burning matches. Sulfur dioxide (SO_2) is the striking match aroma and flavor. It's a common feature of many European lagers and has antioxidant and antimicrobial properties. Sulfur dioxide can reduce acetaldehyde production during storage. Winemakers often add sulfites for these positive purposes. Hydrogen sulfide (H_2S) is the rotten-egg aroma and flavor, which comes from fermentation. Unhealthy yeast or nutrient deficiency can cause increased H_2S levels. It is easily volatilized.

Lower SO_2 with warmer conditioning and storage, increased lagering times, and reducing head pressure during lagering. Reduce its formation during fermentation by increasing yeast nutrients in wort, increasing lipids, increasing aeration, having healthy, active yeast, and removing hot and cold break and trub.

Reduce H_2S by increasing lagering temperatures and fermenter height to cause it to be blown off faster. It can also be caused by an infection, so follow proper sanitation practices.

Sulfates in the water, or sulfate additions (Burton water salts, gypsum) can cause the flavor and aroma of sulfur. Some yeast strains produce more sulfur than others (typically lager strains), so choosing another yeast can be a control. Some copper in the boil can help take sulfur out of beer; simply having some copper equipment in contact with the wort during the boil is sufficient. I know some brewers who throw a small copper plate into the wort to achieve this effect; my false bottom is copper, so I naturally have this on my system. Note, however, that adding copper to finished beer is a mistake that can negatively impact its flavor and appearance.

Vegetal. Perceived as the flavor and aroma of cooked, canned, or rotten vegetables (cabbage, celery, onion, asparagus, parsnip). Can be caused by DMS (see DMS), an infection by wort spoilage bacteria, or oxidation of ingredients.

Encourage a fast, vigorous fermentation (use a healthy, active starter to reduce lag time; this is often due to bacterial contamination of wort before yeast becomes established). Follow proper sanitation practices. Check for aged, stale, or old ingredients (especially old liquid malt extract, which I perceive as a tangy vegetal flavor). Avoid oversparging at low temperatures.

Vinegary. Caused by acetic acid and perceived as vinegarlike sourness in the flavor and aroma. *Acetobacter* infection is the cause, but oxygen is necessary for vinegar to be produced, since the bacteria is aerobic.

Control sources of *acetobacter* and avoid oxygen uptake. Follow proper sanitation practices. Check your equipment for nicks or scratches that can harbor bacteria. If you make *lambics* or otherwise intentionally use acid-producing bacteria, segregate your equipment. Select a different yeast strain. Avoid using barrels or putting wood in your beer.

Yeasty. Perceived as a bready, sulfury, yeastlike, or glutamate flavor and, to a lesser extent, aroma. Some of these flavors are due to young, fresh yeast still in the beer, while others are caused by too long a contact with the yeast.

Young yeast character can be controlled by using a more flocculent yeast strain, allowing yeast sufficient time to flocculate, filtering the beer or using clarifying agents, and avoiding carrying over as much yeast during transfers. Aging the beer longer can also reduce the fresh yeast character.

Autolysis is a character that can come from beer being held on the yeast too long at too warm a temperature. I perceive it as an umami or glutamate flavor (like MSG). Glutamates can remind people of soy sauce, mushrooms, Parmesan cheese, or other similarly strongly flavored foods. Despite being termed "savoryness," it's not a desirable flavor in beer. I've heard it described as "rubbery"; I don't perceive it that way at all. When a beer develops autolysis character, its pH rises after fermentation has completed; that's one confirmation that it's present.

To control autolysis, rack your fermented beer off the yeast as soon as the yeast has reduced the green fermentation flavors. Don't store your beer on the yeast for a long time, particularly at warmer temperatures. If it needs additional conditioning, rack to a secondary fermenter to reduce the quantity of yeast in contact with the beer.

For the longest time, I thought autolysis was a myth, since I never tasted a rubbery flavor in beer. However, once Gary Spedding taught me that it was a glutamate flavor, I could then taste it in several beers (even a few of my own, unfortunately). It caused me to rethink my conditioning practices.

Style-Related Faults

A beer can have no obvious technical flaws yet still not seem right. When this is the case, it is often a *style-related fault*—that is, one that has to do with the balance and drinkability of the beer, or how the beer compares subjectively against commercial examples, reference style guidelines, or simply the taster's own expectations. These faults are often more difficult to identify and isolate, since they are necessarily based on a subjective assessment by a taster and are based on a comparison with a possibly arbitrary standard.

Let's set aside any argument about beer styles; those are covered in Chapter 5. Assume the brewer accepts the reference style description, and that the beer has a noticeable difference when compared against the standard. Style knowledge and structured tasting skills are necessary to isolate and describe the problem in relation to the reference beer style description.

Style-related faults can often be traced back to recipe formulation, ingredient selection, or process selection. Correcting these faults may involve some of the same corrections as would be used to address technical faults.

Low Gravity

A beer with a lower starting gravity than expected will often have the wrong malt-to-hop balance, with the bitterness seeming high. For stronger beers that have noticeable alcohol, lower gravity will make the beer seem more mundane. Lower gravity beers might also seem watery or lacking malt presence.

Gravity-related issues are usually traceable to poor efficiency or improper measurement of boil volumes. Start by checking the malt; is it slack (damp) or does it have any insect damage? Those can reduce the potential extract. Then check the crush of the grain; you're looking for intact husks but flour the size of coarsely ground black pepper. A finer crush will convert faster and give a higher efficiency and vice versa; make sure you are leaving enough time for full conversion (do a starch test if unsure). Doughing-in (hydrating your malt before raising it to a mash temperature) can also improve efficiency. Stirring the mash improves efficiency.

Checking the mash chemistry is next on the list. Did you supply sufficient calcium? Did the mash pH settle in the 5.2 to 5.5 range? Consider step mashing to improve efficiency. Make sure your measuring tools (thermometer, pH meter, hydrometer) are calibrated. Add a mash-out step to increase efficiency. Cut a checkerboard pattern into your mash with a long, thin spatula prior to sparging. Slow the lauter flow and sparge longer.

Measure your starting volume and gravity accurately before beginning the boil. Use a calibrated measuring stick for your system. Determine your final boil volume to hit the target gravity before beginning the boil. If your volume is correct but the gravity is low, add more fermentables (malt extract or sugary adjuncts) to the boil. If your volume is low but the gravity is correct, shorten the boil. If your volume is low but the gravity is high, dilute the wort with water. Based on your system's evaporation rate, decide on the length of the boil to hit the target volume. It's much easier to correct these issues before the boil. Remember that you can adjust several variables (boil length, starting volume, starting gravity) to achieve the target result.

Incorrect Attenuation

Attenuation affects how dry or sweet a beer tastes and, to a lesser extent, the amount of body present. Errors in attenuation can greatly impact the balance, drinkability, and style fidelity of a beer. Dryness accentuates bitterness, and sweetness masks bitterness, so a change in attenuation will alter the impression of bitterness even if the measured IBUs are the same.

Attenuation is driven more by wort composition than yeast strain, so first look to your grain selections and your mashing techniques. Yeast strain can play a secondary role, but most yeast will fully attenuate given the proper conditions. Less flocculent yeast strains and longer conditioning times can improve attenuation.

Try to determine the composition of the extract remaining in the beer. Does it have a malty or sugary sweetness, or is it dry? Sugary sweetness indicates unfermented sugars remain, while a dry beer suggests that dextrins are the cause. Sugary sweetness can be reduced by encouraging continued fermentation, while dextrins remain unfermentable by traditional beer yeast.

Dextrins can add body and raise finishing gravity but not add sweetness. The sweetness often clashes with bitterness, so aim for dextrins for body, not residual unfermented sugars. Too many dextrins make the body full and can hurt drinkability. Certain styles need some residual sweetness, but many are fully fermented.

If you did not get the attenuation you desired, lower your primary saccharification temperature or use a step mash. Adding sugar will increase the attenuation. Starting with a lower starting gravity will result in a lower finishing gravity, which may make the beer seem drier (and hence more attenuated) even if the degree of attenuation is the same.

If your beer attenuated too much, take the opposite steps. Mash higher, remove sugars from the recipe, increase the starting gravity, use more crystal malts, add starchy adjuncts, use dextrin malts, and shorten conditioning times.

Boil-related Issues

The length of the boil can affect several factors in beer. If Pilsner malt or other malt with a significant amount of SMM is used, then a 90-minute boil should be used to reduce the DMS in the finished beer.

The strength of the boil affects the evaporation rate and the final volume. If the final volume target is missed, the original gravity and the BU:GU ratio are likely to be off, which will change the balance of the beer.

Long boils (more than 90 minutes) can extract more harshness from hops, in addition to more bitterness. If you use a long boil, don't add the hops until the last 90 minutes or less. Long boils also can increase the color of the wort and add caramelized flavors; this is desirable in some styles, but not others. Don't use a long boil unless you are looking for these side effects.

Harshness

Harshness is a common problem with beers that use a lot of hops. In my experience, hop-derived harshness comes from four factors: the quantity of hops used, the amount of time the hops are boiled, the water chemistry, and the chemical makeup of the hop varieties used. The more hops you use and the longer they are boiled, the harsher your beer can be. Large amounts of hops can give vegetal flavors, and long boils can extract harsh compounds. Brew water with a high pH, high carbonates, or high sulfate content can lead to harshness in a pale, hoppy beer. Hops with low cohumulone (check the varieties against data from places like HopUnion, "low" is under 30 percent) are known to have a smoother flavor.

All-late hopping can reduce harshness. Avoid post-fermentation oxygen pickup, since oxidized hops can give a harsh bitterness. Sulfates accentuate bitterness but can lead to harshness (particularly if used with noble hops). Using lesser amounts of high alpha hops can cut the harshness by reducing the vegetal mass. Certain hops (such as Magnum) are prized for their clean bitterness without harshness.

Dark grains can also cause harshness when used in long mashes and boils. Using cold-steeped dark grains can reduce this, as can adding the dark grains only at mash-out.

Excessive alcohol can cause harshness. Reducing the gravity of the beer, and hence the alcohol level, can help, as can cellaring the beer for extended times to smooth out the alcohol that is present.

Aftertaste Issues

The aftertaste of beer is particularly important, since that's the flavor left in the taster's mouth after the beer has been tasted; it's the lasting impression. Some of the issues previously discussed (harshness, attenuation) affect the aftertaste, but there are other potential problem areas as well.

A muddy, dull, or indistinct aftertaste can sometimes by caused by using too many ingredients (flavor clashes), using old or lower-quality ingredients, or by having a high pH (above 4.5).

Lingering grassy and vegetal flavors could come from dry hopping. Try adding hops at knockout, in the whirlpool, or in a hopback to reduce the raw character, or reduce the length of time dry hops are used to less than a week.

If the aftertaste doesn't seem dry enough, the problem might not be attenuation alone. It could be the pH is too high, or that not enough sulfates were used. Some styles, such as Irish and Scottish ales, use a little bit of roasted barley to add dryness to the finish.

The relationship between attenuation, dryness/sweetness, and bitterness affects the overall balance and drinkability of the beer. Bitterness and sweetness give a bittersweet flavor, which tends to linger. Excessive sweetness in the finish makes a beer difficult to drink, as does a full body. The lack of a crisp finish tends to make beers more suitable to sipping than drinking.

Clarity

A cloudy or hazy beer can be off-putting and can even affect body and flavor. First try to determine the source of the haze: starches, sugars, yeast, or proteins/tannins. Starch haze usually indicates a mashing problem. Sugar haze usually is due to an incomplete fermentation. Yeast haze is a flocculation problem. Proteins and tannins are usually caused by not having a good hot and cold break or by carrying over excessive break material to the fermenter.

Clarifying is discussed in more detail in Chapter 8, but keep in mind that avoiding cloudiness is preferred to removing it later. Adopt proper brewing practices to convert starches fully, have a good hot break and cold break, fully ferment the sugars, and to have the yeast settle properly. Finings can be used in the boil or after fermentation is complete. Cold temperatures and time tend to improve clarity as the particulates flocculate. Filtering is a rougher way of removing haze-causing particles. Removing haze becomes more difficult once the beer is carbonated, so it's best to handle clarity issues prior to packaging.

CHAPTER 8
finishing beer

All's well that ends.
– Unknown origin

Once you have brewed your beer and fermentation is complete, what's next? Welcome to the realm of the *cold side* of brewing, where your fermented beer becomes something that you will serve. The major goals of this phase are to mature the flavors, clarify the beer, and achieve stability. It includes conditioning, possibly lagering, clarifying, carbonating, and packaging. You have different concerns than you don't on the hot side of brewing, mostly avoiding ruining your beer by oxidizing it or allowing it to become infected.

This chapter discusses general tips and process control points for getting your finished beer into peak serving condition and keeping it that way. If it isn't exactly what you intended, I'll talk about methods of adjusting and blending to change the character or to compensate for earlier problems. These techniques can also help maintain your beer for longer periods of time.

Factors Affecting Beer Stability

The most important steps you can take to preserve the character of the beer for as long as possible are to avoid introducing oxygen post-fermentation and store the beer at cold temperatures. Avoiding frequent large swings in temperature, keeping the beer stored in a dark place, and keeping it from excessive physical handling (shaking, vibration) also have smaller, beneficial effects on beer stability.

Oxygen can ruin your beer—period. Once oxidized, there is nothing you can do to fix it. So you must avoid it at all costs. Some darker beers with natural antioxidants can take some oxidation and produce desirable dark fruit and sherry flavors. Likewise, sour beers can develop more fruitiness, which is also desirable. However, most beers will simply become dull, stale, tasteless, and eventually papery, harsh, and sour. Paler and lighter beers are less stable than darker and stronger beers; antioxidants help preserve them as they do red wines, which age and store better than white wines.

Low temperatures reduce the rate of chemical reactions (like oxidation) by two to three times for every 10° C (18° F) cooler a beer is stored. So a beer at 0° C (32° F) can be held two or three times longer than a beer at 10° C (50° F). The effect multiplies, so there is a huge difference between storing at near freezing and storing in a hot garage that might get to 40° C (104° F). Warmer temperatures can help a beer naturally carbonate and help it finish conditioning, but it can also cause it to go off quickly unless care is taken with cold-side handling and packaging.

Yeast can help limit the impact of oxidation; they take up any oxygen present at pitching. Sulfites and antioxidants are often used in winemaking, in which the yeast has been mostly separated. These might work for beer, but I worry about adding flavors or other side effects. Better methods exist, such as purging storage vessels with CO_2 or nitrogen to displace any oxygen. Keeping the beer on yeast (bottle conditioning) helps stabilize it, as long as it's not stored too warm.

We've been talking about cold-side problems, but many brewers are concerned with hot-side aeration (HSA) causing a decrease in stability and shelf life. While this condition is possible, and oxygen should generally be avoided in all phases of brewing except immediately before pitching yeast, I think the impact of HSA is overstated. It's much more important to avoid introducing oxygen after fermentation; this is where the more immediate damage is done, so focus on that aspect first. I talked earlier about not wasting effort on areas of low return when more important issues remain. Only tackle HSA if you have good packing and storage procedures, and then only if you notice problems. Yes, when possible, avoid oxygen on the hot side, but don't obsess about it.

Lower pH helps keep a beer from becoming infected. Commercial brewers generally test their beer to ensure it is at pH 4.5 or less. The lower the pH, the more microbiologically stable the beer will be. However, flavor stability (and flavor quality) tend to suffer as the pH drops. A tradeoff between flavor and microbiological stability exists concerning final pH. I tend to favor flavor stability and use other techniques to avoid infections. I like to keep beer in the 4.3 to 4.5 range for best flavor, although this does vary by beer style.

Conditioning

Conditioning is the phase of brewing immediately following fermentation, during which green beer flavors are reduced and the beer becomes ready for consumption. Several other steps, such as clarification, stabilization, and natural carbonation can take place during conditioning, but I'm going to treat those as separate topics.

Homebrewers often refer to this phase as secondary fermentation, which is really a misnomer. A secondary fermenter is essentially what breweries call a conditioning tank or a bright tank. Professional breweries tend to keep their beer in the fermenter for short periods of time, so moving the beer off quickly gives them the ability to use the fermenter again. In this case, the secondary is important for clarification and for maturing the flavor of the beer (reducing acetaldehyde, diacetyl, and other green beer flavors that can result from premature separation from the yeast).

Homebrewers typically leave their beer in the primary fermenter longer, waiting until the yeast drops out. In that case, the primary fermenter has also acted as the secondary, so a secondary fermentation is likely unnecessary. If your beer does not have green beer flavors, you can proceed to packaging.

Secondary fermenters also allow the homebrewer to continue to manipulate the beer without risking autolysis or off-flavors from the yeast and trub in the primary. For example, dry hopping, oaking, adding fruits and spices, or other flavor alterations can take place in the secondary. A secondary also can be used as a holding area for beer awaiting packaging (for example, if not enough bottles or kegs were clean and available); in this case, the beer is bulk aging.

You can condition the beer in a carboy or a keg, depending on whether you want to observe the clarity or not. To transfer it to a secondary, purge the receiving container with CO_2 first, then rack gently from the primary fermenter, leaving all trub and yeast behind. You can observe the clarity of the beer in the racking tube and stop transferring when you notice an increase in haze or suspended particulates.

Fermented beer doesn't have to be immediately racked from the primary; it can condition for a few weeks, as long as the ambient temperature isn't too warm. It's acting sort of like a big bottle-conditioned beer at this point. However, if this were to continue for an extended period of time, or if the temperature got warmer, autolysis could result. The larger the yeast mass, the more likely the problem (so beware of long primaries with repitched yeast). Autolysis has a glutamate, umami flavor, and it can ruin the flavor profile of your beer.

Fermentation's completion is your first chance to do some quality control based on the flavor of the finished beer, and to decide if you need to do additional work. Smell and taste beer before racking from the yeast to determine if it should condition longer (look for diacetyl and acetaldehyde; if they're present, it's too soon to rack). Don't separate from the yeast if you still need the yeast to do something. Taste for development of autolysis flavors (which indicate the beer has been on the yeast too long). Taste for other things that can be fixed (like dry hopping to increase hop aroma). Check the gravity to make sure it's done. Look for beer to drop bright. Obviously check for off-flavors that can't be fixed, such as infection, papery oxidation, chlorophenols, etc.

If you are going to fine the beer to clarify it before packaging (especially kegging), then a secondary makes sense. If you are going to prime and carbonate the beer at the same time you want to clarify it, you can add finings and priming sugar at the same time (this is the traditional method for English cask ales where isinglass is added). I keg my beers, so I usually just bulk age them in carboys until they're fairly bright and then keg. I like my house beers to be unfiltered since a little yeast in the keg adds to stability and scavenges oxygen. The yeast and any remaining trub that settles out typically can get pushed out of the keg with the first pour. If I know I'm going to be moving the keg and then serving, I'll filter or fine the beer so it doesn't look murky.

Lagering

Lagering is a traditional brewing technique for mellowing flavors and cold conditioning beers, reducing green beer flavors like acetaldehyde, hydrogen sulfide, and diacetyl. It is conducted cold, generally near freezing, and generally using yeast suited for this treatment (lager yeast). Other beer styles like *altbier* and *Kölsch* can be cold conditioned, which is similar to lagering and achieves similar results. Beer flavors mellow, final attenuation is reached, and the yeast settle out. Lager beer can be fined or filtered during this period for best clarity.

Watch for esters, sulfur, and diacetyl as clues as to whether you're done lagering; these qualities should be reduced below threshold. When the beer is right, try to stabilize it (rack, chill, and package). Even if you do perform a secondary fermentation, there is typically plenty of yeast present to condition the beer and reduce green fermentation flavors.

Traditional German brewing methods, as described by Kunze in *Technology Brewing and Malting*, recommend one week of lagering for each degree Plato of original extract. For best results, reduce the temperature slowly from fermentation temperature to lagering temperature (a few degrees a day). You're trying to avoid stunning the yeast and causing them to drop out early. Lagering does not start with crash cooling! Using a refrigerator or freezer with an adjustable temperature control makes this task much simpler.

Clarifying

Clarification can take place in the primary fermenter, or while the beer is conditioning or lagering. Longer conditioning times at lower temperatures can aid sedimentation of yeast, which improves clarity. Fining agents or mechanical means can also be used to clarify the beer. Many brewers prefer to serve their beer unfiltered and may choose particularly flocculent yeast strains to aid in this presentation. Carbonation should be done after clarification, since the carbonation can interfere with the beer dropping bright and with filtering.

A simple way to clarify beer is to keg it, crash cool it (take it from a warm room and store it near freezing), and leave it alone for several weeks to allow particles to settle out naturally. I pour beer until it starts pouring bright, then I jumper the keg to another sanitized and purged keg (connecting beer out to beer out) using a clear hose. I then push the beer from the original keg to the target keg, watching the clarity in the clear hose as I transfer. I'll often use a flashlight to backlight it. I'll stop transferring at the moment when haze starts to show up, and the target keg will usually be very clear. This process can also be used when fining in the keg and when transferring finished beer when making *eisbock* or another partially frozen beer. I also use this technique when transporting a keg to a party, so I don't wind up with cloudy beer.

If a more aggressive approach is needed, fining agents can be used. There are several types, depending on the type of particles that are to be removed (yeast, proteins, or tannins). The traditional technique for removing yeast from ales is isinglass; gelatin is most often used for lagers, since it works at cooler temperatures. Isinglass is traditionally added to cask ales to help flocculate the yeast in the cask.

Biofine Clear is a silicate-based liquid; add it to the beer as you rack it to the secondary. Polyclar (PVPP) removes tannins from beer; use it the same way. You can also use mead fining agents, such as Sparkolloid, Super-Kleer K.C. (two-stage liquid fining, containing kieselsol and chitosan, which are also available separately), and bentonite.

I like to fine rather than filter, since filtering seems like a very mechanically abusive way to treat your beer. There is a lot of setup when filtering, and it can strip out desirable elements, such as body, color, and flavor. I try to use good brewing practices to make clear beer and only clarify something that is competition-class. Time and gravity assist clarifying agents, but often so does cold; chilling to near-freezing can often help filtering agents to settle more readily. I'm looking for them to pack down, so I have as little loss as possible. Some are more "fluffy" than others (Sparkolloid is notorious for this) and take more time to settle out (and also rouse more easily). Be gentle and use good racking practices to avoid picking up any particulates. You will have some volume loss with any of these approaches, so be mentally prepared for that. Do not use excessive amounts of finings, either; they can also strip desirable elements from beer if overdone.

I've used a lot of clarifying methods over the years. Today I mostly let nature take its course and naturally clarify. I'll do the jumper-two-kegs trick and watch for clarity as I rack. Do this after the beer has been sitting for a while in very cold temperatures and without jostling the kegs much. That's good enough for most beers. For pale beers, especially ones where clarity matters (like *Kölsch*) or where I'm using a more powdery yeast, I tend to use Biofine Clear or Super-Kleer K.C. As a last resort, I'll use a coarse plate filter. I'll try to use gelatin on lagers when they're almost done lagering, but I often forget this step and then use these other ones. Isinglass is useful when I'm making cask ales, but more often than not, I'll just use the Fuller's strain (Wyeast 1968, White Labs WLP002), which is the most flocculent yeast I've ever seen. Just chill it below 65° F (18° C) and it drops out quickly.

Stabilizing

Stabilizing refers to removing proteins and tannins that can combine to form hazes that shorten the shelf life of beer. Much of the work in stabilizing beer happens before fermentation, including following proper brewing practices (milling grain properly, getting a good hot break, racking off the break material, not carrying over trub). Copper finings (clarifying agents added to the kettle) can enhance protein and tannin removal; use additives such as Irish moss, Whirlfloc, or Breakbright.

Post-fermentation, fining agents such as silica gel and Polyclar can help remove protein-tannin complexes. Super-Kleer K.C. also is quite effective in this role. Filtering while chill haze is present is the final method, although this can also strip desired flavors and body from the beer.

If you follow good brewing practices and use copper finings, you are less likely to have chill haze. If you don't have the problem, then don't try to correct it. If you use fining agents post-fermentation, be sure to rack off them before packaging.

Carbonating and Packaging

I'm discussing these topics together, since they are closely related. In general, you can either bottle or keg your beer. If you keg it, you can subsequently choose to bottle it or to remove larger portions for sampling (serving into growlers, soda bottles, etc.). Depending on the choices you made previously, some carbonation options might not be available.

If you are going to bottle the beer, you should make any final adjustments and do whatever blending you might think is necessary (see the next section for more details). If you keg it, you can defer these adjustments until you are going to bottle or serve.

I mostly keg all my beer, because of the convenience, simplicity, and time savings when compared to bottling. I'll still bottle condition some beers when I think it will make a difference. For example, Trappist-style Belgian ales have more authentic character when bottle conditioned (it's actually a requirement for true Trappist beers; the Belgians call it "refermented in the bottle"). For big beers that I intend to save for a long time, I may bottle condition, as well. The yeast in the bottle adds to stability, and I also find the carbonation to have a finer texture.

I'm assuming you all know how to **bottle** beer; it's a basic step. Rack beer from the fermenter into a bottling bucket, add priming sugar, and then siphon into bottles. Cap, and let naturally carbonate at room temperature for a week or two, then chill to serving temperature. It takes me about two hours to bottle five gallons of beer, so I prefer kegging (which takes about 10 minutes).

Priming sugar is normally corn sugar, but any sugary fermentable can work (brown sugar, dried malt extract, honey, Lyle's Golden Syrup, etc.). Corn sugar ferments quickly and leaves little residual character, so it's the top choice. If you want to add additional flavors to the finished beer, this could be a method. *De Dolle Stille Nacht* is primed with honey, for instance. I've primed with molasses, brown sugar, invert sugar, and honey on occasion, but since I've switched over to kegging, I normally use those only as adjuncts.

Using a **keg** to package and condition your beer is what most advanced homebrewers do. When your beer has dropped bright, simply rack it into a sanitized and purged keg, pressurize with CO_2, chill overnight, and then force carbonate. I force carbonate by hooking a chilled keg to CO_2 at about 30 psi, then gently rocking the keg back and forth (I hold it by either end and rock it, listening for the gas to bubble in). I probably rock it 50 or so times, then put it back in the refrigerator to cool. I leave it alone for several days before venting the excess pressure and sampling it. If the keg is overpressurized, I'll attach a pressure-relief valve to the gas-out stem. If the keg is underpressurized, I'll repeat the carbonation process. I tend to keep my kegs slightly overcarbonated, since it makes it easier to maintain carbonation if I transfer to bottles or growlers.

If you keg your beer, you can also go for natural carbonation by priming the keg as you would a bottled beer. You will wind up with more sediment in the keg, but if you prefer the more natural approach, this one will work. You can then leave the beer in a keg for serving, or do something else with it, like rack it to a second keg to keep it clear, bottle it, or transfer it to a cask.

You can bottle your beer from a keg. This approach differs from bottle conditioning in that the beer is already carbonated and bright when put into the bottle. This is how most commercial breweries bottle their beer. The beer can have less of a shelf life than bottle-conditioned beer, so it's very important to avoid oxygen pickup and to store the beer very cold. You can use a counter-pressure filler or (my favorite) the Blichmann BeerGun to bottle from a keg. I use this method when I want to have archive-quality beers for later competition use, or if I need to bottle off a keg in order to have the keg available for a new batch.

More frequently, I'll transfer beer from a keg to a growler or two-liter soda bottle for transport. I vent the keg pressure, then serve, using a keg faucet. I'll put a carbonator cap onto the soda bottle if it needs to have some additional pressure. I sometimes put a hose on the keg faucet to fill the bottles from the bottom and cause less foaming. The same approach works with a cobra (picnic) tap, but I like the keg faucets because of their larger diameter.

Kräusening is a traditional German method for conditioning and carbonating beer. It involves adding actively fermenting beer to the fermented beer. It can be done before or after lagering, depending on whether it is meant to help with flavor maturation or just carbonation. I've never used this approach, since I don't care about complying with the Reinheitsgebot, I don't want additional yeast to remove, and I can prime and carbonate in other ways. Germans might also prime with unfermented wort (spiese) as an alternative to kräusening. If you use the same wort as the finished beer, an advantage to both approaches is that you aren't diluting the flavor or changing the finished profile of the beer. The fresh yeast can reduce green beer flavors, if those are present. But it's a more complex method; you have to save wort from your original brew (or make another batch) and essentially make a starter. It's also harder to calculate the amount to add when compared to simply priming. Again, this is too much trouble for me on a regular basis, but I might consider it as a solution to a finished beer that still is showing a green beer character.

Cask conditioning is another option for packaging your beer. There are two ways to do it, depending on how soon you are serving the beer and on how authentic you wish to be. The phony way is to condition and carbonate the beer in a keg, transferring it to the cask only for serving. Advantages to this approach are that you can have it ready on demand, you can move the cask around at will, and you don't have to adjust the carbonation level to serve. The CAMRA people are probably reaching for their torches and pitchforks right about now, so let me tell you the real way to do it.

After the beer has finished fermenting but before it has been conditioned, rack it into a sanitized, purged cask. How you treat the beer depends mostly on its condition entering the cask. If the beer is at terminal gravity, then it must be primed; this can be skipped if the beer still has fermentable extract remaining. If the beer has not dropped bright, it should be fined (although you might skip this if you used a very flocculent yeast strain). If you want additional late hop character, you can dry hop it as well (hop plugs are designed for this purpose).

Fining and carbonation work at cross purposes, so you may wish to allow the beer to carbonate and then fine later, or you may wish to allow the beer to drop bright and then prime it. The former is probably more traditional, but I like the convenience of the latter. Isinglass is the traditional fining agent in cask ales. Priming can use any sugar source, but corn sugar is the easiest to use.

Once the cask is sealed, condition at fermentation temperatures to allow carbonation to develop. Transfer to cellar temperatures afterward to condition and mature. If you do fine the cask, avoid moving it too much afterward. Finings are less effective the more times they have to clear the beer. Too many times I see cask beer mishandled in the United States; bars often move casks around daily to serve, or leave them on the bar at room temperature. Both practices abuse the beer. The same occurs when transporting casks to festivals, where they are set up on the day of service. If you're not going to handle the casks properly, use the phony cask method. Real cask beer is best served from the cellar, after it has been rested.

If you're going to use casks at the homebrew scale, the pin cask is the easiest size to use, since the volume is similar to a 5-gallon Corny keg. A firkin cask is twice as large but normally is a better price per volume. You'll just need help moving it. Modern casks are normally made of stainless steel, not wood. A variety of parts and supplies are needed, all with unusual names (shives, spiles, bungs, and keystones). They are basically the plugs and fittings used to seal the cask and to manage the gas coming in and out of a vented cask. Taps allow the beer to be served (either via gravity or with an external beer engine). A cask breather can help preserve the beer if it isn't going to be consumed in a few days; it provides a blanket of CO_2 at atmospheric pressure to keep the beer from spoiling. U.K. Brewing Supplies (*www.ukbrewing.com*) is my favorite supplier for all things cask-related.

Barrel aging is an option for maturing beer. Storing in an oak barrel, or a barrel that has been previously used to age wine or spirits, is a growing trend. I'm not going to discuss this method, other than to note it as an option. Reread the introduction if you want to know why.

Final Adjustments

A good chef always tastes each dish before it leaves the kitchen. If something is wrong (such as, it is underseasoned), does (s)he send it? No, (s)he fixes it. Does (s)he throw it out? Not unless it is unrecoverable (burned, for instance)—that would be wasteful. The same lesson applies to brewing. Yes, it's always best to make beer exactly as you intended, but do you always achieve that goal? If not, do you dump the batch and start over? You shouldn't. You also shouldn't have to accept mediocrity and drink it, either. You should instead learn how to fix it.

If you know how to taste your beer critically (skills we discussed in Chapter 5), then you should be able to identify correctable deficiencies. Obviously, the first step is to quickly sample the beer to triage it—is it ready to serve, is it fatally flawed, or can it be fixed? The first two choices have clear consequences (serve it or dump it); the third alternative is what we consider in the remainder of this section.

Using structured tasting, evaluate your beer and identify all technical and style flaws. Quantify the magnitude of each problem, and prioritize them—which are most severe, and which, if fixed would make the beer significantly better? Use the troubleshooting information from Chapter 6 to help identify potential causes and to understand if certain solutions can be applied once the beer has been made. Most balance issues can be corrected, as well as some minor technical errors. Some errors can be covered up or made less noticeable, which will improve the perception of the beer.

So what errors are fatal? I would dump a batch that had any of these faults in noticeable quantity: infection, chlorophenolic (medicinal), light-struck (skunky), metallic, oxidized (papery type), phenolic (some types), burned/scorched, autolyzed, or vegetal. One surprising fault I wouldn't immediately dump is vinegary. Depending on the base style, it could develop into something interesting. I actually medaled in the first round of the National Homebrew Competition in 2010 with an old *doppelbock* that had developed an acetic infection; I entered it as a Flanders Brown, and it was fairly close for the style.

In a pinch, you could adjust a beer to mask some off-flavors, but that's not really desirable. I remember the commemorative beer for the Chicago National Homebrew Conference, a bourbon barrel imperial stout that had developed a lactic infection. It was dosed with calcium carbonate, lactose, and vanilla to try to neutralize acidity, balance it with sweetness, and cover it up with flavor. This was better than dumping a 53-gallon batch, but the result was certainly not going to be an award winner.

Some other faults can sometimes be fixed with additional work. Acetaldehyde, diacetyl, and esters can sometimes be cleaned up with additional fermentation. Kräusening is a faster way than simply repitching yeast; the active fermentation and unfermented sugars to sustain the fermentation gives fresh yeast a chance to clean up those problems. For problems related to tannins, like astringency, harshness, and grassy qualities, I would try fining the beer with Polyclar. Just be sure to rack afterward, because it's not food-safe.

Some faults can smooth out with age, such as alcohol heat and sulfury and yeasty flavors. Some faults can change (and possibly improve) with age if they oxidize, such as esters, fusels, and sourness. Other faults that are more style- or balance-related (low hops, low bitterness, too sweet, etc.) can often be adjusted either directly or balanced or covered with blending. Recognizing when to start over and what can be saved is something of a skill and can be improved with practice and experience.

If your beer is packaged in a keg, it is easier to adjust. You can often make the adjustments directly in the keg (usually after you have tried them on a smaller scale). If you need to adjust bottled beer (say, for a competition), you can decant the bottles into a two-liter soda bottle, make adjustments there, and rebottle. Obviously, any transfers should be done into sanitized containers, and with CO_2 displacing air from containers. The following discussions describe some last-minute adjustments you might make to your beer.

Adjusting Finished Beer pH

This is not an adjustment most brewers will make, but it can help with some specific problems. If your beer has too high a pH (above 4.5), it is more prone to infection. Proper mashing and fermentation should lower it into the correct range, but if you have fermentation problems it might not make it. Also, if your yeast autolyze, the pH can rise. Lowering the pH won't solve the flavor problems associated with these issues, but it can help the beer from becoming worse.

Most beer has a finished pH between 4.0 and 4.5, although some styles (*lambics* and other sour beers) are obviously lower. Personally, I generally like the flavor better if the pH is on the higher side (4.3 to 4.5), and I've read German textbooks that recommend the 4.2 to 4.4 range. Generally, if your beer is no higher than 4.5 and tastes good, don't worry about it.

You can test the flavor impact of pH adjustment on beer in a small glass. If you have a beer above 4.5, it will probably taste heavier, harsher, and lacking in freshness. As you lower it, the flavor will even out and taste better. As it gets below 4.0, the taste begins to thin out and starts to taste tart.

You can lower the pH using food-grade 10% phosphoric acid. It's safe to drink, since it's used in soft drinks as a flavor enhancer. Lactic acid can add off-flavors that remind some of infections. Unless your pH meter has automatic temperature compensation, raise the beer's temperature to 60° F (16° C) to make adjustments, so your meter reads accurately. Add some acid, stir, measure, taste. Repeat until it is at a level you enjoy. When in doubt, stay on the high side.

Raising pH is a little trickier due to flavors added by common chemicals and the difficulty in handling the more neutral-tasting ones. Calcium carbonate and potassium carbonate can raise the pH of an acidic solution, but only if dissolved. They can leave behind some unwanted flavors, so you may want to try either of them in a small sample and see if it is an improvement. Potassium hydroxide solution can raise the pH without adding significant flavors, but it is a powerful base and is not generally available.

Adjusting Salts for Flavor

Brewing salts can be added at any point, even after fermentation. Mash salts should primarily drive the mash pH to a proper range. Kettle salts are added primarily for flavor. If you add salts after the beer is fermented, solubility can be an issue. Food is better when seasoned while cooking rather than at the table; beer is the same way. Nevertheless, you can add calcium chloride, calcium sulfate, magnesium sulfate, and sodium chloride for flavor purposes.

I'm not a fan of excessive water adjustment, so I don't really use this method. If I add salts, I usually do it in the mash and boil. However, if you don't think the flavor profile of your beer is right, you might experiment with salts and see if it makes a difference. In general, sulfates enhance hoppy beers and chloride accentuates malty beers. Be aware of adding too much of any salt, lest your beers actually taste salty.

I've seen recommendations that lagers have no more than a 2:1 ration of chloride to sulfate, and that hoppy beers go no higher than 8 or 9 to 1 of sulfate to chloride. Your mileage may vary, as they say. Season to taste in a sample glass, and see if you sense an improvement. Stir well but avoid aerating the beer. If you make significant changes, make notes, so you can adjust the water the next time you brew.

Adjusting Color

If you need to add a dark color and smooth roasty flavor without bitterness or harshness, you can use Weyermann SINAMAR, which is essentially liquid Carafa Special II extract. It's packaged sterile, so you don't need to boil it if you just open it and use it. If it is opened, add it to the late boil to sterilize it. Store it in the refrigerator or freezer. Experiment with different additions to see the color contributions. A very light touch of something dark often gives a reddish hue.

If your beer is too dark and you need to lighten it, you're pretty much relegated to blending (discussed later) or dilution (which rarely is worth it).

Adjusting Carbonation

If your beer is undercarbonated (and kegged), simply force carbonate it for additional time. If it is bottled or is taken from a keg for other adjustments, pour it into a two-liter soda bottle, put a carbonator cap on the bottle, chill the beer to near freezing, and shake CO_2 into it at 30 psi for 10 to 15 seconds.

If your beer is overcarbonated, keep it at room temperature and vent off pressure every hour until it's at the right level. You can gently swirl the keg or soda bottle to speed the process. If the beer is kegged and massively overcarbonated, you can take a more aggressive approach. Open the keg, insert a mix-stir on a drill, and drive out some of the carbonation (this is actually what a mix-stir is designed to do—drive carbonation from wine). Since you are doing this under the surface of the liquid, it shouldn't aerate it. Don't do it forcefully enough to form a vortex.

Adjusting Clarity

Clarification is discussed earlier in this chapter. However, if you notice that your finished beer is still hazy, or if it develops haze at a later point, you can use some mead techniques. Try fining it using Super-Kleer K.C. or Sparkolloid. These are meant for wine but work with beer, mead, and cider, as well. It's best to use these in bulk in a carboy or keg, but you can use them in smaller quantities in soda bottles, too. I've only had one occasion where one or both didn't work, and that was cleared using bentonite first, followed by Sparkolloid a few days later. These can take some time to work, although I've had them do their thing in a couple of hours. Wait for them to clear (chilling helps), and then decant off into another container. Carbonate if necessary. Note that you'll lose some beer in the transfer, so start with extra volume. You can filter the beer as a last resort, but that abuses the beer more than finings. It tends to strip flavor and color and can introduce oxygen if not done right.

Adjusting Balance

If your beer is lacking some key component, you can try blending with another homebrew. For example, if it needs more hop character, mix in a little IPA. If it needs a richer malt character, try adding some Scotch ale or *doppelbock*. If it's too sweet, blend with a drier or hoppier beer. If you brew beers that are too malty, hoppy, roasty, caramelly, or estery, don't throw them out—save them for blending. Blending two batches of the same beer can often add complexity. You often have to make multiple small-scale trials to get it right. This topic is covered in great detail in the next section.

Blending

Blending beers is a time-honored tradition vital to producing several styles of beer, most notably *lambics* of today, as well as several other fermented beverages, such as wine, Champagne, and Scotch. Guinness blends soured beer in its stout to achieve the signature "tang." Newcastle Brown Ale is a blend of a higher-gravity and a standard-strength beer. English brewers employing the parti-gyle system regularly blended their gyles to produce different beers; Fuller's still uses this method today. Historic beers were blended in the pub cellar or at time of dispense; think of stock ales, "three threads," and other stories of customer preferences driving the blending of beers. Even today, the black-and-tan is an example of a blended beer produced at the tap.

Commercial breweries often blend their products to produce consistency from batch to batch. They blend multiple batches in a single fermenter, multiple fermenters into a single aging tank, and blend aging tanks prior to packaging. The same is essentially true for wineries, which have a much larger problem with consistency of source ingredients. Wineries are concerned about lots, blocks, varieties, and vintages; they may blend to achieve consistency or to develop complexity that's impossible to achieve with a single source alone. These two reasons apply to homebrewers who blend, as well.

The American craft beer industry is currently fond of collaborative brews, where two or more breweries combine their beers to produce a joint product. This method has been employed with American and European breweries working in concert as well. Some breweries produce their beers using high-gravity brewing with subsequent dilution. Others may blend old and new beers of the same type to produce more complexity. The solera sherry tradition of repeatedly taking off a portion of an older blended batch and replacing it with a new batch has been used successfully by homebrewers.

So while many critics of the concept of blending will sniff that "blending is only used to disguise inferior batches" or "blending is cheating," it's clear that the concept of blending beverages has a long history and is considered in most fields to be an advanced topic. I wholeheartedly agree; blending is certainly more of an art than a science, and it's easier said than done.

Why Blend?

I came to learn blending not through beer but through mead. I have a long background in meadmaking and have had considerable success in that field (I won the Mazer Cup in 2002, and won several medals for meads in the National Homebrew Competition finals). My observation in working with meads is that some of the best ones are produced through blending and adjustment. A good base mead can be turned into several different styles of mead, and meads of different ages can be blended for complexity. Meads can be improved through slight adjustments to produce the desired balance. One day I thought, why not use these methods with beer?

Before we can tackle the particulars of how to blend, we first need to understand the goal. There are certainly several valid (as well as some questionable) reasons for blending. The amount of effort put into the blend, and the criteria for success, will change depending on the objective. If you're trying to win a competition, then you'll be pickier than if you're just experimenting or just want to make a weak beer drinkable.

Fixing a broken beer. Trying to correct problems through blending is a common thought among brewers, and one that is widely criticized. Truly flawed beers can rarely be fixed through blending. Some faults might be masked, or at least made less offensive. The goal is typically to make something that's drinkable so that you don't have to dump out a batch. I look at this as "last resort" blending and not something that is a serious practice. Typical approaches might include adding a new flavor to balance an off-flavor, or adding a stronger flavor that partially obscures the off-flavor. Those "fixes" might introduce problems of their own, so the judgment is always whether the cure is worse than the disease.

Making a new style. Blending beers can create brand-new styles. This could be for your own interests or for increasing the number of entries you have in a competition. You may not wish to have a full batch of a style you don't really like, but you might want to serve it at a party or enter it in a competition. Judges in competitions don't see the recipe; the beer is only judged based on what is presented. If you're blending beers to create a different style, then the style guidelines are the reference. If the blended beer is an experiment of your own creation, then your imagination is the only guide.

Extending the useful lifetime of a beer. All beers have natural lifetimes; the goal is to consume each beer at its peak flavor. The length of time of this flavor peak can vary widely. Blending is an approach that can allow beers to change but still keep them near their peak flavor. This practice extends their useful lifetime and is a technique that I sometimes use to have more beers available for competition. If you taste a beer and find it isn't as good as it once was, you might be able to correct that deficiency long enough to consume the rest of the batch.

Tweaking it for style considerations. When I blend, I mostly do it for style reasons. I'm usually trying to enter a competition or provide a beer for a festival, and I want it to match style expectations. You could also take this approach if you have a very specific expectation for your beer and want it to taste that way. You are comparing your beer against a written reference and trying to make it exemplify that description. If you are preparing it for a competition or festival, this expectation is harder to match, since it involves unknown third-party tasters. When I blend this way, I take careful notes, so I can adjust the recipe the next time the batch is brewed.

Consistency across batches. Not many homebrewers will blend for this reason, but it is a consideration for larger brewers with well-established products. Consumers will often demand that a certain beer taste a certain way; if it isn't the same as the last one, they might reject it. Homebrewers and craft brewers often embrace the variability as one of the fun aspects of brewing. Homebrewers might go this route if they are trying to recapture the flavor profile of a previous, award-winning batch, however. In all cases, an established flavor profile is needed in order to provide a target or reference standard for blending.

Complexity not possible with a single batch. This is another reason I blend. Sometimes you can't get certain flavors in a single batch. For example, I often blend an old barley wine with a new one, so that I can get that wonderful aged character but still have a splash of fresh malt and hops. Some high-gravity beers will develop certain malt flavors and esters that are difficult to mimic in a standard-strength batch; blending can take the best of both batches to produce something unique.

Experimentation with recipe formulation. Don't overlook this approach. I recommend blending to brewers who are working on a specific recipe and trying to master it. Rather than doing multiple test batches, you might be able to do a single batch and blend it several ways to test the alternate methods. Take note of the outcomes you like, so you can adjust your recipe accordingly. This might help you converge on a final recipe faster.

Another way of thinking about blending is that your source beers for blending are your ingredients in a greater recipe. If you're a cook and have ever attempted a recipe by Thomas Keller (of The French Laundry fame), you'll find you often have to make several recipes within a single dish. They are a lot of work but produce unique creations. Used properly, you can achieve similar results with blended beers. Keep thinking of how the beers are components in an even larger picture, and what role they fill.

The old adage, "You can't make a silk purse out of a sow's ear" certainly applies to blending. To be successful at blending, you have to start with decent beers. They can have minor balance or style issues, but they shouldn't have real brewing faults. Blending a beer to cover a fault is more like an exercise in diluting. Commercial operations might do that for cost purposes, but it's not a great idea at home. Dump bad batches; blending can't really help.

Conceptualizing Blended Beers

The individual characteristics of the beers you have at your disposal for blending ultimately determine the range of outcomes possible for your blended beers. Each beer will contribute its own character. The hard part is to visualize the end result. The problem becomes more complex when you have to choose between a wide selection of possible source beers to include in the final blend.

When selecting beers to blend, be sure they are finished fermenting and conditioning and have a somewhat stable flavor profile. If the source beers for blending are moving targets, you won't really have a stable result. Depending on why and how much you are blending, this might not be a problem. If you intend to consume your blended beer quickly, then you can safely ignore this warning and shoot for the profile that tastes good now.

Finding Beers to Blend

I'm always on the lookout for ingredients that can deliver a distinctive note of some sort. I'll often make a test batch with a new ingredient to see how the finished flavor tastes. If that is a distinctive flavor, I'll save some of that beer for future blending. I once made a beer with a lot of cold-steeped chocolate malt; it had a beautiful chocolate flavor but was unbalanced. I saved this beer and use a splash of it whenever another beer needs a little more chocolate character. It works great, since I only need to use a small amount. Single-varietal malt and hop experiments are also good sources for blending.

It makes sense to save some of each batch of beer as potential source material for blending. If you keg, you don't have to make this decision right away. However, before you kill the keg, you should decide if you want to save some for future blending. I use two-liter bottles to store these beers in my blending archive. I try to use older two-liter bottles that are thicker for longer-term storage, as these are less oxygen permeable. I always store the beers under pressure and check the bottles regularly to see if there is pressure loss (just squeeze them and see if they feel firm). For very long storage, I also use glass growlers with some CO_2 blown on top.

Don't automatically dump beers if they are off-target; they might emphasize something you can use for blending later. Even acidic beers can be useful to add more bite to a blend. This approach might work better than adding acids, since it can also add other flavor components.

Finally, if you don't have a suitable beer in stock, you can always brew one that fits your need. If you have an overly sweet beer, for example, you might brew a similar beer that is very dry. Having beers complement each other is a very common blending approach.

Matching components from individual beers is somewhat tricky and requires practice. Review the material in Chapter 5 to understand how to develop your palate and critically taste beer. Being able to break down a beer into its component parts is an important skill for blending. If you can characterize the relative intensity of a beer's components, you have the basis for blending.

When pairing flavors, there are several possible outcomes: the flavors can be additive (one enhances or accentuates the other), they can balance (one offsets the other), they can clash (one flavor doesn't taste right in the presence of the other), or they can be complementary (they go in different directions, but in a pleasant way). Each of these is a potential outcome when combining two flavors, and not all are desirable.

Clashing flavors should be avoided at all costs. I've previously mentioned dark malts and citrusy hops as a clashing flavor. To me, adding acidity and citrus notes to something that is coffeelike or burnt brings to mind the flavor of overcooked coffee. Any combination that produces harsh flavors is undesirable. Some flavor combinations might appeal to some people but not others; use your palate as the first test and involve others if it passes muster with you.

Complementary flavors are interesting, and often lead to appealing beers. Certain fruits (cherry, raspberry, orange) combined with chocolate are an example. They aren't reinforcing the chocolate or countering it; they are providing another dimension. Adding dark fruit flavors from CaraMunich or Special "B" can complement the rich maltiness in Munich-type malts, for example. Think synergy as the desired outcome from this type of flavor combination.

Additive and balancing flavors are best described at the same time. A great reference for this subject is Randy Mosher's *Tasting Beer*—he covers the topic in detail. Flavor combinations from food are a great way of illustrating these examples.

Think about the heat you'd get from adding chile pepper (say, a roasted jalapeño) to beer. If you added this flavor to a bitter beer, the effect would be enhanced; the heat from the pepper is additive with the bitterness of the beer. However, if you added this flavor to a sweet beer, the effect is balancing; the heat from the pepper counters the sweetness from the beer. Depending on the outcome you want, you might choose either path.

If a beer is too sweet, you could add chile peppers for heat, fruit for acidity, oak for tannins, blend it with a drier beer to reduce the concentration of sugar, or blend it with a bitter beer to offset the sweetness. Tannins, bitterness, heat, and acidity all balance sweetness. Fruity esters (not acidic) and malty richness enhance sweetness.

The same approaches that can be used in pairing beer with food also can work with selecting beers for blending. As long as you can break down the sources into component flavors, you can visualize how well the flavor combinations work. If a potential beer combination mimics what can be found in food, then you have a natural analogy to tell if that blend will work.

Blending beers to adjust balance is often the easiest form of blending. For example, beers in need of sweetness, bitterness, hop flavor, malt flavor, and fruitiness are fairly easy to adjust. If you save single-theme beers for blending, the job is even easier. Otherwise, you'll have to check your available source beers for those that have the most components you need, and the least components that will clash or have other negative effects. If you don't have the right type of beer for blending, you might have to brew a batch specifically for blending or defer blending of the original beer until you have something suitable.

Strategies for Blending

The specific strategy you adopt will depend on your overall goal. If you are trying to adjust a minor style balance issue, then your best bet is to use the source beer and add a small amount of something to balance or accentuate the characteristic that needs adjustment. If your beer has multiple minor issues, you can use multiple beers, but take it slowly. Adjust one characteristic at a time before moving on to the other. You may have to repeat steps, but don't add multiple beers at once without tasting for the effect.

If you are shooting for a new style of beer, or a beer with a specific flavor profile, then you should taste all the source beers and envision the profile of the finished beer. What proportion of flavors does it seem to have? If you are unsure, then you can do several small samples. Adjust the proportion of two beers in side-by-side samples, and taste them consecutively to determine which is closest to your goal. Repeat if necessary on a finer scale to home in on the target.

In general, I've found that blending works best with one dominant beer. It seems to have a better synergy than a blend of equal parts—those often have a muddier flavor. However, the specific results will always depend on the beers you choose to blend. Aggressive or distinctive beers should be used like spices in recipes; just add a little for complexity, but don't add too much, or they'll dominate the final beer. It's all right to use multiple character beers to add complexity, but just work on one at a time.

It's hard to start blending beers expecting to have an epiphany. Creating new flavors not evident in the source beers is possible, but somewhat rare. Even if you do create new flavors, those are not always desirable. This is best done as a casual experiment in mixing flavors, and if you do get a wonderful fit, then record that combination. Trying to invent a specific flavor that isn't present in any of the source beers is nearly impossible.

If you are trying to fuse multiple beers into a more complex style, it's helpful to have a basis for integration. Pick a theme for your blended beer—identify the common element they should share. If the beers are totally different, they are likely to clash, unless you're lucky. Typically, this is a flavor profile element—sweetness, maltiness, hoppiness, fruitiness, acidity, etc. This allows the common elements to be additive, while the differences in the individual beers will add complexity.

You should always have a reason for adding another beer to the blend. It must have some component you desire, otherwise you risk making clashing or muddy flavors rather than complexity and synergy. Keep track of your milestones along the way. If you add something you don't like, recreate your previous good blend and try again. Think about adding accents rather than major additions. A lighter touch is usually better, so go slow when making changes. Remember that you can also use adjustment techniques (described earlier in this chapter) in conjunction with blending.

As you are learning how to blend, there is significant trial and error involved. Experience makes a difference, but you won't learn it overnight. You can be lucky, but don't equate luck with skill. See if you can recreate a blend before undertaking a full-scale replica. If you are having trouble evaluating the beers or identifying good blends, seek the help of others. They don't have to understand brewing; they just have to have a good palate. You can supply the style knowledge and vision. Tasting beer is subjective, so it doesn't hurt to have multiple opinions. Remember that blending is more of an art than a science, and that you will have failures along the way.

Methods for Blending
Tasting and retasting is at the heart of any blending method. Your palate is the only instrument that matters, and continued tastings will let you know how close you are to your goal. If you find that your palate is becoming

fatigued, take a break, have some water and bread or crackers, and revisit the beer later.

Take good notes of your blending experiments. Keep record of successes and failures. If you are just casually experimenting, just keep track of the combinations you tried. If you are being serious, start measuring using a graduated cylinder. However, keep in mind that as you blend and taste, the volume of beer in your glass will change (as will the volume of the added components). It's difficult to take good notes during repeated tastings without recreating the base blend. When trying to record the results in a rigorous manner, it's often a good idea to create several side-by-side comparisons with slightly different percentages, then pick the one you like best.

Casual experiments are easy to do in a drinking glass. You can mix beers when you're pouring. Add beers to taste, and stop when you have something you like. If you need to recreate this for a competition or scale it up to a full batch, you can use the previous rigorous approach to determine the exact percentages involved. I often use this method when looking for a wider variety while drinking. If you note a good combination, be sure to write it down for further investigation.

If you are practicing blending, play with commercial beer examples. See if you can find a beer that has a character you'd like to change and blend in other beers as an experiment. Try to create a new style; blend an IPA and a *schwarzbier*, and see how close that is to a black IPA. Add some barley wine to a pale ale, and see if you like it as an old ale. You can use this approach as a training method for creating new styles, fixing flaws, adjusting balance, and correcting style problems.

When blending small batches for competition or for tasting, I generally use one- or two-liter sparkling water or soda bottles, not kegs. The small size lets me waste little beer and more easily see the proportions being used, since the bottles are clear. I can also pressurize the containers to keep out oxygen and can make other adjustments (like clarifying the beer) in the same container.

If I wanted to blend a whole keg, I'd certainly use the measuring approach on a small scale to find the right proportion and then scale it up. Measuring volume can be difficult in a keg, although I often chill a keg and then move it to a warm room to get an idea of how full it is. Condensation will form on the lower part of the keg, containing beer; the empty part will be clear. Measure the distance from the bottom of the keg and use algebra to determine the volume based on that proportion of height. Another method is to weigh a full keg and an empty keg and judge the volume based on the proportion of the difference; however, keep in mind that some beers will weigh a bit more than others.

Whether I am transferring beer to a bottle for blending or doing the blending in a keg, I always make sure to blanket everything with CO_2 to keep it from getting oxidized. Any time the beer is exposed to air, it should be hit with CO_2 afterward. It has been my experience that blended beer doesn't always hold up as well as unblended beer, so it helps to blend as close to the time that you need the beer as possible. If you are blending for competition, a beneficial side effect is that you are tasting beer that is likely very similar to what the judges will taste. Deferred bottling and judging can improve your results.

A common question asked about blending is, how hard is it to replicate? The knee-jerk answer is to say that it is easy to replicate a blend if you take accurate measurements of the sources you are blending and scale them accordingly. However, that answer is naïve. Even if you measure percentages, those component beers will change over time. Your goal isn't to replicate the percentages of the blend, it's to replicate the taste. Never forget that your tongue is the best guide to the final blend. You can use your original measurements as a starting point, but you likely will have to tweak it further. If you are blending in a fixed-sized container, keep this in mind, since you'll want to leave room for future adjustments. Always use your palate as the final arbiter—you're not done blending until it tastes right.

CHAPTER 9
competition brewing

Thou Shalt Not Bring It Weak
–"The Brewer's Code," Justin Crossley, The Brewing Network

What's the difference between cooking for yourself and cooking for guests? Usually, you do many of the same things, except that you pay closer attention to details, you use better ingredients, you might pick a fancier recipe, and you serve on your best china. You are cooking primarily to please others and derive your primary satisfaction from seeing your guests happy. Competition brewing is much the same; you are trying to put your best effort forward and are trying to please judges. Actually, I consider *competition brewing* to be a specific case of *special occasion brewing*. You might be making a special batch of beer for a wedding, a party, a festival, or simply a gift for good friends. Are you going to just grab whatever is lying around, or are you going to do it right?

I'll discuss these two cases separately—first, the more general case of special occasion brewing, then the more specific issues concerning brewing for competition. Special occasion brewing entails brewing first and foremost for quality. I'll summarize the main points about making the best beer possible, which obviously also applies to brewing for competition. The competition brewing section discusses how competition judging works and how to get your beer to the competition in the best possible condition. I'll also describe ways to have more beer available for your special event needs.

Brewing for Quality

In many ways, this chapter is the capstone experience of the book. Everything has been building towards this moment. It's how you take all that you've learned and apply it. If you think you can brew better beer, now is the time to prove it.

In general, you want to do the obvious things: brew clean beer, use proper technique, pay closer attention than usual to your processes, don't cut corners, and don't skimp. Increasing the number of measurements you take and observing more process control points can keep the beer on track. Pay particular attention to the transition between major brewing phases; for example, don't let your beer hang out too long on the yeast after fermentation is complete. Taking more frequent measurements lets you know when different phases are done, and you're ready to tackle the next step.

Here are some specific tips for improving the overall quality of your beer:

- Competition entries are evaluated against style guidelines, usually the most current BJCP Style Guidelines. Before brewing a beer, always check the guidelines to make sure your recipe fits the style. Most recipe software will check the basic gravity, bitterness, and color parameters of your recipe, but that only gives you the most superficial indication of style fidelity. You really need to dig into the individual aroma, appearance, flavor, and mouthfeel sections of the descriptions to get the full picture. The comments, history, and ingredients sections often provide important clues.

- If brewing to style, make sure that your recipe targets something squarely within the style guidelines. Make sure the overall impression of your beer is clearly recognizable as the intended style.

- Consider the tastes of the intended consumers. Judges may be attracted to a more aggressive entry, but wedding reception guests may want something more accessible. Know your audience, and plan accordingly.

- Choose maltsters, brands, or types of ingredients that are the best tasting and are the most appropriate for the styles you are making. Pick the more expensive German malt for that lager; don't use the cheaper but blander domestic substitute.

- Select ingredients at their peak of freshness. Store them in a way that keeps their condition the longest (cool, dry environment for malt; frozen, oxygen-free environment for hops). Use yeast with a recent production date, or bank seasonal yeasts so that you have them available when you need them.

- Smell and taste your ingredients before you use them. Even if you believe the ingredients are fresh, confirm it with your own palate. Smell the hops, look at their color. Look for signs of spoilage.

- Select techniques to optimize the flavor of the ingredients, like no-sparge brewing (or at least sparging less at the expense of efficiency) or using all-late hopping to minimize harshness.

- Use whatever techniques that you like, that give you what you think are the best results, and that you are able to execute cleanly. If you've never tried a specific technique before, you may not want to use an important batch as a learning experiment. Repeat something that you know will work.

- Keep the style of beer in mind when selecting techniques; pick the ones that are best suited to the style and ingredients. However, don't be afraid to try something in a new way if you think it will emphasize a character you're seeking. For instance, if you want a maltier beer, try using a decoction mash even if you're not brewing a style in which it is traditionally used.

Once you have produced the beer, you need to condition it properly, so it reaches its peak flavor for serving. Store it cold with as little oxygen as possible once in proper condition, so it maintains its freshness. Think archival when packaging your beers; you want them to be stable throughout storage, and to taste right when consumed.

Taste your beer in advance of when you need it. If you are brewing for competition, taste and judge the beer against the style guidelines before entering it. If there's something wrong, decide if it can be fixed or if it's not worth entering. Follow a similar process for special event beer; judge it against your expectations, but don't use it if it's not right or can't be fixed. If the problems are minor, fix them if you can. See Chapters 7 and 8 for detailed discussion on troubleshooting, adjusting, and blending. If you note problems and have sufficient lead time, you might also be able to re-brew the beer.

If you are using the beer for multiple events at different times, be sure to repeat this process before each time it is used. In some cases, considerable time might have elapsed between events (such as the first round and second round of the NHC).

Often the difference between brewing well and brewing the best possible beer is simply focus, desire, and resources (time and money). The skill levels and raw talent required are similar. Commitment and desire drive the ability to focus and to put in what is necessary to brew the best beer. Understand all the key process control points and make sure they are hit; don't lose focus on key tasks—do it the way you know is right.

Timing Is Everything

Competition brewing is having great beer ready at the right time. Your beers should be made with a specific goal in mind, such as a style that you trying to meet or a concept that you are trying to realize. If you always try to brew quality beers (competition-quality brewing), then you will most likely have good beer available. While most of the work is in brewing the best beer possible, all is for naught if the time for the event arrives and the beer either is not ready or is past its prime.

Advance planning and scheduling can help you time your beers for when they are needed. Using an actual calendar helps during this process, since it can help you consider the lead times, and also allow you to record when you have to take certain actions. Know the dates when you need your beers to be ready and plan accordingly. If ingredients are only available during certain times (seasonal yeast strains, for instance), mark those on your calendar, too. Your goal should be to have your beers peak in front of judges or when consumed by your target audience.

If you are brewing for a specific event with a known date (special occasion or specific competition), think about the best age for the style of beer, and take that into account when planning your brewing calendar. Beers that are paler, lower in gravity, and less hoppy will not store as well as stronger, darker, hoppier beers. Some styles are known to go off quickly, like *hefeweizen*. In a competition with multiple rounds, figure out which beers can be re-brewed.

If you don't know when your beers peak, you should keep better records. I like to look at tasting notes and competition results for additional information. If you ever dump a batch because it has gotten too old, record that information as well. There will be batch-to-batch variability, so make sure you look at records from multiple batches to draw the most meaningful conclusions. I try to determine the peak age range for my beers and group them for easy recall. I'm interested in how long it is before a beer is drinkable, at what point it is best, when it starts to decline, and when it is too old to drink.

Some beer styles age very well and can be stored for several years. Bottle these carefully (or designate longer-term storage kegs) and put them in **archive storage**. Treat them well, keeping them cool, dark, and undisturbed. Higher-gravity beers will often develop much better complexity over time. If you are concerned about drinking your beers before they are ready, adopt a laddered brewing approach. Brew replacement batches for your high-gravity beers before you need them, so you're always using your oldest beers while replacing with fresh beer that will age.

Brewing for Quantity

Special events and competitions often require more beer than you'd ordinarily brew for yourself. Additional planning is needed to have enough beer to meet demand. If you can't brew as frequently as you'd like, or if your normal processes won't give you as much volume as you need for your planned event, then you should try to get the most out of each batch you do brew. Use every opportunity in the process to multiply and transform the batch. This section discusses strategies for increasing your supply and having more beer ready when you need it. You still have to time the individual beers for the specific events.

If you have a large brewing system (say, a half-barrel), then make double batches. I typically make 5- to 6-gallon (19- to 22.7-liter) batches on my half-barrel system, because I like to have a wide variety of beer available and have time to brew. If you double the quantity (making 10- to 12-gallon/37.9- to 45.4-liter batches), then you can easily split the batch and process each half differently. While that isn't the same as making separate batches, it is different enough to get distinctive beers. Here are some ideas on ways to handle your split batches:

- You don't have to make 5-gallon (19-liter) batches of finished beer. Do you have any 3-gallon (11.4-liter) fermenters? You could split a 10-gallon (37.9-liter) batch four ways with those. This gives you even more options.

- Adding different late hops can be done in a split batch. You can run off half and then add more hops. You can run off each through a hopback loaded with different hops. Splitting the beer before chilling it allows both batches to get different hop varieties in the whirlpool.

- The same beer can be dry hopped differently or can receive other conditioning or aging treatments. One beer can be aged on oak, for instance.

- If you want to make two beers of similar gravity, run off the full volume for two beers into one vessel, then split them into separate vessels. Otherwise, use the parti-gyle technique to create different ratios. I'm not a fan of making a beer with nothing but second runnings; I find it to be excessively grainy. Adding some of the first runnings will smooth it out. The gyles can be blended at the time of boil, at the time of fermentation, or when fermentation has completed.

- One technique that I have used several times is to top mash. I run off one beer from the mash, add extra grains that don't need to be mashed, recirculate, and then run off a second beer. Since second runnings are often too grainy-tasting for me, I like to use this along with the parti-gyle technique and blend in some first runnings, as well.

- You can also steep grains directly in the brew kettle of the second batch, as if you were making an extract beer. If you are concerned about carrying over grain husks this way, you can do a mini-mash with your specialty grains and add it to one of the fermenters.

Three Beers From One Base Beer by Steeping Specialty Grains

The American ale styles are closely related, so it's quite easy to change the character of the beer into a related style simply by adding specialty malts and sugars. Commercial American brown ales aren't typically as bitter as American pale ales, but most homebrewed versions are quite aggressive. You can also make these beers using the capped mash technique, but this way is easier and results in a cleaner-tasting beer.

Triple Threat—American Pale, Amber, and Brown

Use a relatively clean pale ale recipe without a lot of added crystal. Target the starting gravity at 1.050 or so. Maybe 80% two-row, 10% Munich, 5% CaraVienne, 5% CaraPils. Mash-in at 150° F (66° C). Don't use overly aggressive or piney hops, maybe Amarillo and Simcoe would work.

For a 5-gallon (19-liter) batch, steep separately:

5 oz. (142 g) chocolate malt

1 oz. (28 g) Kiln Coffee malt

2 oz. (57 g) Special "B" malt

1 oz. (28 g) Carafa III malt

1 lb. (454 g) crystal 60° malt

1 lb. (454 g) brown sugar

Steep as in a mini-mash (1 gallon or 3.8 liters water, 155° F or 68° C), strain, boil for 5 minutes, cool, add to fermenter.

Use separate yeasts, if you want. I like Wyeast 1272 and 1056 and White Labs WLP060.

Can also create an American amber ale the same way: use 1 lb. (454 g) CaraMunich, ½ lb. (227 g) Carafoam, ½ lb. (227 g) Carahell, and 2 oz. (57 g) Special "B." Or try 1 lb. (454 g) CaraMunich and 1 lb. (454 g) crystal 40° for a 5-gallon (19-liter) batch.

- A variation of the parti-gyle technique is to do high-gravity brewing. Make a higher-gravity beer, then dilute one of the batches with water. Be sure to account for IBU dilution as well (less utilization in stronger beers, then adding more water—like in the old days of making extract beers with concentrated boils). This isn't my favorite approach, but it can yield additional gravity-induced flavors (such as more esters and richer malt expressions).

- The split batches can get different sugars added to the boil, during fermentation, or post-fermentation. If you add sugars late, be sure to boil them, cool them, and add them while there is still active yeast to ferment the sugars. Sugar can also be used for priming. Honey is used to prime *De Dolle's Stille Nacht*, for instance.

- Pitch the worts with the same yeast strain, but then ferment the two batches under different conditions. For example, you could compare how Wyeast 3787 yeast works when pitched cool versus pitched warm.

- Once in the fermenter, the worts can be pitched with different yeast strains. This can be done to compare yeasts for making the same style of beer, which is the most common usage. However, if the yeasts are quite different (ale vs. lager, American vs. English, American vs. Belgian, etc.), then the beers could turn out as different styles.

Two Beers From One Mash, Using Different Yeast

This example uses a single mash and boil, which is then split into two fermenters, diluting one of them to lower the gravity and bitterness slightly. One is fermented as an ale, the other as a lager. They can be made in 3-gallon (11.4-liter) fermenters, which is handy in warmer weather since these beers don't age well; it's best to consume them fresh. Enjoy the cream ale while the other beer lagers.

Double Header—Cream Ale & Standard American Lager

Recipe for 5.5 gallons (20.8 liters), based on a recipe originally from Curt Stock

8.5 lbs. (3.9 kg) continental Pilsner malt (I normally use a mix of Durst and Dingemans)
2 lbs. (907 g) flaked corn
1 lb. (454 g) corn sugar
¾ oz. (21 g) Crystal whole hops, 4% alpha acid, at 60 min.
¼ oz. (7 g) Crystal whole hops, 4% alpha acid, at 5 min.
Mash-in at 152° F (67° C).
Boil for 75 minutes.
Cream ale:
OG: 1.052

FG: 1.012

15 IBU

5.2% ABV

Lager:

OG: 1.045

FG: 1.008

4.8% ABV

Split into 2.6-gallon (9.8-liter) and 2.9-gallon (11-liter) batches. Dilute the 2.6-gallon batch to 3 gallons/11.4 liters (approximate OG 1.045). Pitch Wyeast 2206 and ferment at 50° F (10° C). Pitch Wyeast 1056 or WLP001 into 2.9-gallon batch and ferment at 68° F (20° C).

- Giving each beer different kettle salt additions (either alone or in conjunction with different hopping) can lead to a very different interpretation of a beer. This could be used to test the impact of "Burtonizing" water, for instance.

- Add flavorings at serving time. Fruit works well, as do sugars, spice extracts (vanilla extract, cinnamon oil, etc.), and spice teas. Making these adjustments is just like blending; you are doing it to taste. You don't have to use fruit; pure fruit juices also work well—I like Knudson's juices, for instance. Think about pairing the fruit or added flavor with the profile of the beer, so that the fruit accentuates or enhances existing beer flavors. Some examples are cherry *dubbel* and plum *doppelbock*. See Chapter 8 for more ideas on blending, and use food pairings or concepts for inspiration.

- Blend a melomel with a beer to make a fruit beer. This seems counterintuitive, but it works very well. If the mead is sweet, then the fruit character will have a natural taste to it. Fermenting fresh fruit often results in too dry a finished beer; this approach compensates for that problem and can be done at the last minute.

Making a Fruit Beer Using Mead

This beer is called "Thanks, Curt," because Curt Stock first introduced me to the concept of making a fruit beer by blending a melomel with a base beer. It allows the fruit and sweetness levels to be matched very carefully with the base beer. Comments from previous NHCs said it was too sweet, so I lowered the amount of mead in the blending. Third time's a charm; this beer took a gold medal in the fruit beer category at the 2009 NHC.

Thanks, Curt—Blackberry Baltic Porter

All-grain recipe for 5 gallons (19 liters)

2 lbs. (907 g) Maris Otter malt

2 lbs. (907 g) Pauls Mild malt

2 lbs. (907 g) Golden Promise malt

3 lbs. (1.4 kg) Durst dark Munich malt

1 lb. (454 g) British crystal 90° malt

1.5 lbs. (680 g) British crystal 26° malt

.75 lb. (340 g) British chocolate malt

.25 lb. (113 g) British black malt

1 lb. (454 g) British brown malt

1 lb. (454 g) Special "B" malt

1.5 lbs. (680 g) wheat malt

1 oz. (30 ml) black treacle at 1 min.

1.3 oz. (37 g) Northern Brewer whole hops, 8.5% alpha acid, at 60 min.

0.5 oz. (14 g) Hallertauer whole hops at 10 min.

0.5 oz. (14 g) Hallertauer whole hops at 2 min.

WLP 810 SF Lager Yeast

Step mash: 105° F (41° C) for 10 minutes, 135° F (57° C) for 5 minutes, 158° F (70° C) for 90 minutes. Mash-out at 170° F (77° C). Collect 7 gallons (26.5 liters). Boil hard for 90 minutes. Chill, oxygenate, pitch, ferment at 65° F (18° C). Keg. Cold condition at 35° F (2° C) for 6 months. Force carbonate for serving.

OG: 1.080

FG: 1.024

7.3% ABV

Blend to taste with a sweet blackberry melomel before serving (or sending bottles to the competition, in this case):

Mead recipe for 5 gallons (19 liters)

15 lbs (6.8 kg) fresh blackberries
15 lbs (6.8 kg) tupelo honey
Lalvin 71B yeast

Ferment at 65° F (18° C), age 6 months, back-sweeten with tupelo honey to a subjectively sweet, still, standard-strength mead taste.

- A beer can always be given the *eisbock* treatment to increase gravity, body, and flavors. Watch out for overconcentrating the beer or adding off-flavors. You don't have to start with a strong beer to *eis* it. This technique can be used to increase the gravity of any style. An interesting way to make a standard strength beer is to *eis* a light beer. This is like the opposite of diluted high-gravity brewing.

- Blending different beers is always an option for creating new styles. This topic is covered in great detail in Chapter 8.

When analyzing beers for the split batch treatment, think about where in the process the different beers diverge. Visualize a family tree diagram, and think about ancestors. This will help you understand what beers have in common and how far you can advance in the brewing process until you start treating the "child" batches differently. Maybe you can mash a higher-gravity pure Pilsner malt beer. You can use this technique repeatedly to split a batch multiple ways, each with a different character.

Winning BJCP Competitions

As a homebrewer and beer judge, brewers often ask me how they can improve their chances for winning in a competition. After I give them the tongue-in-cheek answer—"brew better beer"—I usually start talking about how judges assess beer and what separates an average entry from one that medals. The more you can anticipate how a judge will evaluate your beer, the better chance you have of providing an entry that will score well.

This section really isn't about brewing, per se; it's more about planning, analysis, and troubleshooting. Let's assume that you have read the BJCP Style Guidelines, that you understand how to brew good beer, and that you can recognize a fresh beer from a stale one. What else can you do? What are your control points? Can you realistically improve a beer already brewed?

Understanding Competitions and Judging

It's time to rethink some conventional wisdom and be aware of how competitions work and what judges do during judging. You may be able to improve your results if you can avoid some common mistakes. At the very least, you will be able to better understand how your beers were treated and why they did or didn't win. Even if you just learn to adjust your expectations, you will have gained some peace of mind.

How Competitions Really Work

Unless you are a judge, you probably don't know how homebrew competitions operate. Even if you do judge, you may not know the behind-the-scenes work that takes place unless you've organized and run competitions. Let me review the typical way competitions work, and then I'll describe some of the less-than-ideal issues that sometimes arise.

Brewers decide they want to enter a competition and register their entries. Most of the time this is done online, but some competitions still use paper entry forms. It is up to the entrant to determine in which category to enter the beer and how to describe it. Certain styles require supplemental information that helps judges decide how to evaluate your beer properly.

Competition organizers take the entry information and organize the beers into judging categories. Depending on the number of entries and judges, individual style categories may be judged by themselves, be grouped with other styles, or be split into multiple flights. If a category is judged by multiple panels, then a mini-BOS (best-of-show) is used to select the winners from the combined flights. Other categories directly award winners.

Judging panels normally consist of two to four judges, some of whom should be BJCP judges. Competition organizers like to put BJCP judges on all panels, normally so that higher-ranked judges are spread around as much as possible. If a competition can't draw enough BJCP judges, they may use whomever they can find who claims they can judge beer. Hopefully, these people will be brewers or at least beer aficionados, but it's up to the competition organizer and judge director to decide who can judge.

Judges are given information about their flight by the organizer. They normally are told the entry number, the style of beer (BJCP category, typically), and any special information provided by the brewer. Judges decide the order in which beers will be judged, but they tend to follow the ordering of categories in the BJCP Style Guidelines.

Judges taste the beers and fill out scoresheets, assigning a consensus score to each beer. They repeat this for every beer in their flight, then select the top three beers for medal purposes and send the top-ranked beer to the next round (typically, the best-of-show panel). Beers are judged against the criteria in the style guidelines and are evaluated for style fidelity and technical merit.

During the best-of-show round, the top beers from each panel are judged again. Scoresheets are not prepared during BOS judging. Judges typically kick out beers one by one until they have a small number left, then discuss the relative merits of each and pick the best one for overall winner.

So what are some of the problems that might arise, and how might they impact the judging?

- Entrants might not supply necessary information (such as with specialty beers, not identifying what makes the beer "special"), or the information might not get passed to the judges. Even if the information is supplied, the judges might not understand it or know how to interpret it. If this happens, the beer is unlikely to be judged properly and often won't win even if it's a good beer. Make sure you put yourself in the judges' position and give them the information they need to understand what you intended to do.

- The order of entries within a flight might impact judging. It shouldn't make a difference, but it sometimes does. Judges may not give the first beer a high score, since they are "leaving room" to award higher scores later. Judges might find one of the first beers or last beers particularly memorable. If you have a subtle beer, early might be good. Later in the flight, palates might be tired, so assertive beers might do better. It's hard to "game" this system, since results depend on the specific panel of judges you get.

- BJCP style categories may be combined into a single judging category if there aren't enough entries to justify a single flight of a given style. If this happens, your beer could be judged against something completely different, as in the BOS. If you have a subtle style and it's judged in the same flight as something more aggressive, then you may be disadvantaged unless you have more experienced judges.

- In the National Homebrew Competition, categories aren't combined. You are always judged against beers in the same major style category per the BJCP Style Guidelines. Subcategories with an earlier letter will be judged before later ones. You might take this information into consideration, although the limitations identified in the last bullet point still apply.

- Entering early in a competition tends to give you lower entry numbers, and vice versa. This might be used to influence your order in the judging, although note that some competitions do randomize entries.

- Competitions have varying bottle requirements, so you might send anywhere from one to three bottles per entry. It's helpful to know if a competition will be using the mini-BOS format, since if you only send one bottle for the initial judging, then the same bottle will be used for mini-BOS. If this occurs, issues regarding how long the bottle sat open, whether the bottle was tightly capped, whether it was chilled after judging, and how it was handled will come into play. It's difficult for a beer to retain its character through these conditions.

- When a category uses a mini-BOS, each flight that constitutes that category can send one to three beers forward. Depending on the number of flights, this can mean many beers are ultimately compared during mini-BOS. The lead judge from each flight (up to three) is generally used for this judging. It's another element of subjectivity introduced into the process. Your beers aren't re-scored; they are picked, as in the BOS round.

- Entries can get lost, broken, mishandled, or subjected to extreme temperatures. Your bottles might not wind up in front of the judges in the best condition. If you send bottle-conditioned beers, they might not have a chance to settle after shipping. If a mini-BOS is held with one bottle, the pours during the mini-BOS round might be cloudy.

Based on my experiences entering the NHC, I've found that a very good beer that has no flaws and meets the style guidelines well has about a 1-in-3 chance of medaling simply based on randomness. It's unfortunate that judging is not more accurate, but you have to accept that there is some subjectivity in the process. Yes, the quality of other entries plays a role in your outcome, but this is the ratio I've seen over the course of four NHCs.

How Judging Really Works

Unfortunately, the reality of beer competitions is that judging isn't perfect. Judging is inherently subjective, and judge skill can vary widely. Judge rank is not necessarily the best indicator of judging ability. Not all judges will have familiarity with the styles they are judging. Some outspoken judges can intimidate others into going along with their scores. Competitions are often stressed to find enough judges and will take nearly anyone. Judges in training often judge as a learning experience. Judges can have off days. The competition judging environment may be less than ideal. Beers may be served at inappropriate temperatures.

These issues don't arise at every competition, but they can happen. The BJCP, competition organizers, and senior judges try to mitigate these risks through education, training, standardized reference materials, common processes and procedures, and general peer pressure. We like to think of judging in idealized terms, but be aware of what can go wrong. You can brew a great beer and still get hosed in a competition. It happens to all of us. There's nothing you can do about it, so don't dwell on it.

What you can do is be aware of these problems and try to "drive defensively." If you produce beers that are recognizable as being in-style by a wider range of judges, you will have an advantage. If your beers taste good over a wide temperature range, you are less subject to cellaring and stewarding problems. If you send a clear beer without sediment, then you are less prone to mishandling. If your beer doesn't have typical flaws, judges will give it closer attention.

The style guidelines provide the common link between brewers and judges and form the standard against which your beer is judged. The guidelines are important, but not all judges follow them religiously. Sometimes they are just used to check a certain parameter ("is medium body allowed?"). Judges can't directly measure gravity, bitterness, or alcohol level during the competition, so the numerical style parameters are not checked. The judge can only apply subjective measures ("hmm, I can taste the alcohol, so this must be more than 5%"). It's much more important to get the overall impression of the beer right, such as the malt-hop balance, malt and hop flavors and aromas, color, body, and carbonation.

If your beer is served too cold, then the malt character will be suppressed, and the beer can seem more bitter. Judges can't determine IBUs, so they can only go based on their impression of bitterness. Look at the description of the bitterness level rather than the specs, and be aware that malty sweetness will offset the impression of bitterness. If you aim for the midpoint of the bitterness range, your beer is less sensitive to temperature issues.

Some judges overstate problems or tend to focus on easy-to-find problems, like color, clarity, and carbonation. Don't give them that chance. Make sure your beer is within the allowable color range, preferably hitting the first color described in the guidelines. Hazy beers often get marked down, but this is a real killer for meads and ciders—they absolutely won't win if not crystal clear. If you bottle condition beers, you can get sediment kicked up in transit. Some judges may give you a break. But if your beer is kegged, then there really is no excuse for a hazy beer. Fix it before you bottle it. Carbonation should only be worth a point or two on the scoresheet, but a flat beer can ruin the whole drinking experience and result in deductions in every section of the scoresheet. Overcarbonation is penalized less, since it's easy for a judge to shake out some bubbles.

Unfortunately, some judges look for a reason not to judge your beer. The most common excuses are that it's out of style ("you should have entered it elsewhere") or that it has a fault ("I get DMS"). Then you get a lecture about the other style or the fault rather than an evaluation of your beer. Brewing clean beers that hit the midpoint flavors of a style is a safe bet. However, for styles that are known to have big flavors (e.g., bocks, barley wines, IPAs), it's often better to go big so you get noticed. Avoid ingredients and processes that can introduce faults or be mistaken as faults. Heavy kettle caramelization in a Scotch ale is often mistaken for diacetyl. Using smoked malts (especially peat-smoked malt) can add phenolics. Some yeast produce more by-products than others, and those can be misrecognized by judges. A clean fermentation character is almost always rewarded.

Some styles allow for additional information to be provided. If there is something about your beer that could be confusing, let the judges know what to expect. They want guidance about how to judge your beer. If you don't give them information they expect, they may hold it against you (even subconsciously). For any style that has multiple variations (e.g., Foreign Stout, American Wheat/Rye, Bière de Garde), be sure to give an indication of which version you intended.

Preparing for Competitions

Given an understanding of how competitions and judging work, you can plan your own strategies for entering. In general, you want to have sufficient beers available for entry, taste and analyze your own beers, tweak them if necessary, package them properly for shipment, enter them in a way that suits your goals, and ship them.

If you want to enter certain competitions, plan ahead. Arrange your brewing calendar to give yourself the most options for entering; you'll want a good quantity of high-quality beer. Know how many bottles you'll need for upcoming competitions and reserve them. Re-brew any beers that have gone off.

Taste them and compare them against the style guidelines, and select the ones that best fit. If you don't have the skills to critique your own beer, enlist help from others with good palates and style knowledge. Compare your beers against the same criteria judges will use. Don't misread or misuse the guidelines; it's easy to fixate on certain words or phrases—pay more attention to the big picture and overall balance of the style. Judge other beers, too; it helps to have a frame of reference so you can understand if your beers are good on a relative scale.

Enter wisely; don't enter your beer in a certain style category if it doesn't fit. It doesn't matter what you intended to brew, it matters how the judges will perceive it—select the best match. Understand what competition you're likely to face in specific competitions. You can enter more marginal beers if you know the competition will be weak, or the judges will be inexperienced. In good competitions, only enter your strongest stuff.

If your beer isn't exactly where you want it to be, see if you can adjust it. This takes some practice and skill, particularly a good palate and strong knowledge of beer styles. Package it well and ship it carefully.

Remember that the fun doesn't stop when the brew day is done. You have to finish strong if you want to do well in competitions. Pay attention to each step until the beer is in front of the judge.

Analyzing Your Beer for Competition
I've discussed general evaluation techniques for assessing your own beer in Chapter 5. This additional discussion covers how you apply those skills when preparing for a competition, since you have to keep a potential judge's opinion in mind rather than just relying on your own observations.

The best way to analyze your beer is to train to become a beer judge; learn structured tasting and how to apply the style guidelines. Judge in actual competitions with BJCP judges and observe the process, take part in the discussions, and develop the skills. Judge in different cities or regions to get a better cross-section of judge opinions; don't just talk to the same people all the time. If you are able to review your beer objectively, you have solved the most difficult step.

If you don't have the skills or objectivity to review your own beer, organize a group review with your club or with local judges. They can fill out a scoresheet or just give opinions, but you need to determine if the beer fits the style, if it has any flaws, and get their opinion on how well it would do. If you have multiple batches to choose between, they can help you select the best one.

When you brew a beer, you usually have a style in mind. However, the resulting beer might not be a great example but could fit another style quite well. You aren't being judged on how well your recipe concept was executed, you're being judged on how well your beer fits the style guidelines. Keep an open mind about where something might be entered. Your big American pale ale might score better as an IPA, for instance.

Beer style descriptions are often quite broad (look at Old Ale and Mild), and allow for a wide range of creativity and interpretation on the part of the brewer. Other style definitions are quite narrow (check *Kölsch* and California Common) and can seem like they are clones of specific beers. However, not all combinations of individual components listed in the guidelines make sense for the style. You have to consider all the elements of a beer together to get the overall essence of the style.

The concept and general balance of the style are more important than individual style numbers or specific descriptions. Your beer has to evoke the beer style in the mind of the judges. It has to embody the spirit and the intent of the style, as well as being fresh and well made.

Keep an eye out for easy-to-spot (and easy-to-adjust) flaws, like clarity and carbonation. Try your beers at normal serving temperature but also at fridge temperature, since you don't know how the beers will be served. Try them in a series of beers. Set up a flight of the same style and judge your beer against fresh commercial examples.

Taste the beer and think how a judge would fill out the scoresheet and assign the score. For any areas marked down, can you adjust them? Make notes and try to correct the issues in future batches. If you bottle your beer, this might be one of your only options. If your beer isn't right and can't be fixed, don't waste your money entering it.

Final Tweaking and Packaging

Tips on tweaking your beer are for people who want to change their beer before sending it. Of course, you can just send your previously bottled beer or bottle from a keg. If you bottle "archive quality" beer, then those are likely to be ready to go. If you bottle from a keg, you can use a cobra tap with a tube, a counter-pressure filler, a BeerGun, or a method of your own—I'll talk about my competition bottling approach a bit later.

If you detect small problems after you assess your beer, you may be able to improve them for competition. Clarity, carbonation, and balance can be easily adjusted; refer to techniques in Chapter 8 for more details. If you keg your beers, they are much easier to adjust. If you bottle, you can still adjust them but you first have to decant them into a working container. Depending on how much finished beer I need, I use either one-liter or two-liter soda bottles with carbonator caps.

Whenever you make changes, you will have to taste the beer again. Repeat the adjustments until you're happy with the results; you need to use the same judge assessment criteria every time you taste. Save carbonation for the final adjustment. I like to let the beer absorb CO_2 overnight before testing the carbonation level again. I like to carbonate my beer a touch on the high side when I know I'm going to be transferring it, since it tends to lose some gas during bottling.

When I need to produce a small number of bottles from kegged beer for a special occasion, I'll often use a more fine-grained technique that gives me more direct control over each bottle. This is a variation of my normal keg dispense techniques described in Chapter 8:

1. Dispense the cold beer into a clean one- or two-liter soda bottle, put on a carbonator cap, squeeze the air out, and blanket the beer with CO_2. Sanitize sufficient bottles, drain, and cover with foil.

2. Let the beer reach serving temperature. Taste and evaluate it.

3. Adjust, blend, fine, or carbonate the beer to correct any deficiencies.

4. Chill the beer and the bottles to 32° F (0° C).

5. Slowly vent the pressure on the beer, remove the carbonator cap, and gently pour the beer into bottles that are tilted at a 45° angle. Alternatively, use a tube on the soda bottle to fill the bottles from the bottom. The beer shouldn't foam much if everything is at the same temperature.

6. Watch carefully as the liquid level rises in the bottle. As it nears the top, tilt the bottle upright and leave some foam pushing out the top of the bottle. The headspace should be at an appropriate level; if not, keep pouring the beer, displacing the foam. Judge the final fill level based on the level of the liquid in the bottle; the foam will not add much to the final level once it settles.

7. Cap on foam. If the foam settles too quickly, blow a little CO_2 onto the beer, then immediately cap. The cap-on-foam method drives out any oxygen in the bottle.

If you want to be extra safe, blow some CO_2 into each bottle before filling. This technique takes some dexterity and good lighting. You need to be able to see when the beer is approaching the top of the bottle. Doing this over a sink is also a good idea, because spills are possible. Have a towel handy for bottle cleanup. You'll want to clean and label the bottles after you finish.

This technique is fairly labor-intensive but is well suited for bottling a large number of different beers. If I were to bottle more of a single beer, I'd use a BeerGun or counter-pressure filler instead. But it doesn't make sense to clean such a tool repeatedly when filling three or fewer bottles.

Packing and Shipping

Many brewers rush through this phase, treating it as little more than an afterthought. That's a mistake—this is the place where your great beer can be ruined. Beer isn't inert and can't be treated as simply so many cubic inches of volume to move from one place to another. Be paranoid about beer handling, and plan ahead, assuming that your beer will be mishandled. This can allow you to lessen the impact on your beer.

My first recommendation is to drop off the beer yourself, or arrange for it to be hand-carried, whenever possible. If you can handle it yourself, then you are solely responsible for it. You know that it wasn't mistreated, and you can store it cold (I keep my beer in coolers with ice packs). You also can avoid the excessive packaging necessary for commercial shipment. Finally, you can often see that your beer is properly labeled and stored on-site. If you are a beer judge, competitions will frequently extend you the courtesy of letting you deliver your preregistered beers on the day of the competition. For larger competitions that require entries to be shipped in advance, it's often more cost effective to drive them yourself.

If the competition is not within easy driving distance but still in the same general region, you can look for other brewers who are closer who will be hand-carrying their beers. Perhaps you can arrange to drop off your beer with them, and they will take both sets of beer to the competition. If you take this approach, give a gift of a few of your special beers or offer gas money to your friend. I've taken this approach a few times with the second round of the NHC.

Assuming you can't take this approach, then you can go the commercial shipping route. I see this as a three-step process: building a shipping container, packing the beers, and selecting a shipping method. The methods can vary depending on the time of the year; more care is needed in the hot months, since you are trying to keep your beer as cold as possible throughout its journey.

I normally build a cold box for shipping. I go to an office supply store and get as many cardboard boxes as I need to contain the bottles I'm shipping. For large competitions, I might use a 15-inch-by-22-inch-by-12.5-inch box to hold around 30 bottles. For smaller shipments, such as club-only competitions, I'll reuse shipping containers that I use to receive beer. The total box size shouldn't be too big, or the package handlers may throw it around or drop it. Make it easy to handle.

When shipping in hot weather, I'll get rigid foam insulation (like you use to insulate a house) and thick plastic sheeting from a home center. I'll line the box with the plastic sheeting first, then cut the foam insulation to fit. The insulation is used to build a box inside the sheeting (foil-side facing out); gluing or caulking the joints will keep air out. The goal is to make an airtight box that will retain cold. When I'm ready to ship, I'll seal and tape the box shut in layers: first the inside box, then the plastic wrap, then the cardboard box.

If the weather isn't hot, I'll skip the airtight seals and just use Styrofoam. This will provide some cushioning and crush-resistance to the box. Lining the box with plastic (even a heavy garbage bag) will help in case there are any broken or leaking bottles. You don't want any liquid to seep out of the box, which might cause it to fail or the shipper to return it to you.

Chill the open box and beer both to 32° F (0° C). You don't need icepacks if you pack your beer cold. There is enough thermal mass to retain temperature for a couple of days if the weather is not too extreme. The box is designed to keep the cold in while keeping any hot air out. Your goal is for your beer to arrive cold.

As for packing the beer inside the box, my primary goal is to not have the beer rattle around while shipping, and my secondary goal is to make it easy for unpackers to handle the beer. I first make sure all the bottles are marked appropriately with whatever competition labels are required. Then I wrap each bottle individually in bubble wrap (the smaller diameter bubble wrap is best). The bubble wrap is perforated in one-foot sections, typically; I use one section per bottle. I don't tape or put rubber bands around the bubble wrap. I roll a bottle in bubble wrap and fold the bottom and top of the bubble wrap around the bottle, then put the wrapped bottle in the box.

Pack the box very tightly. Press the bottles together. See if you can wiggle them around. As long as the glass of the bottles doesn't touch, the bottles won't break. The bottles can shift around during shipment, so press hard when packing them together. If there are any gaps left in the box, fill it in with more Styrofoam or use wadded newspaper. Do not use Styrofoam packing peanuts—unpackers hate these! If you make them angry, they might not treat your beer as well. Once the beer is in the box, I leave the lid open and chill it to near-freezing temperatures.

When shipping your beer, pay attention to the weather. Use faster shipping methods during hot weather (I typically send my beer two-day), and avoid long truck rides. Understand how long it will take to ship, and allow sufficient time. It's better to ship during the week rather than letting your beer sit in a warehouse or truck over the weekend.

Not all shipping companies will transport beer, so you may need to find a shipping site that doesn't ask a lot of questions. Don't mark your package as containing alcohol, and avoid mentioning beer-related terms in the address. If asked what your package contains, don't lie but don't be particularly forthcoming. I might say something like "perishable foodstuffs" or "gifts." Don't say "yeast samples for evaluation" as some have suggested—that sounds suspicious. You can also try printing out packing labels yourself on the Internet and arranging a direct pickup. You might also try dropping them off at a packing company that deals with multiple shippers—they can quote you prices for different shippers and delivery times. If you are a regular customer, you also are likely to get less scrutiny. If you've packed your beer properly and you don't act shifty, you likely won't have any problems.

CHAPTER 10
conclusion

I may not have gone where I intended to go,
but I think I have ended up where I needed to be.
– Douglas Adams, Dirk Gently's Holistic Detective Agency

The wisest mind has something yet to learn.
– George Santayana

We've reached the end of the book, but you're still not done learning. I'd like to leave with some closing thoughts I call *Living the Dream.* I don't think of brewing as simply a set of skills to learn; it's more of a lifestyle. To get the most enjoyment and reward out of brewing, I think you have to immerse yourself in it and make it a part of your daily life.

Learning how to brew isn't a one-time event. Even if you've mastered the skills, you still have to maintain them. You have to use those skills and work at your craft in order to maintain your level of performance. The body of knowledge used by brewers isn't static, either. Staying abreast of new developments keeps you involved and current.

I often find teaching others about brewing is one of the most personally rewarding aspects of brewing. I don't think you can call yourself a master in any subject if you aren't actually helping others. What is the point of amassing knowledge and then hoarding it? Sharing ideas, contributing to the body of knowledge, teaching others, and returning something to the community are all ways of paying tribute to those who helped you along the way.

As you interact with others, you'll learn that you don't know it all. You always have something new to learn, so be humble. Some days you'll be the teacher, and other days you'll be the student. Keep an open mind, and remember to share and enjoy.

Expanding Your Knowledge

I've written about channeling influences from other parts of your life into brewing. Expanding your knowledge and branching out into new interests can provide new influences for your brewing. Similarly, brewing may also be able to provide influences on those other interests of yours. It's somewhat of a random path approach to learning, but those journeys can also be rewarding.

If you haven't become a beer judge yet, you should seriously consider doing it. I consider it the single best thing I've done to improve my brewing. The skills you learn as a beer judge directly affect many aspects of your brewing. You gain an appreciation of beer styles and how to critically assess beer. You investigate the relationship between source materials and finished products, and how the brewing process transforms the ingredients. You learn how to detect faults and troubleshoot beer. The skills you develop as a brewer help you to be a better judge, so the disciplines are certainly complementary.

Think about developing your palate. You may be able to do this in unusual ways. Take advantage of any opportunity to do a structured sensory evaluation, whether it be with food, wine, whiskey, or some other product. I've learned more about structured tasting during wine appreciation classes than any other place—I call it "cross-training." Learning from someone with a good palate will give you that basic training—identification, description, discrimination— that can be applied to any tasting situation.

Developing cooking skills is a good idea. Much of brewing uses similar skills, and the knowledge of ingredients, process control, and tasting is good experience for brewing. Brewers typically make great cooks, and I always enjoy going to parties where brewers are bringing food. They tend to appreciate big, bold flavors, and put the same care into their cooking as they do into their beer. If you can cook and make beer, you will always be welcome at any party.

Travel and experience life; don't just stay in your small community (whether real or virtual). You can learn a lot about brewing and beer by visiting the historic locations and breweries where world-class examples and styles were developed. Even if you don't leave the country, you should travel to different regions and experience the differences. You'll be surprised at how much variation there is in different areas.

When I travel on business or on family vacation, I always do some advance research and see what the region has to offer. Make a list of brewpubs, breweries, styles, or commercial examples you'd like to try. Stop at local beer shops to see if you can pick up a different selection of beer than you can get in your local area. If you can get examples closer to the source, compare those beers against what you have tried at home—you may not have really understood the style otherwise. My trips to England to understand mild and bitter, to Belgium to understand *saison* and *tripel*, to Germany to understand *altbier* and *Kölsch*— all of those led to me re-evaluating my opinions of the styles.

Get out and engage with others in the community. Have discussions about beer, share experiences and passions, and try to learn. Participate, don't lecture. Keep an open mind about what you know, and be prepared to learn new things. If you can help others with what you know, do so. Every time you help someone else, you are repaying those who helped you.

While picking up new information and skills, be sure to take the time to reflect on what you have learned and what it means. In addition to just remembering the skills themselves, think about how they fit into the general framework of what you already know. Do they confirm things you believed? Do they contradict something you previously learned? Does it change your outlook on anything? Understand the process of learning, and make sure your knowledge is consistent. Context is important; make sure you aren't just collecting random trivia but understand the meaning behind the information you learn.

Staying Current

As a proponent of lifelong learning, I constantly am trying to increase my knowledge and understanding of topics of interest to me. In brewing, new ideas come up all the time, whether through published research papers, new books, Internet postings, experimental results, or other means. Take advantage of learning from others, and keep looking for cool new tips and techniques to add to your brewing toolkit. Remember, a master doesn't have to invent every method he uses—a wise man knows when to borrow a superior skill from another master.

When you read new technical brewing papers, you may only pick up one or two new ideas to try. Much of the information might seem academic and not immediately practical for homebrewers. If you can get specific recommendations, try them in practice. If it's something that makes a difference for you, decide if it's worth the effort. Some papers simply confirm things you believed to be true. Other papers are simply a waste of time—but don't look at it that way. You should at least be informed as to what other people are discussing. But it's up to you to decide if you want to use information or not; keep what adds value to you and discard the rest.

Keep your own repertoire simple and manageable; continue to build your own personal style. Don't be afraid to add techniques or concepts championed by others; you don't have to be original in individual methods, but your overall approach should reflect your preferences and attitude.

Final Advice

I hope you've learned some methods and techniques for brewing better beer. Rather than summarizing these topics, I'd like to close with some final advice on how to think about brewing. These lessons have been useful to me; hopefully, you'll get some value from them, too.

- Use abstraction to simplify the mental model of processes, ingredients, systems, and techniques. Manage the complexity of your work, so you don't have to think about all the little details of brewing all the time.

- Learn to predict what your outputs will be. Develop a feel for how your system works and responds, so that you will have an innate grasp of your results.

- Know what's important, and where to focus your energy, time, and thought. Some aspects of brewing have more of an impact on your finished beer than others; master those first and give them your undivided attention when brewing.

- Brew with economy of motion. Make it easy on yourself; hobbies are supposed to be fun, after all. If you're constantly thrashing while brewing, then you haven't thought your process sufficiently through. Think more; do less.

- Learn what to keep and what to discard in your processes. You want to choose the simplest set that works for you. Eliminate redundancies, and structure your processes to remove extra work. Don't spend time on tasks that don't add value to your finished beer.

- Everyone brews differently. You can learn from others. Don't be a hermit.

- Don't think you know it all—you don't. Even if you did master everything about brewing, the subject will change over time. Besides, you'll be no fun at parties.

- Be creative, try new things, and bring in influences from other parts of your life. This is the key to keeping your brewing fresh and being able to stay satisfied over the long term. Try to continually evolve and mature, but when you need a new inspiration don't be shy about reinventing yourself.

- Think but don't overthink. You don't want to be completely *laissez-faire* about brewing—*relax, don't worry, have a homebrew* is fine for beginners but a bit too simplistic for advanced brewers. On the other hand, don't be so obsessed with details that you find yourself overemphasizing trivia. Seek the balance where you are doing what is necessary, but no more.

Technical information will change over time, but these lessons will always apply. Keep them in mind as you master the art of brewing. If you can successfully incorporate them into your brewing routine, you will be able to adapt to change and use your own style to brew better beer.

Staying Alive

You can't enjoy the lifestyle if you can't go the distance. Alcohol does beat up your body. Your ability to bounce back diminishes as you age. Over the years, I've found certain survival strategies that have changed the way I drink. Keep in mind I'm not a doctor and this isn't medical advice, but I hope you find my experiences useful.

- **Water.** Stay hydrated. Have some water before you drink, alternate water with beer while you drink, and have two glasses of water when you're finished drinking. Most ill effects of alcohol have to do with you being dehydrated, and your liver needs water to help break down the alcohol.

303

- **Propel.** A sports drink or "vitamin-enhanced water beverage." OK, this one may sound a little silly but it works. It contains vitamins, minerals, antioxidants, and water, all of which are good for you when drinking. I get the powder so I can mix it to taste; sometimes it's a little sweet, but it seems to work well for avoiding hangovers. Have one before you go to bed, and one when you wake up.

- **Vitamin B complex.** I take one multivitamin, normally labeled as a super or mega vitamin B tablet, that contains 1000 percent RDA of multiple B vitamins. This is liver insurance, since B vitamins will get depleted when your liver is working hard.

- **Ibuprofen.** A pain reliever that works much better than acetaminophen (Tylenol) when drinking. Tylenol can beat up your liver, which you don't need. It also breaks down into chemicals that can aggravate a hangover. Ibuprofen beats up the kidneys, so don't take high dosages for long. This can help you avoid a headache; take at bedtime or when you get a headache.

- **Acid reducer.** I use Pepcid AC or the generic equivalent. This turns off acid production in your stomach for 12 hours and can help prevent waking up with acid reflux or a sour stomach. When I drink a lot of strong, highly hopped, or sour beers, this is an absolute must. It doesn't help if you already have an upset stomach, so take it before drinking. I used to use Pepto-Bismol as a preventative stomach-coater, but this works better.

- **Food.** The Belgians have it right; they always have food with their beer. Food can slow the rate of absorption of alcohol, especially proteins and fats (a steak works great). Food can also help you pace your consumption and provide some nutrients your body needs.

recipe list

index